Computer Networks And Communications (Set of 2Vol.)

Computer Networks And Communications (Set of 2 Vols)

V.K.Jain
Naveena Bajaj

CYBER TECH PUBLICATIONS
4264/3, Ansari Road, Daryaganj New Delhi - 110002 (India)
Phone : 011-23244078, 011-43559448, Fax : 011-23280028
Email : cybertechpublications@gmail.com

CYBER TECH PUBLICATION
4264/3, Ansari Road, Daryaganj
New Delhi - 110002 (India)
Phone : 011-23244078, 011-43559448,
Fax : 011-23280028
E-mail : cybertechpublications@gmail.com
Website : www.cybertechpublications.com

Computer Nwtworks and Communnications

First Edition : 2019

ISBN 81-7884-072-7

Printed at :

New Green Print Solutions, New Delhi 110078

Preface

Communication is the most important aspect of the business. These days the good business skills are based on good communications. For communications, you need good means of communicating. The most important means of communications these days is through networking.

This book tackles the various aspects of the networking through the following topics.

- Networing Technology
- Network Architecture
- Network Administration Securty
- Client Server Computing
- TCP/IP
- Network Troubleshooting Techniques
- Designing the Network
- Network Connectivity
- Wireless Networking
- LAN Databases
- Protocol Suites

I am indeed debited to the staff of Cyber Tech Publications for their suggestions and encouragement in producing this book in this form.

Suggestions for improvement are always welcomed.

Author

Contents

1

Communications Technology

Introduction

It is not that the Personal Computers are for personal use only. They can be used for sharing of information too with others having similar type of equipments. Logically it sometimes is fisible to have a number of PCs then having a bigger computer which can give the same thoughput as the number of PCs. But, overall it becomes a expensive proposition and sometimes is not fisible, specially for individuals and small businesses or small companies.

Another problem arises for those who are physically placed at a distance. They would need to send messages and receive messages, or use the same data at, or share program at, many different locations. One answer to this problem is to keep separate data files at each location, but this approach is very costly and potentially a dangerous solution. It is very expensive to maintain these redundant files of data and difficult to ensure the continuing accuracy of data at any one location. The solution of both, the need for more power and the ability to receive, send messages and share data, are found in data communication technology.

Communicating Data

When you send data from one location to another using any electronic means, it is called Data communication. Linking one computer to another permits the power and resources of that computer to be tapped. It also makes possible the updating and sharing of data at different location. Computer that are located in the same room office building, can communicate data through a direct cable link. For example, in a multiuser system, a single processing unit is linked by several dumb terminals through direct cables. Since multi-user systems link inexpensive terminals instead of the more expensive personal computers used with other systems, multi-user systems provide cost savings for small companies purchasing a complete system or adding users to a system currently in operation. In general, multi-user systems are most appropriate for companies requiring a shared data base for extensive data input and output. Computer located far away from the processor use a special form of data communication – telecommunication or telegraph. For example, teller and point-of-sale terminals are spotted in location away from computers: airlines, car-rentals, railway reservation systems and hotel reservation systems have thousands of terminals located many miles from the processors. In these cases, the process of using communication facilities such as the telephone system and microwave relays to send data between computers is a form of data communication, sometimes referred to as telecommunication, or tele-processing.

Dr. George Stibitz was the first to link computer and computing devices and send data way back in 1940. He used telegraph lines to send data files from Dartmouth College in New Hampshire, USA to a Bell Laboratories calculator in New York City, USA. An early large-scale business application was the Sabre passenger reservation system, developed in late 1950s and early 1960s by American Airlines. Hundreds of terminals were linked to the central processing unit. Communication usage has grown steadily since then.

Now-a-days minis and larger machines are in constant communication with outlying terminals. With available attachments, computers can use telecommunications channels to link up with information retrieval services, banks and electronic bulletin boards. An electronic-mail message can be sent from one place to another and an answer can be returned by electronic mail as soon as it is received. This service eliminates the hassle of continually trying to return a call, or long mail delays.

Data Transmission Techniques

Telephone lines are used for sending human voice. They were never planned to send Data. So to send data through telephone lines you have to convert the data into the format which can be read by telephone lines. These are called analog signals. For data communication between computers to take place over a telephone line, the digital pulses of the data to be transmitted must be converted to an analog signal before they are transmitted.

After its journey over the telephone lines, the analog signal must be re-converted to digital pulses so that it can be used by the receiving computer. The process of converting digital pulses to an analog signal is called modulation. And the process of re-converting an analog signal to digital pulses is called demodulation. The device that accomplishes modulation-demodulation process is called a modem.

There are 3 basic types of modems used in microcomputers.

Acoustic Coupler Modem

This is used to provide the necessary interface. The acoustic coupler is attached to a portable terminal and a standard telephone handset fits into rubber cups located on the coupler. The acoustic coupler modem sends data through the mouthpiece and receives data through the earpiece of the handset. The digital pulses produced by the terminal are converted into audible tones that are picked up by the handset receiver. The signals from these tones are then sent to the processor location where another modem converts them back to digital pulses.

External Direct-Connect Modem

It is external to the computer and connects directly to computer via RS-232 serial interface cable and to the telephone line via a modular phone jack. An external direct-connect modem may be equipped with microprocessors, storage chips and specialized communication chips. Such intelligent modem is programmed to automatically perform dialing, disconnecting functions, check the operating status using status lights and speakers, self test to verify the modem's ability to correctly transmit data, respond to commands from a communication program and change the speed at which data are transmitted.

Internal Direct-Connect Modem

It has all the needed communication circuitry on a plug-in board that fits into one of the expansion slots inside the computer. Internal direct connect modem also links directly to the telephone line via a modular phone jack.

These modems have many of the same special features as the external direct connect modems.

Communcation Channels

It is actually the media through which data is transmitted from one place to another. There are 3 types of communication channels.

Wire Cable

These are the most popular and widely used channels to transmit data from one location to another. This is so because it is cheaper and easier to use. Wire cable includes telegraph lines, telephone lines and coaxial cables. An advantage of wire cable is that the technology used to transmit data over wire cables is standardized, thus reducing the compatibility problems.

A disadvantage of wire cable is that it is subject to electrical interference making it less reliable than other types of communication channels. Another disadvantage is that wire cable must transmit data in analog form. Therefore, digital data must be converted to an analog signal before they reach the wire cable. This conversion not only needs special hardware, i.e., modem but also slows down the transmission of digital data.

Various items used are:

Telephone Lines

Telephone lines may be used to transmit computer data using the modems. The lines themselves may be either leased or switched.

Leased Lines

A leased line is a telephone line that is leased for the express purpose of maintaining a communication channel between two computers. The line is not shared with any other users and is available at all times for data communication between the computers. A leased line is similar to a telephone connection that is always open. Both computers are always listening for a signal to start the communication. Leased lines are used in computer networks where computers or terminals in the network must be in constant contact with one another. For example, leased lines are used in a network employing point-of-sale terminals, as the terminals must be in constant contact with the main computer. Leased lines are often conditioned to limit the level of noise on the line. Conditioned leased lines are usually necessary to carry on high speed data communication. Security requirements often require that leased lines be shielded from outside interference and unauthorized snooping.

Switched Lines

A switched line can be used for either voice or data communication and is switched from user to user, as requirements dictate. When switched lines are used, one computer must establish contact with the other by dialing a telephone number. After the transmission has been completed, the connection between the computers is broken, just as if a telephone receiver were hung up.

Twisted Pair Cable

Twisted pair [YP] is a common scheme for using copper wire as telecommunication cable. Because copper is such a good conductor of electrons, copper wires do not constrain electromagnetic signals well. When two copper wires conduct electric signals in close proximity, a certain amount of electromagnetic interference occurs. This type of interference is called cross-talk. In addition, because of the electromagnetic range used, TP transmits and receives unwanted signals from other sources. Twisting the copper wires reduces cross-talk and signal emissions. Each intertwined strand conducts a current whose emitted waves are cancelled out by the other wire's emissions. Twisted pairs are formed by two insulated 22 to 26 gauge copper wires that are twisted about each other. When one or more twisted pairs are combined within a common jacket, they form a twisted pair cable.

The two types of TP cables are:

Unshielded Twisted Pair Cable

This type of cable is composed of a set of twisted pairs with a simple plastic encasement. You may be familiar with UTP because it is commonly used in telephone systems. It is widely available and has been largely standardized. The Electrical Industries Association (EIA) popularized a category labeling scheme for five different qualities of twisted pair cable.

Category 3 and Category 5 UTP are commonly used in computer networking. While Category 3 is suitable for most contemporary computer networks, Category 5 included some enhancements, such as more twists per foot and a higher grade insulator, to improve the transmission media performance. Category 5 installations also require compatible equipment and more exacting installation techniques. Due to its voice telecommunication heritage, computer network UTP is often installed in the same manner as most telephone installations. A user device contains a port which accommodates a modular RJ-45 (4-pair) or RJ-11 (2-pair) telephone connector. The cost of UTP is extremely low compared to other transmission media. It continues to be mass produced for telecommunications and has become a popular computer network medium.

Some network integrators use existing spare wires from telephone cables to significantly reduce the already low implementation costs. However, this practice is not recommended if the existing UTP cable is lower than Category 3, if the cable drops exceed 100 meters, or if significant crosstalk is already present between the voice wires. UTP installation equipment is also inexpensive, easy to use and widely available.

Installation techniques are so simple that the cable can be adequately installed with very little training. Because voice telecommunication connection techniques have been optimized for easy moves, adds and changes, UTP is easily managed and reconfigured. Using current and emerging techniques, UTP may support data transfer rates from 1 to 100 Mbps at distances up to 100 m. Ten Mbps is the most common transmission rate in use today. All copper wire suffers from rapid attenuation when used as a communication medium. UTP is no exception.

Current technology restricts the effective range of UTP to hundreds of meters.

The copper cable used in UTP is very susceptible to EMI. Although the twists greatly reduce crosstalk, a certain amount of interference exists between pairs of wires.

Also, signals on the pairs are easily influenced by outside emitters of electromagnetic waves. External devices can also be used to intercept signals that are emitted from the pairs, breaching the security of a network.

Shielded Twisted Pair Cable

Though most of the cable is unshielded, but some forms of Shielded Twisted Pair (STP) is also used at some places. STP is insulated cable which included bundled pairs wrapped in a foil shielding. Various transmission media specifications from Apple Computer and IBM use STP cable. STP is more difficult to install than UTP.

Like coaxial cable, an electric ground, created by special connectors and installation techniques, must be provided for the shield. However, STP is more difficult to install than coaxial cable. If you use standardized and pre-configured cables, it makes installation simple. Bulk STP is moderately expensive. It currently costs more than UTP but is less expensive than thick coaxial or fiber optic cable. With the reduction of outside interference, STP can use higher frequencies and more bandwidth-efficient signaling techniques.

It is capable of greater transmission speeds, up to 500 Mbps at 100 m, but has not been widely implemented at data rates higher than 155 Mbps. The most common transmission rate is 16 Mbps. The biggest difference between UTP and STP is the reduction of interference and EMI emissions provided by STP's shielding. However, STP still suffers from relatively low immunity from interference. STP suffers from attenuation at a rate similar to UTP. Current technology also restricts the effective range of STP to hundreds of meters.

Coaxial Cables

This type of cable come in protective cover which shields the cable from physical dangers as well as from electromagnetic interference. Within the cover, the various cables are shielded from interference with one another. Coaxial cables are used in communication networks that require many simultaneous communication links. Each coaxial cable can provide more than 5000 links. The initial installation of coaxial cable is relatively simple. However, current installation techniques usually use a single strand of cable, which may become difficult to manage and reconfigure.

Local drops may be connected to the base cable to make device connections easier. Using current technologies, coax supports data transfer rates between twisted pair and fiber optic cable, although the typical data rate in use today is 10 Mbps. Much greater data rates are available. However, these higher rates are only infrequently used in computer networking. It is important to note that coaxial cable's bandwidth potential increases with the diameter of the inner conductor.

The cost of coaxial cable increases with the diameter and composition of the conductor. The cost of thin coaxial cable is relatively low (less than STP or Category 5 UTP). Thick coaxial cable is moderately expensive (more than STP or Category 5 UTP). Both are more expansive than Category 3 UTP (all comparisons are made in reference to bulk cable with no connectors).

As a copper wire media, coaxial cable suffers from high attenuation, but at a much lower rate than either variety of twisted pair. Using current LAN technology, the effective range of coaxial cable is in the low thousands of meters. While copper wire generally is a poor resistor to EMI, the shielding provided by coaxial cable greatly reduces its effects.

There are two types of coaxial cables: baseband and broadband.

A baseband coaxial cable transmits a single signal at a time at very high speed, while a broadband coaxial cable can transmit many simultaneous signals using different frequencies. A baseband cable transmits a single stream of digital data at a very high communication rate (millions of bits per second) but must be amplified every 1000 feet or so. It is mainly used for local area networks. A baseband coaxial cable can carry only an analog signal, so it must be used in conjunction with a modem. It is more complex to use in a network.

Fiber Optics

They are very reliable communication channels and they transmit data in digital form. They use light impulses that travel through clear flexible tubing (tiny threads of glass or plastic). A single glass fiber is thinner than the size of a human hair and it can transmit all the characters in dozens of books of the same size of this one across the country in a single second. It would take about 21 hours to send the same information over a copper telephone line. Since thousands of these fibers can be fit in the same amount of space required for one wire cable, the future cost of broad band transmission capability should be within the reach of small organizations and individuals.

Fiber optics can transmit data at very high speed with no errors. Unlike wire cables, fiber optic cables are not subject to electrical interference. They do, however, require repeaters to read and boost the signal strength because light pulses will lose signal strength over long distances. Optical fibers support extremely high bandwidths because they are limited by the high-frequency photon properties of light rather than by lower frequency properties of electrical systems.

Current technologies allow data rates from 100 Mbps to over 2 Gbps, at distances from 2 to 25 km. The data rate of a given fiber optic system is dependent upon the fiber composition (glass or plastic), the mode and the wavelength of the light transmitted. The most common LAN installations include glass multi-mode fiber and 850 nm wavelength LEDs. This configuration can sustain a transmission rate of 100 Mbps at distances of approximately 20 km. Historically, bulk fiber and connectors have been relatively expensive compared to copper wire, but these costs are falling rapidly.

However, the extreme cost of installation far outpaces the cost of materials. The nature of fiber optic cable poses installation problems. Every fiber junction, splice, or connection must be made with extreme care to ensure that the light path is unobstructed. Installers must be careful not to excessively stretch or bend the fiber. Fiber optic cables have extremely low attenuation rates. The amount of attenuation varies depending upon the operating wavelength, but effective ranges are usually measured in kilometers. Therefore, fiber optic cable attenuates much less than any copper wire transmission medium. Due to the use of the light spectrum, fiber optic cables do not leak signals and are immune to electromagnetic interference and eavesdropping. Also, the light spectrum does not require electrical grounds, so fiber optic cables do not suffer from potential shifts to the electrical ground not do they produce sparks. These characteristics make fiber ideal for hazardous, high voltage, or eavesdropping sensitive environments.

Microwave

This is also a type of analog communication channel. Microwave signals are transmitted through the atmosphere rather than through wire cables, similar to the way radio and television signals are transmitted. Microwave signals must be transmitted in a straight line, they do not bend around corners or around the curve of the earth. Transmitter stations redirect and boost the signals. The data may be beamed to a communications satellite that acts as a reflector by accepting signals from one point on earth and returning the same signals to some other point on earth.

The satellite appears from the earth to be stationary target for the microwave signals because its precisely positioned 22,300 miles above the equator with an orbit speed that matches the earth's rotation. Dozens of satellites are now in orbit to handle international and domestic data, voice and video communications.

Compared to wire cable, microwave has a much lower error rate, making it more reliable. Also, because there are no physical links between the sending and receiving systems communication links can be made over large distance and rough terrains. The only disadvantage is the high cost of ground stations and satellites to support a microwave network.

Bandwidth Channels

The bandwidth, or grade, of a communication channel determines the rate or speed that data can be transmitted over a channel. The term **bandwidth** is often shortened to **band**.

There are 3 bands for communication channels.

Narrow-band

The narrow-band channel is used where data volume is relatively low and which transmits data at a rate between 40 to 100 bits per second (bps). Telegraph lines are an example of narrow-band channels and their transmission rate is slow.

Voice-band

The voice-band channels are able to speed up the transmission rate between 110 to 9600 bits per second. Telephone lines are an example of voice-band channels. In many cases, a terminal operator at a remote location uses the regular dial-up telephone switching network, calls a number at the control processor location and enters the data. For large volumes of data, it is cheaper for an organization to acquire its own dedicated or leased line which can be used for both voice and data transmissions.

Broad-band

The broad-band channels are used where data volumes are large and which transmit data at rate upto several megabits per second. Microwaves, coaxial cables, fiber optics and communications satellites are examples of broad-band channels.

Data Transmission

The 2 forms of data transmission are discussed below.

Analog Data Transmission

Here the transmission of data is in a continuous wave form. The telephone system, for instance, is designed for analog data transmission.

Waves are measured using one or more of the following 3 characteristics.

Amplitude

You can consider the amplitude of a wave as the signal strength compared to some reference value (measured in volts). Analog signals are based upon amplitude, or strength, shifts which vary constantly from positive to negative values. Amplitude is commonly expressed in volts when measuring electrical potential, amps when measuring electrical current, watts when measuring electrical power, and decibels when measuring the ratio between the power of two signals.

Frequency

The frequency of a wave is the time it takes for a wave to complete one cycle. In other words, if a signal takes one second to make a transition from high amplitude to low and back to high, the frequency of the wave is one second. Frequency is typically measured in hertz[Hz], or cycies per second.

Phase

The phase of a signal refers to the relative state of the wave when timing began. Two signals cross at a slightly different time. Signal phase is measured in degrees. As with digital signals, analog signals can be modulated on encoded to represent binary data.

Current State

The most common analog current state strategies use different signal amplitudes or frequencies to represent data. These are two type of analog signal encoding schemes:

Amplitude-shift keying (ASK)

Amplitude-shift keying encodes binary data by varying the signal's amplitude between two or more levels. For example, a binary 0 might be one volt and a binary 1 might be three volts.

Frequency-shift keying (FSK)

Frequency-shift keying encodes binary data by varying the signal's frequency between two or more values.

For example, a binary 0 would be one frequency or group of frequencies and a binary 1 would be some other frequency or group of frequencies.

Network devices, using current state analog signaling, periodically measure the signal's amplitude, frequency, or both simultaneously.

State Transition

Transitions from one analog phase to another can also encode data on an analog signal. This method of analog signaling is called Phase-Shift Keying (PSK). This encodes binary data by varying the phase of the signal to indicate a value. For example, a 180 degree phase shift could represent 1 and no shift could indicate 0. Network devices periodically measure the analog signal to determine if a phase change has occurred.

Digital Data Transmission

It is the transmission of data using distinct **ON** and **OFF** electrical states. Computer circuitry represents data as a pattern of **ON** or **OFF** electrical states. These two states are represented by a 1 or **ON** and 0 for **OFF**. Digital data communication is faster and more efficient than analog. All the data communication between the computers is in digital form as the computers understand and work only in digital forms.

However, telephone system, an analog data transmission system, is used for a great percentage of data communication because it is the largest and the most widely used communication system in the world. The modem, sometimes referred as interface element, is used to bridge the gap between digital and analog data transmission, or to allow the digital data to be transmitted/received over from the telephone lines.

Buffers and Protocols

Before data are transmitted, a set of traffic rules and procedures, called protocol, must be established. The same protocol must be followed by all devices participating in the communication session. These rules may vary depending on the devices being used. Prearranged signals defining the protocol to be followed when transmitting and receiving data are sent between computers in an exchange called handshaking. Data communication between computers takes place independently of the CPU through the use of buffers at both the receiving and sending ends.

A buffer is a section of RAM which holds the data being transmitted or received. When the sending computer's buffer is almost empty, the CPU is interrupted and asked to refill the buffer. At the receiving end, the receiving buffer interrupts the CPU when it is full and the data are moved to their ultimate destination such as screen, printer or disk.

If the buffer size is large or the communication rate is slow, the buffer may be manipulated without interrupting the transmission of data. If the buffer size is smaller the communication rate is high, the sending and receiving modems use a protocol or prearranged sequence of signals, to interrupt the transmission while the buffer is filled or emptied. When the receiving computer's buffer is full, the receiving modem sends a signal to inform the sending computer to stop. When the buffer has been emptied, the receiving modem sends another signal to inform the sending computer to resume sending.

Error Detection

A number of methods have been used to detect errors while transmitting data. The most popular method for detecting errors is inserting a parity bit alongside the data bits for a character. When the receiving modem detects an incorrect parity bit, it can request the sending modem to retransmit the character.

Serial and Parallel Interface

A parallel interface is the one that uses eight wires to transmit all 8 bits in a byte at the same time. Therefore, parallel interfaces are faster and more expensive than serial interfaces. An interface connection is often called a port. The program instructions used by the computer to communicate with other devices is called driver program. In other words, most data are organised into 8 bit bytes. In some computers, data are further organised into multibyte words. Sometimes data are transmitted, a byte or a word at a time. This is done by using many wires, with one wire carrying each bit, which is known as parallel communication.

Unlike parallel interface, in a serial interface, the 8 bit bytes are lined up into a single stream for bits for transmission to a peripheral device. That is, a serial interface transmits only one bit at a time and hence it is slow. Parallel communication is used primarily for transferring data between devices at the same site. For example, communication between a computer and a printer is mot often parallel, so that an entire byte can be transferred in one operation. Communication between computers is almost always serial.

Rate of Data Transmission

The speed at which data travel over a communication channel is called the communication rate. It is also known as the transmission speed. The rate at which the data are transferred is the baud rate. Baud rate is the number of time per second that the signal being transmitted changes (modulation or demodulation). Baud is often equated with bits per send (bps), however, this comparison is not entirely accurate because a signal does not always carry one bit.

Although higher speeds are possible, typical data transmission speeds are 300, 1200, 2400, 4800 and 9600 bps. Modems used with microcomputers typically use 300, 1200 or 2400 bps. Larger computer systems used for communication in business typically transmit data at speeds of 4800 bps or higher using high-speed modems.

Methods of Data Transmission

There are 3 main methods of data transmission.

Asynchronous Transmission

Here one character is transmitted at a time. The transfer of data is controlled by start bits and stop bits. Each character is surrounded by bits that signal the beginning and end of the character. These characters allow the receiving terminal to synchronize itself with the receipt of data on a character-by-character basis. Asynchronous transmission is often used for low-speed transmission of data in conjunction with narrow-band and few slower speed (less than 1200 bps) voice band channels where the transmitting device operates manually or intermittently. It is least expensive of the two methods. Because the bit strings are relatively short, timing errors between the two device's clocks will not cause the receiving device to mistake the start of a frame.

This type of transmission is often used when characters are generated at random intervals, such as when a user types at a terminal. The start and stop bits not only indicate when a receiver should measure for the presence of bits, but also indicate the beginning and end of the data stream.

Synchronous Transmission

This transmission of data is a method in which blocks of characters are transmitted in timed sequences. Rather than using start and stop bits around each character, each block of characters is marked with synchronization characters. The receiving device accepts data until it detects a special ending character or a predetermined number of characters at which time the device knows the message has come to an end.

Synchronous transmission commonly uses the faster (greater than 1200 bps) voice-band and broad-band channels and is usually used when data-transfer requirements exceed several thousand bits per second. It is much faster than asynchronous transmission. Synchronous transmission is used in direct computer-to-computer communication for large computer systems because of the high data-transfer speeds required. The special characters used by asynchronous (start/stop bits) and synchronous (synchronization characters) transmission to alert the modem when data are being send and when the transmissions are finished are called message characters.

Synchronized transmissions resist timing errors much better than a synchronized transmission because both the transmitter and receiver use the same clock. To maintain framing when no data is being transmitted, synchronous transmission systems use fill bits. The sender can then maintain the integrity of the transmission timing. As with asynchronous transmission, synchronous transmission can perform error detection.

A method known as Cyclic Redundancy Check (CRC) is often used the CRC process subjects the block of data to an algorithm. The result of the computation (called the CRC) is appended to the block of data prior to transmission. On the receiving side, the same algorithm is used and the results are compared with the CRC field. Any difference is assumed to mean frame damage occurred during transmission. CRC is less vulnerable to multiple bit errors than asynchronous error-detection methods.

Isochronous Transmission

These methods use a constant fixed-frequency transmission clock to create set time slots. A clock signal is generated by a designated network device and is passed to all other devices on the network. Using the prescribed media access rules, the network devices monitor the network for free space within the slots and insert data as needed.

Multiple frames can be inserted into each slot until the slot is full. By using this method, a clock signal is not provided for every frame like asynchronous, or provided by the sender at the beginning of a string like synchronous. Rather the clock is provided at a constant rate by a single device for all other devices on the network.

Communication Channel Configurations

The two main communication channel configurations are as follows:

Point-to-point

In a point-to-point channel configuration, a device is connected directly to another devices by a dedicated communication channel. This communication channel configuration can be inefficient and costly if a terminal is not active enough to keep the line busy.

Multi-point

In the multi-point channel configuration, three or more devices, e.g., a terminal or computer, are connected to the same line. Compared to point-to-point configuration, multipoint channel configuration is more efficient and less costly because it reduces the amount of intercabling needed.

Communication Processors

A number of communication processors are used by network designers to achieve their goals. They increase the efficiency of a communication channel. These processors are used for a number of purposes, some of which are as follows:

Multiplexing

It is the process of combining the transmission, character by character, from several devices into a single data stream that can be transmitted over a single communication channel. A multiplexer is a device that produces multiplexing. It is also used at the receiving end to separate the transmissions and send them back in their original order for processing. A multiplexer allows the communication channels to transmit much more data, at any one time, than what a single device can send. Multiplexers are more efficient and less expensive. The equipment that multiplexes and demultiplexes is sometimes called a multiplexer or mux.

The following methods are used by multiplexers to allow multiple devices to communicate concurrently.

Frequency-Division Multiplexing

It uses separate frequencies to establish multiple channels within a broadband medium. To do this, the mux creates special broadband carrier signals that operate on different frequencies. Data signals are added to the carrier signals and are removed, at the opposite end of the media segment, by another mux. FDM is used in broadband LANs to separate different direction traffic on the cable and to provide special services like dedicated connections between machines.

Time-Division Multiplexing

These systems divide a single channel into short time slots. Bits, blocks of bits, bytes, or frames can be placed into each time interval is not exceeded. Time division is a multiplexing technique that you can use on baseband systems. You can also use it on an individual channel of a broadband FDM system. Conventional TDM systems are sometimes called synchronous TDM because the time-divisions are fixed when the muxes are set up. The time slots are always of the same length and are assigned in the same order.

Statistical Time-Division Multiplexing

Conventional synchronous TDM systems waste bandwidth if many of the time slots are left unused. Statistical time-division multiplexing (StatTDM) solves this problem by dynamically allocating time slots to active devices on a first-come, first-served or priority basis. A control field identifies the owners of each slot's data so that the receiving mux can appropriately split out all the individual signals.

Concentration

Very often, it is required to connect more devices (or terminals) to a computer so that the communication channel can handle all at once. Concentration is the process of connecting and serving these devices. A concentrator is hardware that provides concentration. The data are stored in the buffer of concentrator for later transmission, when the number of devices transmitting exceeds the capacity of the communication channel. However, today's micro-processor equipped multiplexers perform much like concentrators. Compared to concentrators, multiplexers are less expensive.

Message Switching

The message switcher receives and analyzes data messages from points in the network, determines the destination and the proper routing and then forwards the messages to other network locations. If needed, a message can be stored till an outgoing line is available.

Front-end Processing

The front-end processor is a computer, which is usually located at a central computer site. It handles all the data communication control functions while the Central Processing Unit (CPU) of the front-end processor handles all the communication tasks. Its purpose is to relieve the main computer – called a host computer – of a number of the functions required to interact with and control the communications network. The two processors interact only when data need to be passed between them.

A typical front-end processor might control scores of communication channels of varying types and speeds coming from a number of diverse remote terminals. The functions of communication processors differ from one network to another and there may be an overlapping of functions. A message switching processor, for example, may also function as a remote concentrator; a front-end processor may perform message-switching function; and, in less complete networks, the host computer may perform most or all of the functions of the front-end processor.

Transmission Modes

Data transmission may occur in one of the following 3 modes.

Simplex Mode

In this mode, data can be transmitted in one direction. A device using the simplex mode of transmission can either send or receive data, but it cannot do both. Simplex mode (circuits) are seldom used because a return path is generally needed to send acknowledgment, control or error signals.

Half-duplex Mode

Here, data can be transmitted back and forth between two stations, but data can only go in one of the directions at any point of time. An example is a citizens band radio where the user must either talk or listen, but cannot do both at the same time.

Full-duplex Mode

The full-duplex mode allows a device to receive and send data simultaneously. A full-duplex mode is faster, since it avoids the delay that occurs in a half-duplex circuit each time the direction of transmission is changed.

Communication Procedures

All communication between computers are managed by data communication software. The precise procedures used depend on the particular software, but the following account outlines the general procedures.

Communication Between Two Microcomputers

A small business that uses microcomputers has accumulated information that it wants to send to a customer who also uses microcomputers.

The procedure used to send the information is as follows:

1. Both the business and the customer start the communication program, which gives them a menu of options.
2. Both the business and the customer choose the same options, including the number of start and stop bits, the type of parity checking, the communication rate, full-duplex or half-duplex transmission and so on.
3. The communication link is established. The users decide who will originate the telephone call and the originator enters the telephone number. The communication program then instructs the modem to detail the number and reports to the users if a connection has been made.
4. After the connection has been made, the users can have an on-line conversation. They can type messages back and forth to each other and can record their conversation.
5. When the business is ready to transfer the information, it sets its computer to send;

the customer sets its computer to receive. The business starts, the transfer. The communication program takes over by reading the information from the disk and sending it through the communication link. The receiving computer stores the incoming information on a disk. The transfer proceeds without any further human attention.

6. When the transfer has been completed, the business and the customer say "goodbye" and terminate the connection.

Communication Between Microcomputer and Larger Computer

The procedure for communication between a microcomputer and a minicomputer or mainframe is similar. The only difference is that the larger computer have safeguards that limit access to files and facilities to authorized users. The most common safeguards are the user identification number and the user password. After the communication link has been established, the receiving computer asks for the user's identification number.

This number is assigned to the microcomputer user by the operators of the larger computer. When requested to do so, the microcomputer user types in the user identification number. The receiving computer checks that the identification number is valid. It then asks for the user's password.

A password is a confidential sequence of characters that allows access to the system.

An example of a password is:

S12$T11

The password is required for the user to obtain access to the larger computer. It also determines exactly which files and facilities the microcomputer user is allowed to read. If the typed password is valid, the microcomputer user is allowed access to the large system.

Going On-Line

Before you establish a communication link, you must adjust various settings to match those of the computer you want to connect with. Called communication parameters, these settings vary with different types of computers and programs. Fortunately, most communication programs let you store and retrieve the parameters that apply to various remote systems. When you connect to a remote system such as an on-line information service, you will probably be asked to reply to one or more on-screen questions.

Generally, you will need to provide some kind of identification, such as your name, an account number and a password. This brief dialogue between you and the remote system is often called a logon procedure. Some remote systems compare your identification with a list of paid subscribers. Obviously, if you are not on the list, you would not be able to access the service.

Other systems use the logon procedure as a security measure, protecting valuable records from tampering. In either case, the remote system maintains a record or log of every caller.

Many communication programs support automated logon procedures. When you log on for the first time, the program "records" your entries for later use.

Subsequently, when you access the remote system, these entries are automatically supplied in response to prompts from the remote system. Many communication software packages let you dial, connect and log on to a remote system at the touch of a single function key. Once you have gone through the formalities, the remote system usually welcome you with a greeting and waits for your net command.

At this point, your communication software has turned your computer into a simple video terminal, allowing you to use the remote system's software as if you were connected directly to the system.

File Transfer

Transferring files to and from your disk drive is one of the most common communication applications. These files may be bulletins, electronic mail messages, airline information or even computer programs. In addition to matching communication parameters, file transfer requires that both systems in a communication link agree on a common protocol.

A protocol consists of the technical details that regulate data transmission between computers. Fortunately, you need only a rough idea of how a protocol works in order to use one. The simplest to understand is the text or ASCII protocol. This method sends a file as one uninterrupted stream of ASCII characters.

While this protocol offers transmission of maximum characters in the shortest possible time, it is also the one most likely to produce errors, especially over noisy telephone lines. To combat flaws in file transfer, most protocols offer error correction. Specific methods vary from protocol to protocol, but the basic error correction scheme is the same; breaking up a file into small blocks and then comparing the received blocks to those that were sent to make sure they are identical.

Each block includes an extra character mathematically derived from the ASCII values of the characters it contains. If the receiving computer comes up with a different value for that character after it receives a block, it assumes an error has occurred and requests that block again. While this procedure reduces throughput, error checking and correction virtually assure error free file transfer.

Common error correction programs now include more advanced session level protocols that check for errors throughout an entire communication session, not just during file transfer.

Choosing Parameters

Before loggin on, you must make sure that you and the remote system are using the same communication parameters – the various settings that regulate the means of communication. To clarify this point, baud rate, parity, stop bits and echo are further discussed. Baud rate refers to the rate or "speed" of data transfer. In common parlance, this means the number of bits per second (bps) sent or received.

Technically, baud rate refers to the rate of the phase-shifting method a modem uses to transmit information – which is not necessarily the same as the bps rate. However, most modem manufacturers use baud rate to describe bps and this corruption of the technical term is now commonplace. Since transmitting one character usually takes 10 bits, dividing the baud rate by 10 will give you a rough approximation of how many characters per second are being transferred. Which baud rate you use depends on the capabilities of your modem, as well as the equipment used by the remote system.

Most modems for personal computers transfer data at 300, 1200 or 2400 baud. Whatever baud rate your modem supports, it has to be seen that the rate for your modem and the remote system must be identical. Sometimes a remote system will have different phone access numbers for different baud rates. In general, you should communicate at the highest baud rate possible, since this reduces the amount of connect time you are charged for.

However, some commercial information systems charge premium rates for communication at higher baud rates. Even so, the time saved makes using higher baud rates more economical when transferring large files. Parity refers to a scheme using a single bit along with each character to test for accurate data transfer. The most popular configuration for PC communications uses seven bits for data and the eighth bit for even parity. Using even parity during data transfer means that the eight bit always makes the 1 and 0 bits within a character add up to an even number. If the receiving computer detects an odd number, it either requests re-transmission or ignores the character completely.

Sometimes, however, eight bits are used for data and an additional bit is used for parity, resulting in other common setting; eight bits and no parity. Other parity schemes, such as odd number, space and mark are also used, but they are rather uncommon in PC communications. Stop bits refer to the variable number of bits used to mark the end of each character transferred. Often, you may see parity, the number of data bits and the number of stop bits in one reference. "E-7-1" for example, means even parity, seven data bits and one stop bit.

One stop bit is used almost universally in personal computer communication and many communication programs automatically use this setting unless you specify otherwise. Echo refers to a remote system's practice of sending back the characters you transmit, giving you on-screen verification that the characters have been received.

Mainframe computers and commercial information services often use this procedure, while most PC link-ups omit echo. When you are on-line, it is easy to determine whether to turn the echo function on or off. If you see no characters on the screen as you type, turn echo on; if the characters you type appear in duplicate, turn echo off. Most communication programs let you adjust the echo setting while you are engaged in a communication session.

Logging Off

When you have finished a session with a remote system, you need to formally log off. Usually, the system displays a message on screen confirming that log off procedures have been properly completed. Standard log off commands include log out, Bye, Quit, Off and Exit. If you disconnect without formally logging off the system, the remote system may be fooled into believing that you are still connected.

When you are using a commercial service that charges by the minute for connect time, this can be quite an expensive mistake. Therefore, it is a good idea to watch for the remote system's log off confirmation on screen.

Applications of Data Communication

The applications of data communication fall into one of 4 categories.

Electronic Mail

A business depends on the efficient exchange of information between different parts of the business and between the business and the outside world. Much of this exchange has been traditionally carried out through paper documents, delivered by secretary, mail or messenger service. With the growing use of personal computers, a more efficient alternative has emerged, i.e., electronic mail. Electronic mail is usually used to exchange messages and data files. Each user is assigned an electronic mailbox.

Using the appropriate command, the user can scan a list of messages in the mailbox, display the contents of a particular message, send a message to another user and so forth. To send a message, it is not necessary for the recipient to be present at the computer. The message resides in the mailbox until it is read. The sender may restrict delivery of the message to authorised readers by using a password. That is, the recipient must "sign" for the message by typing his or her identifying password. Many other features of standard mail delivery are implemented in electronic mail systems.

For example, mail can be forwarded, stored for delayed delivery and sent to anyone at a particular phone number. In addition, electronic mail systems implement many new features. An electronic mail system can deliver copies of a message to all individuals listed in a certain file. It also allows merging of standard data (from a data file) with a particular message. Now-a-days, several companies have started subscription to electronic mail services. These services are accessed through a modem and allow users to communicate with other subscribers to the service. The service may also accept a message and transmit it to its destination city. There the message is printed out and delivered with the next day's mail. This technique can be used to communicate with people who are not subscribers to the network.

Using External Databases

The most important applications of data communication is the ability to access external databases. There are literally thousands of databases containing information on almost every conceivable subject. Users can subscribe to many of these databases at a cost of the initial fee and a charge for the amount of time spent accessing the database. Users can locate information in an index or can just browse through the database as they would brows through books at a public library.

The types of information available through services vary greatly, as can be seen in the following examples.

The Dow Jones News Services provide current news, current stock and commodity prices and securities research data. The stock prices are very nearly the same up-to-the-minute prices that are simultaneously crossing the tape at the major stock exchange. This allows users to use the service for the data on which they base trading decisions. A number of subscription services supply on-line transactions. For example, a number of banks now allow subscribers to bank through a communication link to a personal computer.

Some services even allow users to pay bills in this way. Personal computers may also be used to execute stock trades through several on-line brokerage systems. Transaction-oriented services are in their infancy. In the years to come, they will certainly grow in number and sophistication. A number of multiple-listing real estate services offer on-line options.

This allows a broker to find all homes meeting particular criteria, price range, neighbourhood, size and so on, to match client demands. Also in the real estate field, services supply on-line listings of currently available mortgage money, interest rates and restrictive terms. These services allow a prospective home buyer to shop the entire country to obtain the best mortgage terms.

Sharing Data Files

Probably no single data communication application is as important to a large business as is the link between its micro-computers and its mainframe computers. In the last few years, businesses have purchased millions of personal computers to increase their employees productivity. The initial applications of personal computers were stand alone activities, such as word processing and the use of spreadsheets.

To increase productivity further, businesses are taking the additional step of making data stored in mainframe computers available to microcomputer users. The savings including financial ones can be huge. With data communication and networking, the tasks of data collection, analysis, decision making, report writing and data distribution can be integrated into a single, efficient system. In effect, the entire office (or even the entire company) becomes one large communication network.

Bulletin Board Systems

A bulletin board is a communication system that allows users to call in and either leave or retrieve messages. It is similar to an electronic mail system, but there are no private mailboxes, only a single large mailbox. The messages may be directed to all users of the bulletin board or only to particular users. But all messages can be read by all users. Some computer equipment manufactures maintain bulletin boards that users may call to determine the status of company products, corrections to programs and the like. Users may report problems, ask for literature or place orders.

Some computer user groups maintain bulletin boards for notifying members of meetings and other group activities. Other bulletin boards are maintained by individuals are meeting places for like-minded people.

Communication Processing

Communication processing is the collective term for all the activities that help to ensure the successful entry, transmission and delivery of information. Just as data processing involves taking raw data and adding value by changing the inherent information content, communication processing adds value to the raw message by ensuring that the message arrives at its destination in a timely manner, in the proper form, at the proper speed, in the proper language and without errors.

The basic responsibilities of communication processing can be divided into three major areas: editorial, conversion and arbitration. Editorial functions include formatting of the message, editing the data and controlling errors. Conversion functions include translating transmission speed and code.

Arbitration functions involve network control and message routing. Communication processing can be performed in any intelligent device, using the storage and processing capabilities of that device. In the microcomputer based of LAN, most communication processing occurs within the micro-computer itself. Within a network, communication processing is implemented as protocols, the rules that govern the transmission of information.

The following are sample communication processing services:

- Accommodating different video display characteristics such as screen size, line strength and paging.
- Translating data into the standard network format and subsequently re-translating the data to meet the requirements of the receiving station.
- Controlling the sequence in which messages are sent.
- Assembling and transmitting messages on the basis of time interval, order received, receipt of particular character or other characteristics.
- Alerting users to error conditions and possible problems.

Packets

It is neither practical nor advantageous to transmit long messages as a single entity. Therefore, for the purpose of data transmission, particularly in local area networks, messages are broken down into segments, called packets. Each packet normally contains five parts.

- A start frame, identifying the beginning of the packet.
- A header, containing information for maintaining control of the packet and the network.
- An information field, containing a segment of the total text information or data to be communicated.
- An error control field, permitting the system to verify packet integrity.
- An end frame, signifying the end of the packet.

The control information contained in the header includes the source address, which identifies where the packet originated; the destination address, to which the segment is to be delivered; the packed sequence number, which helps insure that the packets can be reassembled in proper order; and a control block, which helps prevent duplication, loss or looping (in which a packet is routed back and forth in an endless circle) of the packet.

Additional information to insure proper operation of the network under various overload or impaired operating conditions also may be included. Overhead is the additional information that must be transmitted through the network in order to facilitate the proper transmission and delivery of messages. It is created by the system's need to maintain control of all transactions.

A percentage of overall network capacity is dedicated to this control information. Overhead information exists on the network in two basic forms; data appended to each user packet, such as the control and error-checking fields named above. The amount of data appended to a basic message varies from one system to another and itself contained acknowledgment and control packets, which are transmitted from one device to another.

These packets keep the system advised of the status of the components.

Communication Software

Most computer applications, including data communication, require both appropriate hardware and software. Specialised data communication software is required to set up a communication link between two computers and to transmit data. Data communication software performs a number of jobs.

One is to send data at the proper speed; if the receiving and sending computers do not agree on the communication rate, the receiving computer will not be able to understand the communication. Another job is to monitor signals from the receiving computer that indicate any transmission errors. The communication program you choose plays a key role in data exchange between computers. If you are on the receiving end, communication software lets you decide whether you want to save data to disk, send it to a printer or simply let it scroll off the screen.

When you transmit data, most programs let you choose between sending it form a disk file or typing it directly from the keyboard. Software for communication also stores telephone numbers, modem commands and other critical settings. Usually, these parameters reside in a dialing directory, so you do not have to re-enter them each time you want to hook up with a remote system.

A well-designed communication program makes it easy to select a remote system from the directory and begin connection procedures. Many communication programs direct modems to dial, hang up and answer incoming calls automatically.

While it is modem that actually performs these tasks, the software provides the appropriate instructions. For example, when the program sends the modem a dial command and a phone number. The modem automatically goes off-hook (the same as lifting a telephone handset), waits for a dial tone and proceeds to generate click pulses or tones that dial the number.

Most modems provide an audible indication that dialing is in progress, followed by a signal that a connection has been made. You will hear the modem beeping out tones like fast fingers on a touch-tone phone.

Then, if all goes well, you should hear the remote system's line ring and the remote modem "pick up" the call. The remote modem then generates a high-pitched answer tone, to which your modem responds with a burst of tones of its own. This opening interchange is called handshaking. Once two modems are locked on to each other, most communication programs display a 'Connect' message on screen. In the foregoing paragraphs, we listed the rudimentary features of a communication program but a typical one has many additional features.

Some programs allow users to redial a number repeatedly (if the line is busy, for example) until a connection is made and others allow users to take remote control of the computer at the other end. That is, the program user can control the other computer from his own keyboard. This allows communication with no one in attendance at the other end. Some programs allow users to dial a sequence of numbers one after the other. These are sometimes used to generate recorded advertising calls.

Micro-to-Mainframe Link

Micro-computers can also be connected to large systems in a micro-to-mainframe link to share data and computing power. As the number of micro-computers used in business increases, this connection is being seen more and more. Line micro-to-micro communication, micro-to-mainframe communication can be accomplished via modem and telephone lines or by hard wiring.

However, the connection is not as simple because large systems use different formats for communication and they handle data differently internally. To complicate the problem, the communication and data formats used among the various large systems also differ. Specialized hardware designed for the particular type of computer being used is usually needed to make the data compatible.

For a micro-computer to communicate with a large system, three facts must be known:

1. Type of mainframe to be communicated with;
2. Mainframe's specific data format; and
3. Mainframe's specific communication protocols.

Communication Challeges

The use of data communication is not without its challenges. Data sent over communication channels are subject to various kinds of interference which may alter or destroy some of that data. In addition to ensuring the security of the data, privacy of the data must often be protected.

However, unauthorized access to data files can be limited by the use of passwords and access codes. To prevent highly sensitive data from being accessed and used from the communication channels, the data are often encrypted, or scrambled, based on some code before they are sent. Then they are unscrambled using that same code after they are received.

Suppliers of Data Communication Services

Various kind of Data Communication Carriers are:

Common Carriers

To handle large public telephone and telegraph networks, services of common carriers are availed. A common carrier is an organisation that is licensed and regulated by the government to transmit the data communication property of others at regulated rates. There are thousands of licensed common carriers of data communication.

Specialized Common Carriers

In addition to these common carriers that offer a wide range of facilities, there are specialized common carriers whose public networks are often restricted to a more limited number of services. MCI communication corporation is an example of satellite using organizations.

Value Added Carriers

A value added carrier is an organization that leases communication channels from the common carriers (it may not have its own transmission facilities) and adds extra services over and above what the common carriers provide. For example, Tymnet and Telenet both have computer networks that receive customer data coming in over telephone lines. These data are temporarily stored and organized into 'packets' of characters.

These packets are then routed and transmitted at high speed over the final data destination. At these offices, data in the packets are reassembled into the complete message for transmission to the final destination. The transmission cost of value-added network (VAN) is less than directly utilizing common carrier channels. Telenet and Tymnet are sometimes referred to as packet-switching networks.

Micro-to-Micro Link

Microcomputers are often connected for data communication in a micro-to-micro link so that microcomputer users with incompatible data formats can share data. For instance, data on an Apple IIc disk cannot be used by an IBM PC/XT drive because the data are not saved on the disk in a format that the IBM can read. However, that data, provided they are in a standard format such as ASCII, can be sent via modem and telephone line to the IBM, saved on the disk by the IBM and used in that format.

The reverse, sending data from the IBM to the Apple computer, is also possible. If the two computers are located near each other, another option is to connect directly (hard wire) using a null modem cable. The null modem cable uses a different pin configuration from a modem cable and eliminates the need for a modem by directly matching the data transmit pin from one computer to the data receive pin on the other computer.

The advantages of hard wiring are:

- It allows incompatible computers to transfer data.
- It eliminates the need for modems at each computer.
- It allows data transfer to take place at speeds upto 9600 bps.

However, there are no error dedication capabilities with hard wiring. A small business that uses microcomputers has accumulated information that it wants to send to a customer who also uses microcomputers. The precise procedures used depend on the particular software, but the following account outlines the general procedures:

1. The business and the computer both start the communication program, which gives them a menu of options.
2. The business and computer both, choose the same options, including the number of start and stop bits, the type of parity checking, the communication rate, full-duplex or half-duplex transmission and so on.
3. The communication configuration is made. The users decide who will originate the telephone call and the originator enters the telephone number. The communication program then instructs the modem to dial the number and reports to the users if a connection has been established.
4. When the connection has been established, the users can have an on-line conversation. They can type messages back and forth to each other and can record or capture their conversation.
5. At the business end, if the computer is ready to transfer the information, it sets its

computer to send; the customer set its computer to receive. The business starts the transfer. The communication program takes over by reading the information from the disk and sending it through the communication link. The receiving computer stores the incoming information on a disk. When the transfer of a file has been completed, the business and customer sides computers saying "good-bye" and then terminate the connection.

2

Network Technology

Introduction to Networking

Networking is a concept, where 2 or more than 2 computers are joined together to share information. This can be in the form of data or programs. These computers can be within a walking distance or in the same building of the office or in the same city or even across the cities.

But, why is this needed. Have you ever found yourself rushing from one computer to another in your office or home, attending to several different jobs at various locations? Or do you often find yourself moving files that need printing form a PC that you happen to be working on the PC that is connected to the printer? All of these situations can be made easier by allowing the various machines to communicate with each other – by networking the PCs.

The distance between the computers is narrowed down by the telephone lines. The information from the computer is converted to the media understandable by the communication lines and then transferred from one place to another.

With networking you can not only share data and programs, but can also share the resources like printers, scanners, etc. In PC technology, such a collection of computers, all located within a few thousand feet of each other, is called Local Area Networking.

Networking Basics

Networking several computers together allows data to be transmitted form one machine to another in rapid and easily managed data streams. This sharing of data allows many of the resources that are located on a single machine to effectively become available to all other machines on the network.

These resources can be physically located on the machine, e.g., as files on the hard disk, or connected logically to the machine. An example of a logically connected resource would be a printer that is connected to a PC, but which is then available over the network to other machines on that network.

An alternative situation would be where access to the Internet is available to all the PCs on a network through a special communication device attached to the network. Access to all external and internal resources are thus made available to PC users on the network.

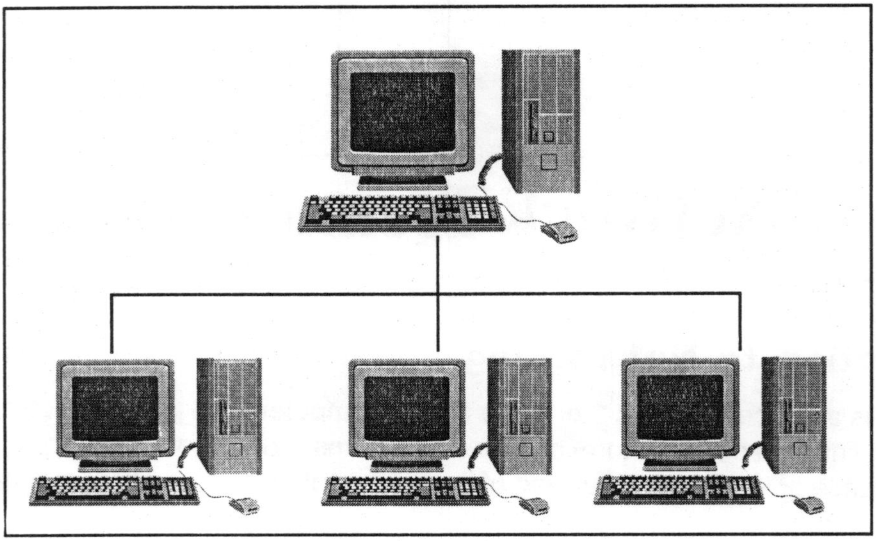

A network server provides network services to a user workstation (server) on the network. Services can range from sharing database and files, printers; communications or other network resources. Thus, the network servers are also called file servers, print servers, communication servers, etc. They can be dedicated to the task of providing network services.

They are then called dedicated network servers. Otherwise, they may be called non dedicated servers. A typical networking is shown on the last page.

Another factor which also favours the networking is the cost factor.

Cost Reduction

If you have 2-3 computers attached in a single networking system, you may go in for a single printer which can be used by all of them. The same goes for other devices like Scanner, Plotter, etc. This results in lots of costs.

The main advantages of Networking can be clubbed as follows:

Resource Sharing

There are two main types of networking systems. The type used for larger networks is known as the Client/Server model. This model involves using a powerful computer that runs a Network Operating System and acts as the 'server'. The Network Operating System then runs the server, supplying network services to the other 'client' computers.

These services might include the management of file transfers, running printing jobs, or even running applications across the network. For example, a word processing software package running on a PC is actually being 'served' form the server across the network, rather than being loaded onto the PC's local hard disk.

The problem with the Client/Server model is that it requires specialised hardware, software and to a large extent skilled networking techniques to configure and maintain the network. All of this can become expensive.

The second model, the Peer-to Peer system or resource Sharing is fortunately a lot easier to implement and maintain and it is this model that we will use in this book.

Resource Sharing is incorporated into Windows 98 and allows all network users access to all resources such as the hard drives, directories, printers or CD-ROM drives that are available on the network. It also allows access to external resources across the network via special intermediary devices.

Resource Sharing involved each computer on the network taking on equal an equal part in the networking process and is ideally suited to smaller networks.

Security

Being able to have complete access to all resources on the network is not always desirable. It is often the case that certain resources may need to be restricted to certain users.

Resources Sharing within Windows allows for this and incorporates the ability to protect access to particular resources with passwords. These passwords can then be stored within the windows 98 configuration files so that access to protected resources is automatically assigned once the user has gained access to the network; the relevant passwords is therefore only entered once during the network login procedure. This function can also be disabled so that a password is required every single time the user attempts to access a protected resource.

Password access can also be configured to allow the user to read but not to change a particular resource or to allow full access, including the ability to write to a resource (which would be necessary for sending jobs to a printer).

Each individual resource can also be configured separately so that different passwords and access rights can be assigned for different resources

Types of Networking

The three basic types of networks are:

1. Local Area Networks or LAN
2. Metropolitan Area Network or MAN
3. Wide Area Network or WAN

Let us see them in details.

Local Area Network

A local area network (LAN) is two or more computers directly linked within a small well-defined area such as a room, building, or group of closely placed buildings. A LAN may be made up of only microcomputers or any combination of microcomputers and large systems.

A LAN usually consists of the following:

1. Two or more computers
2. Peripheral devices such as printers and hard-disk drives
3. Software to control the operation of the computers or other devices connected to the LAN
4. Special cables, usually coaxial or fibre optic, to connect the computers and other devices
5. A plug-in board to handle the data transmissions.

Some computers require that all the computers be of a certain brand, while others allow a variety of brands to be connected. The number of computers in a LAN varies from smaller LANs that typically connect 2 to 25 computers, to large LANs that can connect as many as 10,000 computers.

The length of the cable connecting a computer to a LAN also varies depending on the LAN. Most LANs allow cables of about 1,000 feet, but some allow cables of several miles to be used. The data transfer speeds range from several thousand bits per second to around 10 million bits per second. The programs that control the LANs also vary in the features they offer. Some programs allow the user of more than on operating system; others allow only one. On some LANs file access is limited to one user at a time; on others, more than one user can access a file simultaneously.

Hardware for LAN

The following are the major hardware components/devices for establishing LAN:

1. Transmission Channel
2. Network Interface Unit or NIU
3. Servers
4. Workstations

Transmission Channel for LAN

Generally four types of channels are used for data transmission in a LAN. These are:

1. Twisted Pair Cables
2. Coaxial Cables

3. Fibre Optic Cables
4. Radio Waves

About these you will read in a next chapter.

Interface for LAN

Network interface units connect each devices in the LAN network to shared transmission device. It contain the rules or logic to access the LAN. NIU is also used to implement LAN protocols and for device attachments. Its function depends on the type of topologies (to be told later in the this chapter), used in LAN.

Server and Workstations

One of the major benefits of implementation of LAN is sharing expensive resources such as storage devices, printers, etc. This is achieved through providing servers on the LAN. It is dedicated computer that controls one or more resources. This contains both hardware and software interface for LAN. Three major categories of services used in LANs are:

1. File Server
2. Printer Server
3. Modem Server

In networking, file server is used to share storage for files. Besides providing storage space for files in a LAN environment, it is used for taking periodical backup, and also to provide gateway to other servers with and between LANs. Similarly printer server is used to handle printing works of all workstation connected in the network. In LAN environment also modem is required to get connected to other network or simply to use a telephone. A modem server is used to share this expensive resource by all connected workstations in a network ring.

Software for LAN

LAN operating system is required to operate on the LAN system. It has basically two aspects:

1. Server Software
2. Workstation Software

LAN operating system facilitates :

1. Sharing of expensive resources, e.g., printer, storage space, etc.
2. Security for data
3. Connection to other network

There are various types of LAN operating system. Some popular LAN operating systems are :

— Novel Netware
— Ethernet
— Corvus
— ArcNet
— LAN Server
— Omni Net
— PC Net
— IBM PC LAN
— Etherlink Plus, etc.

Wide Area Networks or WAN

A wide area network is two or more computers that are geographically dispersed, linked by communication facilities such as telephone system or microwave relays. This type of network is usually limited to use by large corporations and government agencies because of the high cost involved in building and maintaining them. A WAN is a network that links separate geographical locations and this network can be a public system or any of the various packet switched services provided by the public telecommunication agencies.

The main difference between a WAN and LAN is under the complete control of the owner, whereas the WAN needs the involvement of another authority like telecom department. LANs are successful and capable of handling very high data transfer rates at low cost because of the small area covered. Besides LANs have a lower error rate than WANs.

Transmission Channel for WAN

Generally 3 types of channels are used for data transmission in a WAN. These are:

1. Radio Waves
2. Micro Waves
3. Communication Satellites

Hardware Requirements for WAN

There are mainly 4 hardware devices which are required to establish linkage between geographically separated computers. These are:

1. Bridges
2. Routers
3. Gateways

4. X.25 Standard Interface

These are explained below.

Bridges

These are used to connect two LANs that use the identical protocols over a wide area. The bridge acts as an address filter which picks up packets from one LAN that are intended for a destination on another LAN and passes these packets on the network. The amount of processing required at the bridge is minimal because all the devices use the same protocols. In case the distance between two LANs is very large then the user is required to employ two identical bridges at either end of the communication link.

Routers

It is a special type of device that can be used to connect networks that may not be similar. Such type of devices provide connectivity between two LANs and two WANs over large geographical distances. These devices operate at the Network Layer of the OSI model. These devices participate in a routing protocol to access the network topology, and on the basis of this information routers compute the best route from a sender to the receiver.

Gateways

These are used to connect two dissimilar LANs. The terms Gateways and Routers are used interchangeably, though there is discriminating difference between the two. A router operates at the network layer whereas a gateway operates on the application layer of the OSI model. A gateway is required to convert data packets from one protocol format to another before forwarding it, as it connects two dissimilar networks.

X.25 Standard Interface

X.25 is a protocol for interfacing to a Public Packet Switched Network. It is not a protocol used for implementing a network. Two systems that support X.25 can't necessarily be connected back-to-back. They can only be connected through a DCE in a Public Packet Switched. International Telegraph and Telephone Consultative Committee (ITTCC) developed X.25 as the standard interface between the Data Terminal Equipment (DTE) and Data Circuit Terminating Equipment (DCTE). This recommendation has been widely accepted as the industry standard for public packet switched networks.

Types of Wide Area Networks

There are mainly two types of WAN:

Public Networks

These are those networks which are installed and run by the telecommunication authorities and are made available to any organization or individual who go for their subscription.

Private Networks

The basic technique used in all forms of private WAN is to use private circuits to link the locations to be served by the network. Between these fixed points the owner of the network has complete freedom to use the circuits in any way they want. They can use the circuits to carry large quantities of data or for high speed transmissions. Private wide area networks can be built using whatever standard technology is available.

Topology

There are ways in which you can connect the various computers for networking. This physical arrangement is called Topology. Different types of topologies are:

The Ring Topology

As the name suggests all the server/nodes are joined together to form a ring. There is no central server in this case. A ring may be unidirectional or bi-directional. A unidirectional ring moves data in one direction only; a bi-directional ring moves data in both directions, but only one direction at a time. In a unidirectional ring, if one computer breaks down, special software is required to keep the network functional. When one node malfunction in a bi-directional ring, a message can usually be sent in the opposite direction still allowing the node to communicate with all the other active nodes in the network.

Advantages of the Ring Network

1. **Short cable length:** the amount of cabling involved in a ring topology is comparable to that of a bus and is small relative to that of a star. This means that less connections will be needed, which will in turn increase network reliability.

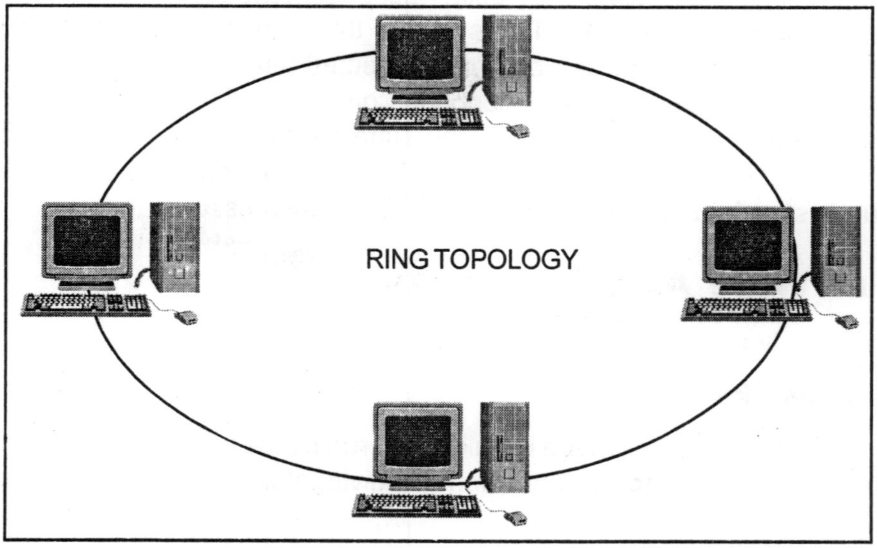

2. **No wiring closet space required:** Since there is only one cable connecting each node to its immediate neighbours, it is not necessary to allocate space in the building for wiring closets.

3. **Suitable for optical fibers:** Optical fibers offer the possibility of very high speed transmission. Because traffic on a ring travels in one direction, it is easy to use optical fibers as a medium of transmission. Also, since a ring is made up of nodes connected by short segments of transmission medium, there is a possibility of mixing the types used for different parts of the network. Thus, a manufacturing company's network could use copper cables in the office area and optical fibers in the factory areas, where electrical interference may be a problem.

Disadvantages of the Ring Network

1. **Node failure causes network failure:** the transmission of data on a ring goes through every connected node on the ring before returning to the sender. If one node fails to pass data through itself, the entire network has failed and no traffic can flow until the defective node has been removed from the ring.

2. **Difficult to diagnose faults:** The fact that failure of one node will affect all other has serious implications for fault diagnosis. It may be necessary to examine a series of adjacent nodes to determine the faulty one. This operation may also require diagnostic facilities to be built into each node.

3. **Network reconfiguration is difficult:** The all or nothing nature of the ring topology can cause problems when one decides to extend or modify the geographical scope of the network. It is not possible to shut down a small section of the ring while keeping the majority of it working normally.

4. **Topology affects the access protocol:** Each node on a ring has a responsibility to pass on data that it receives. This means that the access protocol must take this into account. Before a node can transmit its own data, it must ensure that the medium is available for use.

The Bus Topology

In this case all the server/nodes share a common bus of connecting cables. Every computer can communicate directly with every other computer or device in the network. Each node is given an address.

To access a particular, a user just needs to know its address. This topology is frequently used with local area networks. Going through a hierarchy of nodes is not necessary.

Advantages of the Bus Network

1. **Short cable length and simple wiring layout:** Because there is a single common data path connecting all nodes, the bus topology allows a very short cable length to

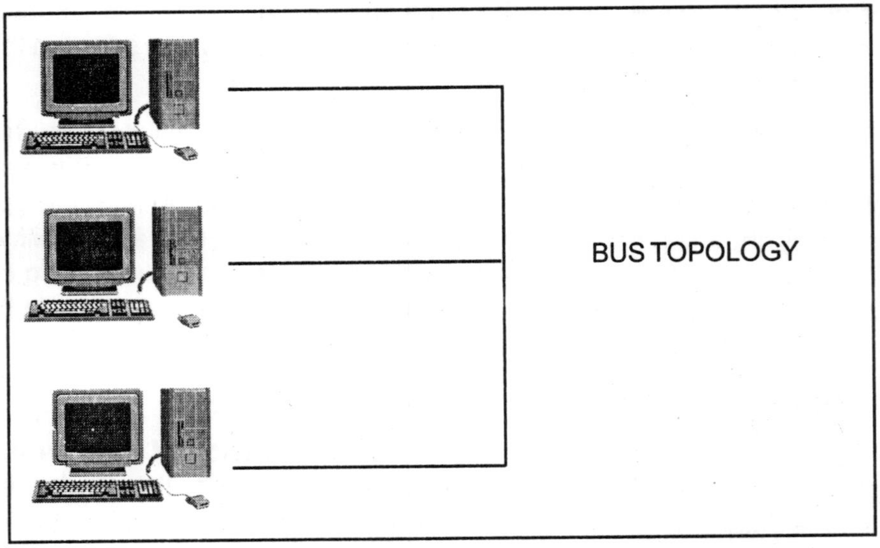

be used. This decreases the installation cost and also leads to a simple, easy to maintain, wiring layout.

2. **Resilient architecture:** The bus architecture has an inherent simplicity that makes it very reliable from a hardware point of view. There is a single cable through which all data passes and to which all nodes are connected.

3. **East to extend:** Additional nodes can be connected to an existing bus network at any point along its length. More extensive additions can be achieved by adding extra segments connected by a type of signal amplifier known as a repeater.

Disadvantages of the Bus Network

1. **Fault diagnosis is difficult:** Although the simplicity of the bus topology means that there is very little that can go wrong, fault detention is not a simple matter. In most LANs based on a bus, control of the network is not centralized in any particular node. This means that detection of a fault may be performed from many points in the network.

2. **Fault isolation is difficult:** In the star topology, a defective node can easily be isolated from the network by removing its connection at the center. If a node is faulty on a bus, it must be rectified at the point where the node is connected to the network. Once the fault has been located the node can simply be removed. In the case where the fault is the network medium itself, an entire segment of the bus must be disconnected.

3. **Repeater configuration:** When a bus-type network has its backbone extended using repeaters, reconfiguration may be necessary. This may involve tailoring cable lengths, adjusting terminators, etc.

4. **Nodes must be intelligent:** Each node on the network is directly connected to the

central bus. This means that some way of deciding who can use the network at any given time must be performed in each node. It tends to increase the cost of the nodes irrespective of whether this is performed in hardware of software

The Star Topology

In this case all the computers and the main server form a star like shape. All the computers are connected to a single main host. All communication first goes through the centralized computer allowing it to control the operation, work load, and resource allocation of the other computers in the network. For example, a bank with branch offices would typically use a star network to control and coordinate those branches. The advantage is relative simplicity, but a problem exists with the single-point vulnerability of the network. If the central computer breaks down, none of the other computers can communicate with each other.

Advantages of the Star Network

1. **Ease of service:** The star topology has a number of concentration points, i.e. at the central node or at intermediate wiring closets. These provide easy access for service of reconfiguration of the network.
2. **One device per connection:** Connection points in any network are inherently prone to failure. In the star topology, failure of a single connection typically involves disconnecting one node from an otherwise fully functional network.
3. **Centralized control/ problem diagnosis:** The fact that the central node is connected directly to every other node in the network means that faults are easily detected and isolated. It is a simple matter to disconnect failing nodes from the system.
4. **Simple access protocols:** Any given connection is a star network involves only the central node and one peripheral node. In this situation, contention for who has control

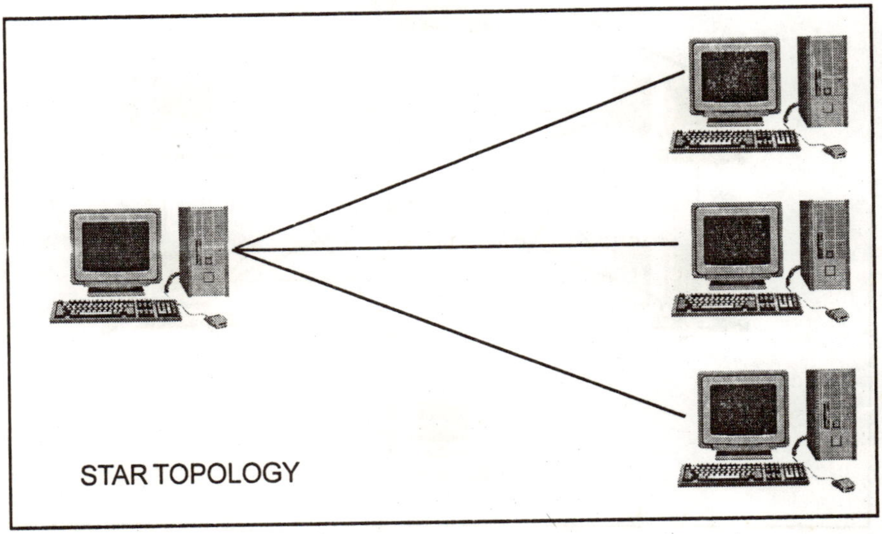

of the medium for transmission purposes is easily solved. Thus in a star network, access protocols are very simple.

Disadvantages of the Star Network

1. **Long cable length:** Because each node is directly connected to the center, the star topology necessitates a large quantity of cable. While the cost of the cable is often small, congestion in cable ducts and maintenance and installation problems can increase costs considerably.
2. **Difficult to expand:** The addition of a new node to a star network involves a connection all the way to the central node. Expansion is usually catered for by providing large numbers of redundant cables during the initial wiring. However, problems can arise if a longer cable length is needed or an unanticipated concentration of nodes is required.
3. **Central node dependency:** If the central node in a star network fails, the entire network is rendered inoperable. This introduces heavy reliability and redundancy constraints on this node.

Mesh Topology

A network topology featuring a direct path between two nodes. The backbone of this topology looks like this, where most major cities have a direct connection to most major cities.

Advantages and Disadvantages of the Mesh Network

- **Units affected by media failure:** Mesh topologies resist media failure better than

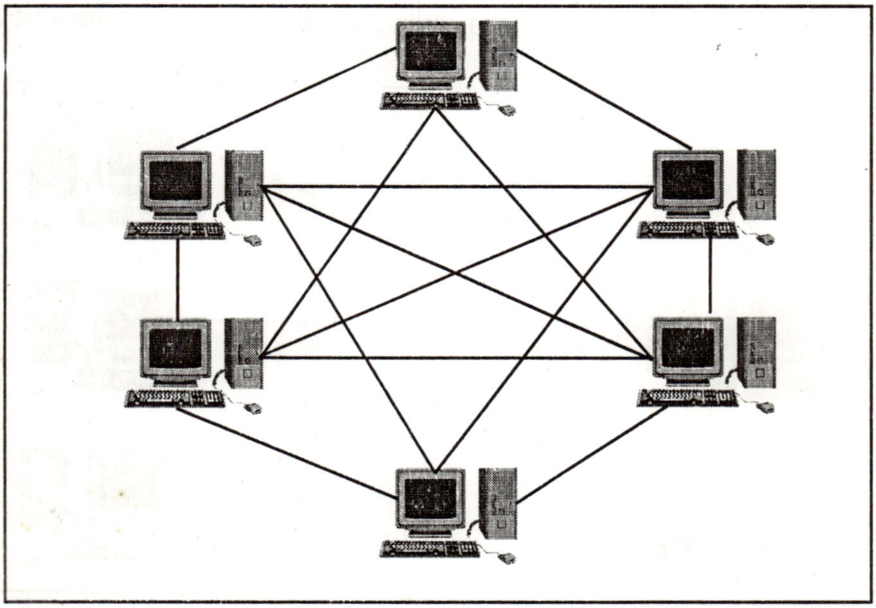

other topologies. Implementations that include more than two devices will always have multiple paths to send signals from one device to another. If one path fails, the transmission signals can be routed around the failed link. Theoretically, no units are affected by media failure. However, if all paths normally use the maximum capacity of each link, some performance degradation will occur are signals are routed around a failed link.

- **Ease of installation:** Mesh networks are relatively difficult to install because each device must be linked directly to all other devices. As the number of devices increases, the difficulty of installation increases geometrically.
- **Ease of troubleshooting:** Mesh topologies are easy to troubleshoot because each medium link is independent of all others. You can easily identify faults and can isolate the affected link.
- **Ease of reconfiguration:** Mesh topologies are difficult to reconfigure for the same reasons that they are difficult to install.

Hybrid Topology

A combination of two or more network topologies. The resultant is a hybrid network. Although the backbone is mostly a mesh network, each local loop is a star network with the central office at each hub.

Advantages of the Hybrid Network

1. **Fault diagnoses and isolation:** The presence of concentration points in the network greatly eases fault diagnosis. If a fault is detected on the network, the initial problems to find out which concentration point in the ring is to blame. The fact that this ring is quite small in relation to the total size of the network makes this problem more manageable. The offending concentration point can be isolated easily, leaving the network in a fully functional state while further fault diagnosis is carried out.
2. **Ease of expansion:** The modular construction of a star-ring network means that new sections may be easily added. When designing the network originally, each concentration can have extra, unused lobes which can be called upon later, if needed. The next growth step involved adding a new concentration point and wiring it into the ring.
3. **Cabling:** The concentration points in a star-ring are connected via a single cable. This simplifies wiring between areas in an installation and cuts down on the congestion of cable ducts. Also, the wiring practices involved are very similar to that of telephone system installation. These techniques are well understood by building engineers and lend themselves well to the prewiring of buildings.

Disadvantages of the Hybrid Network

1. **Intelligent concentration points required:** Depending on the implementation used,

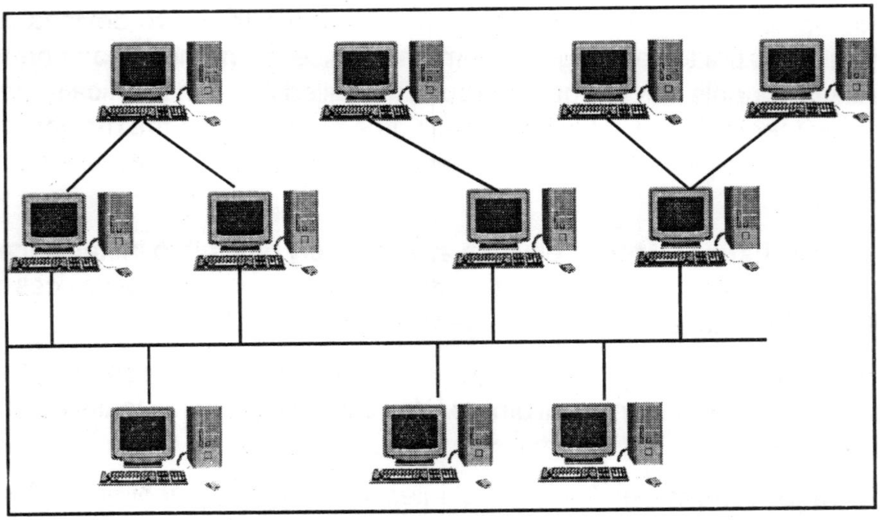

the concentration points may need to have built in intelligence/processing ability. This will be necessary if it is to assist in network fault diagnosis, node isolation or conversion from one form of transmission medium to another.

2. **Cabling:** The intercloset cabling in a star ring is critical to its operation. This may mean that redundant cabling in the form of one or more back up rings may be necessary to meet reliability requirements. The largest section of the network (i.e. between the concentration points and the nodes) is laid out in a star. This means that a considerable amount of cable may be required.

Tree Topology

From a purely topological viewpoint, this network resembles a interconnection of star networks. Individual peripheral nodes must transmit to and receive from one other node only, toward a central node. An advantage of a tree structure is that functional groupings can be created

For example, one branch could contain all the general ledger terminals, another branch all the accounts receivable terminals, and so on. If one branch stops functioning, the other branches in a tree network are not affected. However, data movement through this network can be slow.

Advantages of the Tree Network

1. **Easy to extend:** Because the tree is of its very nature, divided into subunits, it is easier to add new nodes or branches to it.

2. **Fault isolation:** It is possible to disconnect whole branches of the network from the main structure. This makes it easier to isolate a defective node.

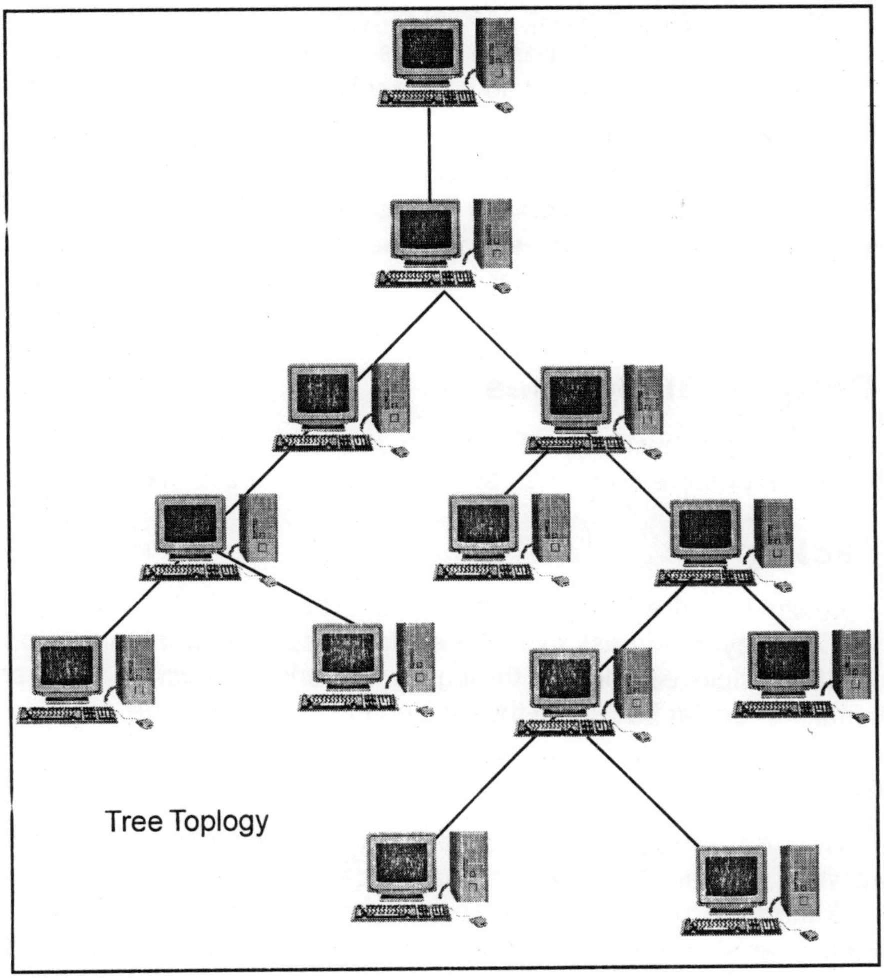

Disadvantages of the Tree Network

1. **Dependant on the root:** If the "headend" device fails to operate, the entire network is rendered inoperable. In this respect, the tree suffers from the same reliability problems as the star.

Applications of Networking

In business, government organizations, universities and many other organizations networks of all types of computers provide tremendous benefits. Four of the most compelling benefits are as follows:

Simultaneous Access

In business computing, most office workers use the same software package. With a network, business can save a lot by purchasing special network versions of the most commonly used software rather than buying separate copies for each machine. When employees need to use the software, they simply load it from a shared storage device into their own desktop computer.

Since a single network copy of the software can serve the needs of large number of users simultaneously, all the employees also save the storage space that the software program would occupy on his computer's disk drive. The same is true of data that multiple employees need access to at the same time. Another major area of computer network advantage is access to remote databases.

Shared Peripheral Devices

The best incentive for small businesses from computers networking is sharing of peripheral devices, especially expensive ones such as laser printer and scanners.

Easier Backup

In business, data can be extremely valuable, so making sure that employees backup their data is critical. One way to address this problem is to keep all valuable data on a shared storage device that employees access through a network. That way, one person can be charged with making regular backup of the data on the shared storage device.

Electronic Mail

Computer networking has helped in increasing the speed of the message transfer tremendously. With the help of e-mail, messages can be transferred through computer network within a short span of time. User can send written message without worrying about whether the other user is currently using his/her computer or not. Over centralized networks, the message is delivered almost instantaneously. E-mail cross time zones, can reach many people with the same message, reduces the paper flood and does not interrupt meetings the way a ringing phone does.

Voice Mail

It releases workers from the tyranny of the telephone. In it, if the person being called does not answer, the called is given instructions to dictate a message to the system. The voice mail computer system stores the message in the recipient's Voice mailbox. Later when the recipient dials the mailbox, the system delivers the message. A voice mail system translates the word of a message into digital impulses, which it then stores on disk, just as any other data. Later this message is reconverted to audio form.

The Ethernet Protocol

Ethernet is the most popular protocol used for LAN communications. In essence it uses a digital 'packet' that can contain any other digital information. Every computer that uses this protocol contains an Ethernet Network Interface Card (NIC) that has a unique address code embedded into a microchip on the NIC. This address is used by the protocol to identify each individual computer. This allows every electronic packet that is sent from one machine to another to contain the destination address for which the packet is intended.

Every computer on the network 'listens' for packets that contain its own address. When a packet is placed on a network, that packet is broadcast to and received by every other computer on the network but only the computer which corresponds to the destination address is allowed to claim that packet and receive the digital information contained within it. Only a single packet is allowed onto the network at any one time, but the process operates at such a high speed that effectively the packet is delivered to the destination within milliseconds, allowing the next packet access to the network almost immediately.

The Ethernet protocol also provides a means of preventing two computers from trying to place packets onto the network at the same time. When a NIC tries to place a packet onto the network, it first 'listens' to see if there is already a packet being transmitted to and from other machines, If so, then it is forced to wait for a random amount of time (milliseconds), before trying again. This continues until a 'gap' is found and then the packet can be successfully transmitted onto the network. The Ethernet protocol provides a means of delivering data from any PC on the network to any other on the same network at a theoretical rate of up to 10 Mega bits per second. Ethernet can also be used to connect remotely located PCs, but this requires special communications links to be set up over specialised equipment.

Fast Ethernet

It is a new standard of the Ethernet protocol, based on the existing 10 Mhz standard, but designed to operate at the much faster data rate of 100 Mhz. Mhz stands for megahertz or a million cycles per second and represents the operating frequency of the protocol. The terms 'Mhz' and 'Mega bits per second' are often used interchangeably, but this is only true where one cycle represents one bit (a bit being a unit of data). For many protocols, this direct relationship holds true, but it is not always the case and so the terms should be used with caution.

The TCP/IP Protocol

TCP/IP is actually two protocols. These two protocols are almost invariably use together, hence the term TCP/IP has come to be accepted as describing a single system. We will be using this assumption here. TCP/IP is the networks protocol that is used throughout the Internet. It was originally developed in American academic institutions as a means of communicating between university computer systems, first locally and then nationally across America and internationally between universities, that formed the basis of what is now know as the Internet.

It is the capability for being used over existing telephone systems that gives TCP/IP (and hence the Internet) its enormous potential for worldwide data communication. Ethernet is designed to run over relatively short distances at a very high data rate, but the physical limitations of the public phone systems mean that this high data rate cannot normally be sustained, except perhaps over the larger truck routes between countries and major cities.

TCP/IP however is independent of the various data rates associated with different communication media and so can be used over both very slow and very high speed systems. Like Ethernet, the TCP/IP protocol uses an addressing system to determine the intended destinations for a data packet, but unlike Ethernet TCP/IP also includes a source address in the data packet. This system of addresses is used to route the data packet across the Internet, very much like the address on a envelope is used to route a letter across the various national postal systems.

However, unlike Ethernet, each packet is not broadcast cross the entire network, but is routed individually using the addressing system to a single destination. This system is known as 'packet switching'.

Packet Switching

When one computer communicates with another using the TCP/IP protocol, it breaks the information it needs to send into 'chunks' small enough for the TCP/IP packet to be handle and then attaches a destination address and a source address. The packet is then sent out across the Internet, containing all of the information it needs to navigate its way to a remote destination. It is a feature of the Internet that each individual packet can then take one of many different routes via the thousands of intermediate computer systems across the world to reach its final destination.

Each computer along the way reads the destination address of he packet and routes it according to certain sets of rules to the next computer system on the Internet. This fragmenting of information and use of many alternative routes means that the receiving computer may well receive the packets in a different order to that in which they were sent. It must therefore have some means of making sure that it reads the incoming packets in the correct order.

The job of the 'TCP' part of TCP/IP is to ensure that each packet reaches its destination intact and that the packets are numbered effectively so that the receiving computer can put the incoming packets back into the correct order. It is the 'IP' part TCP/IP that looks after the addressing. Because TCP/IP packets contain a source address as well as a destination address, the receiving computer system also has a way or replying automatically to the sender by simply reading the source address and then generating another TCP/IP packet using this source address as the destination address for the new packet.

Another feature that is very useful part of the TCP/IP protocol is that because each packet is essentially self-sufficient in its journey across the Internet, many packets from different sources can share a single communication channel, allowing perhaps hundreds of thousands of channels to share a single cable at the same time.

Basic Elements in Networking

All networks require the following three elements:

1. **Network Services**: At least two individuals who have something to share.
2. **Transmission Media**: A method or pathway for contacting each other.
3. **Protocols**: Rules so that two or more individuals can communicate.

Network Services

Network services are provided by numerous combinations of computer hardware and software. Depending upon the task, network services require data, input/output resources and processing power to accomplish their goals.

In the computer industry, the following 3 types of service providers and requestor are as follows:

Servers: Servers are only allowed to provide services.

Clients: Clients are only allowed to request services from others.

Peers: Peers may do both concurrently.

Computer networks are often classified as one of the following two types:

Peer-to-peer

Server-centric

Peer-to-Peer Networks

This type of networks allow any entity to both request and provide network services. Peer-to-peer network software is designed so that peers perform the same or similar functions for each other.

Server-Centric Networks

This network involves strictly defined roles. By definition, a server-centric network places restrictions upon which entity may make requests or service them. Currently, the most popular personal computer networks are server-centric.

Transmission Media

It is the pathway by which networked entities use to contact each other. Computer transmission media includes cable and wireless technologies that allow networked devices to contact each other. Transmission media cannot guarantee that other network devices will understand a message. It can, however, guarantee a message delivery path.

Protocols

A protocol can be one rule or a complete set of rules and standards that allow different devices to hold conversations. For example, human communication would be impossible without language, grammar and cultural rules.

The following is an example of set of rules and standards in which network service requesters and service providers can communicate:

- How is the transmission media physically set up?
- How do network entities contact one another?
- How do network entities know how much data can be transmitted?
- How are network entities guaranteed that a message has been received correctly?
- How is a message passed to the intended recipient(s)?
- How are bits transmitted on the media?
- How do network entities, with disparate languages, communicate?
- How do network entities know when to transmit data?

When you formally agree that you will both use the same language in future communications, you have established a communication protocol.

Value Added Networks

Another type of network is the value added network. This is an established data communication network that owns a leases communication facilities and computers to manage communication. The facilities may include microwave antennas and communication satellites. The owners design and maintain the value added network. They then rent the network simultaneously to many subscribers, who link their own equipment tot he facilities. Using value added network saves organizations the time and cost of designing and maintaining their own networks. The concept of value added common carriers was important in the development of computer networking.

A value added carrier leases communications facilities from conventional common carriers and uses these in conjunction with computers to build a network which offers new types of communications services and tariffs. These are called Value Added Networks (VANs). Graphnet offered services for delivery of documents, often in facsimile form. Telenet built a network for the interconnection of data processing machines, like the ARPA network although the software and hardware mechanisms eventually became substantially different from ARPANET. Telnet delivers packets of data between computers or terminals in a fraction of a second and charges by the packet.

TYMNET offering similar services evolved from a private time sharing network to a value added common carrier. In 1971 the United States Office of Telecommunications Policy recommended a policy of first tier second tier common carriers.

The first tier carriers construct and own telecommunications links and lease channels to their customer. They typically own 50% to 100% of the channel miles in service and lease the remainder from another carrier. The second tier carriers are the value added carriers. They add equipment including multiplexers and computers, to channels leased from first tier carriers and sell services that they create in this way, including message delivery services, computer networks and possibly information retrieval services and computer timesharing devices. It seems likely that second markets will develop in may telecommunications areas. The second tier carrier may minimize investment in terminals by letting the customer provide these. Legislation in favour of second tier carriers has increased the diversity and competitiveness of the telecommunications industry in those countries where it has been passed.

In most countries, such legislation does not yet exist. Telecommunication systems use computer in different ways. Some use them for switching; some for sorting messages which are transmitted; some for processing the data transmitted. At one extreme the computer merely switches the circuits; at the other the circuits are merely linked into a data processing system. The term "computer utility" became used for describing public access to computer networks and in 1966 the United States Federal Communications Commission (FCC) initiated a lengthy inquiry to determine whether public computing services should be regulated.

Hybrid communication services must be completely tariffed and regulated by the FCC. Common carriers may not offer data processing services (hybrid or otherwise) except through a separate corporation with separate facilities, officers and accounting. AT&T has been excluded from offering any such unregulated services under an earlier consent decree. Most countries do not have these legislative problems because the state telecommunications authority rigorously enforces its absolute monopoly over all telecommunications, no matter how bad its service may be.

Public Networks

During the mid 1970's the need for building a public data network was realised by the telecommunication administration of various countries, with two specified objectives. One was to provide better services to the computer community and the other was to earn revenue which was enormous. This is the revenue from the switches, concentrators, multiplexers polling equipment, line control equipment, etc., - the various devices used in the interconnection of machines.

Common carriers operate (this term includes the telecommunication administrations of countries with government-controlled telecommunications – the PTT's) the equipment for switching and routing telephone calls; it seemed natural that they should operate the new equipment for switching routing data.

One computers were used for switching the desire grew to use them for other functions also. AT&T developed its plans for ACS (Advanced Communications Service) in which the nodes would not only switch data but provide a variety of functions which need processing and storage. The British Post Office created its Viewdata scheme (subsequently called Prestel) for operating public data bank accessible with television sets in homes or offices, initially via the telephone network.

Private Networks

Some networks are designed specifically for and used completely by individual organizations. They are called private networks. The communication equipment that forms the network is purchased or leased in the name of the organization. The first WAN to be designed and developed was the private network, ARPANET, a United States network. The objective was to make the interesting and unique computer facilities available in some computer centers accessible to a large community of users.

It has grown from a four-site experimental network to a nationwide communication system interconnecting more than fifty universities and research centers. A few computer networks link computer centers in multiple locations. To operate these multicorporate networks, a separate service organization is usually set up and that organization will take care of creating and operating the network. A leading example is the SWIFT electronic fund transfer network that passes financial transactions between banks. SWIFT (Society for Worldwide Interbank Financial Transactions) is a non-profit organization set up and wholly owned by the banks connected to it.

The objective of this network is to replace mail, cable and telex and work for 24 hours a day and 7 days a week. It handles over a million transactions per day. It is used to send money, messages and bank statements at high speed between banks and the transaction time is drastically reduced.

SWIFT connects about 3000 financial institutions in more than 600 countries. Citibank Corp. in New York, was the first one to opt for the system and over 40 banks in India have joined the network. The computer based terminals of these banks are hooked with SWIFT's access center in Bombay, which is maintained by CMC Ltd.

From here, messages are relayed to the overseas communication center of VSNL and then transmitted to SWIFT's international receiving centers based in London or Singapore, depending on the location of the receiver, through VSNL's GPSS services. The software needed for the operations has been supplied by SWIFT terminal services, a wholly owned subsidiary of SWIFT and the hardware is being supplied by Tata Unisys, Digital Equipment

(India) Ltd. The participating banks finance the system and a tariff structure has been built based on the message, connection charge and annual charge.

Common Network Services

The following common network services are available:

File Services

The network file services improve the efficient storage and retrieval of computer data, they are one of the primary services offered on computer networks. The following file service functions are :

- File transfer – Rapidly move files from place to place.
- File storage and data migration – Use storage hardware efficiently.
- File update synchronization – Manage multiple copies of the same file.
- File archiving – Back up critical data

File Transfer

Before computer networks were widely implemented, users physically moved storage media from computer to computer. This inefficient practice has been called "sneaker-net" (because users hand carried data from machine to machine). Organizationally, it is relatively expensive and time consuming to employ people to move computer storage media. The network file service file transfer refers to any service that saves, retrieves, or moves files for a network client. This service allows you to handle data much more efficiently.

The major advantage of Computer Networks is, file transfers can be performed with relative ease regardless of file size, distance and often even the local operating systems. This service increases the organization's efficienty, as well as it also provided access to data and information that were previously inaccessible. File services may also coordinate access rights because of the increased information access that the file transfer service provides. An organization may allow network transfer of sensitive information, but only by authorized individuals. During file transfer, network file services often use passwords to control access to systems and files. They use data encryption schemes to encode data so that it can only been read by appropriate individuals.

File Storage and Data Migration

The rapidly increasing amount of computerized data has caused the development of numerous online, nearline and offline storage devices. Hard disk drive, tape jukebox and removable storage is an example of online storage, nearline storage and offline storage respectively. Computers store data on a variety of magnetic and optic disks, diskettes and tapes.

Each storage medium exhibits characteristics that make it suitable for a specific use. Because the efficient use of each storage device requires continuous management of multiple devices, network application are well suited to control data storage activities on different storage systems. In addition, if you are working with high end equipment, such as magnetic tape banks or optical libraries, you can use the network's economy of scale to justify the equipment purchase, operation and maintenance.

Using file storage and data migration functions, all networked computers can take advantage of the data storage device that is appropriate for their access time, reliability and longevity needs. As data ages and becomes less used, it can be moved from expensive online hard disk drives to less expensive and longer life offline storage media. Moving data from one storage media or location to another is call data migration. Through data migration, you can set up file services to move files based on age, user, size or various other criteria.

File Update Synchronization

File update synchronization is a service that compares the time and date corresponding files were saved and determines which is most current. It may also keep track of who has a specific file and if intermediary changes have been made. Using this information, it automatically updates all file locations with latest version.

For examples, mobile computers are not always connected or available to the network. If you are a mobile computer user and you want access to a file that is on a network file server, you would normally save a copy of the file to your computer' shard drive. However, someone else may access and change the original file in the meantime. If that person does make changes, your copy now contains out of date information. Somehow you need to recognize when changes have occurred and take the appropriate action.

File Archiving

Many organizations create duplicate copies of important data on magnetic tape or some other offline storage media in case of emergency. This practice is called file archiving or file backup. The original file can be kept in addition to the backup copy, or it can be removed from online storage media so that the offline media contains the only copy. When file storage devices are interconnected on a network, file archiving becomes much easier. Computer operators use the network to traverse great distances, saving the organization time and money.

Print Services

These are network applications that control and manage access to printers and fax equipment. Print services accept print job request, interpret print job formats and printer configurations, manage print queues and interact with networkable printers and fax equipment for network clients.

The following are print service functions:

- Provide multiple access from limited interfaces – Reduce the number of printers your organization needs.
- Eliminate distance constraints – place printers wherever is most convenient.
- Handle simultaneous requests – Queue print jobs to reduce the time your computer spends sending a print job.
- Share specialized equipment – share specialized printers efficiently.
- Network fax service – Computerize the transmission and reception of fax images.

Providing Multiple Access from Limited Interfaces

Reducing the total number of printers can save your organization a substantial amount of money having fewer printers reduces the number of devices to buy, maintain and manage.

Most modern printer provide multiple ports or interfaces. However, the number of interfaces is finite and relatively small. Typically, only two or three computers may be directly connected to each printer. On the other hand, a network connection requires only one interface. Through this interface, many computers may send data to the printer.

Therefore, print services allow numerous clients to be serviced by a single printer. Managing access to printers, or other devices with limited interfaces, is a major use of modern computer networks.

Eliminating Distance Constraints

Printer ports are often based on cable interface specification that limit the distance between the printer and attached computers. Network cable systems and devices allow longer distances for cable specifications. Organizations can use the network to place printers in strategic locations throughout a building or campus.

Handling Simultaneous Request (Queuing)

Print servers can often handle simultaneous request for print services. When two users try to send data to a printer at the same time, both applications compete for the printer's limited ability to accept and store print request. Queuing solves this bottleneck problem. A print queue is the part of the print server which captures and stores computer print jobs. Depending upon each implementation's specific features, print queues can hold, prioritize, and manage print jobs.

When printing with network printing services, your application sends print requests and data to what it believes is a printer. These requests are actually routed to a print queue. The print requests remain in the queue until the desired printer is available. Print queuing increases the efficiency of network print services by organizing the interaction between printers and their clients. In addition, because multiple clients may send data simultaneously to the print queue at full network speeds, each may complete print request rapidly and return to other tasks.

Sharing Specialized Equipment

Some printer are designed for specific use, such as high speed output, large format paper, or color printing. Specialized equipment may be expensive or may not be frequently used by end users. The economies of scale produced by networking each device with numerous clients can reduce the effective cost per user and optimize printer use.

Network Fax Service

Network fax allows users to send and receive faxes using special network hardware and software. This service is becoming increasingly popular because it reduces the time and paper handling normally involved in traditional fax transmissions. Traditional fax machines use computer modem, scanner and printer technologies to send a digital document image to remote locations. Network fax systems use the same computer technologies and computer networks to better integrate fax service with the rest of the network's print and message services.

Message Services

Message services include storing, accessing and delivering text, binary, graphic, digitized video and audio data. Message services are similar to file services. However, unlike file services, message services deal actively with the communication interactions between computer users, user applications, network applications, or documents. Instead of simply storing data files, message services transport data from point to point.

The following are the message services functions:

- Electronic Mail
- Integrated electronic mail and voice mail
- Object oriented applications
- Workgroup applications

Electronic Mail

A business depends on the efficient exchange of information between different parts of the business and between the business and the outside word. Much of this exchange has been traditiOonally carried out through paper documents, delivered by secretary, mail or messenger service. With the growing use of personal computers, a more efficient alternative has emerged, i.e., electronic mail. Electronic mail is usually used to exchange messages and data files. Each user is assigned an electronic mailbox.

Using the appropriate command, the user can scan a list of messages in the mailbox, display the contents of a particular message, send a message to another user and so forth. To send a message, it is not necessary for the recipient to be present at the computer. The message resides in the mailbox until it is read. The sender may restrict delivery of the message to authorized readers by using a password. That is, the recipient must "sign" for the message by typing his or her identifying password. Many other features of standard mail delivery are implemented in electronic mail systems.

For example, mail can be forwarded, stored for delayed delivery and sent to anyone at a particular phone number. In addition, electronic mail systems implement many new features. An electronic mail system can deliver copies of a message to all individuals listed in a certain file. It also allow merging of standard data (from a data file) with a particular message. Now-a-days, several companies have started subscription to electronic mail services. These services are accessed through a modem and allow users to communicate with other subscribers to the service.

The service may also accept a message and transmit it to its destination city. There the message is printed out and delivered with the next day's mail. This technique can be used to communicate with people who are not subscribers to the network.

Integrated Electronic Mail and Voice Mail

Message services that integrate E-Mail and voice mail are also being developed. Voice mail is a service offered by specialized computer hardware and software that answers telephone calls and records audio messaged. Because voice mail systems are simply specialized computers, thy can be incorporated into computer networks. Computer network and voice mail vendors are currently developing ways to make voice mail system cooperate on computer networks. Eventually, user could retrieve messages from whatever type of device is convenient.

Object Oriented Applications

Object oriented application are computer programs that combine smaller applications to accomplish complex tasks. Message services often facilitate communications between objects on a computer network. Messaging application accomplish this by acting as the object's agent, so every object does not meet to contact every other object. The object simply communicates with an agent from the local messaging service. The agent then become responsible for communicating the message to the destination object.

Workgroup Applications

Message service have also been used to create a new class of applications called workgroup applications. The following are common types of workgroup applications:

Workflow management

Workflow management application intelligently forms, route notices and documents among network clients. These service providers are designed to handle multiuser distributed business processes. For example, assume that you want to convert a payroll process using workflow management. The old manual process required that employees fill out a paper based time card. The time card was then signed by a manager and sent to the payroll department. Upon receipt payroll employees entered the information from the time card, calculated the employee's pay and benefits and generated a check. At each point along the path, an auditor verified that the steps were completed correctly and that errors did not occur. In addition, all of these steps had to take place hurriedly to meet employee expectations and government regulations.

Message services are ultimately responsible for making workflow routing and delivery decisions. Workflow management can improve this process by intelligently routing electronic forms to each individual. The form can contain data provided previously by other users that is customized to represent the formats required by each individual. In addition, data can now be moved, stored, manipulated, verified and presented to each user much faster than similar manual processes.

Linked object documents

The computer industry is moving towards the linked object model for creating compound documents. Linked object documents, similar to object oriented applications, incorporate independent data objects into larger structures. For example, a single electronic document could contain text, spreadsheets, graphics, voice and video elements which are linked to other files, objects, or parts.

Although this technology is still in development, network message services may act as agents on behalf of the data objects that comprise linked object documents. Conceptually each object includes the intelligent required to pass messages between a document element and its originating application of file. A single document serves as the integrator of the various pieces.

Application Services

Application services are network services that run software for network clients. They are different from file services because they allow computers to share processing power, not just share data. The two other aspects normally associated with application services are:

Specialization of Servers

The greatest benefit of application serves is that they can employ specialized equipment to increase speed, data integrity and security. However, how much processing should be handled by a server and how much is left to the client? Application servers have more computing power than user workstations and they often use special operating systems that have been optimized to perform a specific operation.

For example, a personal computer user wants to perform a complex mathematical calculation to create a graph. Using a personal computer (PC), the calculation would take an extremely long time. To accomplish the task more rapidly, the PC sends out the math portion of the calculation to be processed by a mainframe computer. The mainframe quickly processes the request and sends back the results. The PC is only required to collect the resulting data set and generate the graph. What would normally take a very long time can now be accomplished much more rapidly.

Scalability and Growth

Network application services can also provide organizations with relatively inexpensive upgrade paths. If more computing power is required, only the network application server is upgraded. For example, assume that you use an extremely complex modeling application and that the application server software currently runs on a minicomputer.

As your company grows, the minicomputer becomes overworked and response time gets worse and worse. To improve response times you simply move the application software to a faster computer, or add another server. You can improve the processing power of your computer while leaving other client and server computer totally unaffected.

Database Services

Network database services provide server based database storage and retrieval that allow network clients to control data manipulation and presentation. A special term has been created to describe database applications that allow clients to request data from these specialized servers: client server databases.

Client server database applications divide and optimize the tasks involved in requesting and providing data. Depending upon the design goal, the client is given a portion of the tasks involved in formulating the request and processing the response, while database servers typically evaluate incoming requests and return data.

Network database provide the following services:

- Optimize the computers which store, search and retrieve database records.
- Control where data is stored geographically
- Organize data logically between organizational departments.
- Provide data security.
- Reduce database client access time.

The following aspects of network database services are:

Coordinating Distributed Data

Large organizations often segregate tasks and information between multiple departments. When data access is shared, concerns arise about who controls what data and where it should be stored. Network database services employ a tactic called distributed data to achieve seamless data sharing.

They divide control over the pieces of the database among the various departments' computer systems. The database management system is responsible for making the database appear as one logical unit while coordinating changes that occur on various computer systems.

Replication

Data from local databases may typically be retrieved much more rapidly than from remote databases. Therefore, users prefer to work on local data. However, when more than two copies of a database exist, organizations run the risk of making decisions based upon out-of-data or incorrect information. Replication creates and synchronizes multiple copies of a database over the network.

Presently, the leading database software uses two different methods to perform replication. One method uses a master database, which is the repository of all additions and changes. The database management system is responsible for making sure that the changes recorded in the master are sent to all copies of the database. The second method gives several local databases responsibility for recording adds and changes. In addition, the local portion of the management system must then coordinate adds and changes with all the other copies.

3

Designing the Network

Introduction

Given the recent surge in networking, it might be possible to believe that you could build a network simply by purchasing the parts and following the instructions that explain how to insert tab A into slot B and so forth. It is possible to purchase the parts and assemble them into a network.

However, if you are working with a business or organizational network, and you want to get started on the right foot, it is necessary to approach the various sets of instructions you will receive, with products, in books, advice from friends, etc.

Identifying the Uses of Your Network

Every network is different. Just as every human being is different. Once created a network grows its own way. No matter what your organization does, its network has to accomplish only one task to be considered successful. It has to ensure that what your organization does, it can do better, faster, more efficiently, and more reliably with the assistance of a network.

If the network does not work do that, it will be a failure, regardless of the quantity of premium technology and quality of service. Keep this is mind as you progress, it is the single most important fact here.

The network is not about technology, no matter how much a techo-fanatic may want it to be. Networks are about getting things done, primarily by people who could not care less whether they do their work on a network or not.

Deciding What Happens at Which Computer

The next step in the network-design process seems obvious. This is knowing which applications and tasks have to preformed at each of the computers on your network. There can be various options under it. Some of them are:

Many-User Computer

Computers used by many users can be built minimally or with all the bells and whistles As with any other system, the amount of power and features depends on the application.

Single-User Computers

It generally occurs in offices. Whether an office is physical or virtual, an increasing number of office workers use computers on a day-to-day basis. This shift in computer has created a new class of office workers called knowledge workers because their currency is dealing with information and formatting, managing, and analyzing data.

Given the increasing focus on high-tech jobs and high-tech workforces, it is easy to lose sight of the fact that knowledge workers are not a homogeneous mass.

Depending on the nature of their jobs, they tend to require higher-end computers to begin with, but they also have widely varying connectivity requirements. For example, some workers may be able to leave their work behind at the end of the day and require no remote access; other users may require two or more computers to be able to do their jobs.

Naturally, this is a rightsizing issue, if you have to provide more than one computer for some users, it is going to affect your capacity planning to a great degree.

Determining the Degree of Centralization

There are times to centralize administration and security, and there are times not to. There are times when it is worthwhile to go the whole nine yards toward establishing a central administrative authority, and times when the return from doing so is not worth the effort or expense. When you are designing a network, you must determine whether or not you want the ability to administer your network from a central point.

Clearly, you would not necessarily want to administer every system if your network consists of only a few computers (less than 10 or so) in the same location. The cost of network management software, that can handle configuration management and software distribution, among other tasks, is altogether too high to justify on a small, local network.

On the other hand, even for a small network, you may want to find some way of centralizing some functions such as file services, security, and backup.

Client/server networks, by contrast, are secure. Their files are usually stored in a central location and backed up on a regular basis. User tends to be controllable. As a result, there are myriad upsides of even basic centralization.

1. Easier access to files
2. Stronger security
3. Easier backup
4. Easier configuration management and standardization of workstations.

Easier access to files

Files stored across multiple workstations can present a problem for network users. If the user has to put together a contract, he or she might have to find a contract file stored on server's machine. To centralize access to files, you have to build a file server, or a server dedicated to sharing its disk space with a collection of users for file storage.

Typically, a file server requires a powerful processor, a lot of memory, and as much disk space as you can afford.

Stronger Security

File servers usually have some security built in so that they can ensure that access to files is limited to those users who should have access to them.

Typically, file server security for PC-based operating systems follow some fairly simple rules:

1. Security inheritance works similarly to financial inheritance; what a parent has can by a child unless it is blocked by third parties. In security a user gets access to a particular directory. Whatever access a user has to this directory is inherited by any and all subdirectories of this directory. Inheritance is a useful tool to ensure that a user has as much access as he or she requires to a given part of the server's disk.
2. In general, uses are limited to 3 levels of access to a given file or directory on a file server:

   No Access, which often means that users cannot even see the file or directory.

   Read-only Access, which means that users can view the contents of a file or directory but cannot modify it.

   Read-write Access, which means that a user has the access rights to view and modify files and directories.

Easier Backup

If all the network user's files are stored on a centralized server, they can be backed up simply by duplicating the server's hard drive to tape. Assuming that your network has 50 user workstations. If all the users store their files on their workstations, you will have to back up all or part of their hard drives to ensure that no data is lost if a system crashes.

Further suppose that each user has 25 megabytes of files on their workstation's hard drives. Backing up this quantity of files across the network for this many users could take 10 or 12 hours and be a nightmare to manage.

On the other hand backing up to a server's drive with an attached tape drive can take as little as an hour or so. Clearly, backing up files from a single server to a tape drive takes less time is more controllable.

Easier Configuration Management

It is an art of using a central console to ensure that user workstations have the correct hardware and software installed, and that the software and hardware are set up according to consensus and preset standards. Its software is however, little complex. It is usually composed of a highly complex database with a proprietary front end that allows a network administrator to view and modify the configurations workstations.

Most management software requires that each system have an agent installed on the workstation, often, agents can be installed automatically as a user logs on the network.

Drawing the Network

By this time you have gained knowledge about:

- ☐ The purpose of the network
- ☐ The specifies of the network's use
- ☐ The quantity of both users and computers
- ☐ Whether or not the network will be centralised or decentralised
- ☐ The network topology you plant to use

Drawing the Logical Diagram

The first drawing you make is the logical diagram. It details the applications that have to run on workstations have to be able to access.

1. Start by drawing a workstation for each type of user (for example, one warehouse floor computer, one analyst's computer, one accounting computer, one secretary's computer and so on).

   Just make a circle for each computer; draw them in a line across the top of the whiteboard or page.

2. Below each computer, list the applications it has to run. This could include word processing, spreadsheets, emails, scheduling and more for a user's desktop computer, or a single application for a dedicated machine, such as a factory or warehouse inventory computer or an in-office computer dedicated to routing email.

3. Make a list of the resources each workstation computer will share. In general, peer networking has a lot of these shared resources (such as printers, scanners, shared modems and so on); client/server networks will have fewer shared resources. No matter whether you've elected to use client/server or peer, add these resources into your diagram.

4. If the system will participate in a network-wide security scheme, note which group of users has login access to the various pieces of the system. For example, business desktop users can log into the file server, warehouse supervisors can log into the transaction server and administrators can log in to anything anywhere. This step helps ensure that you provide the correct levels of security.

5. Add the workstation operating system to the bottom of the list. The Operating System is usually something like MS-DOS, Windows, or Macintosh. Although Unix can be used as a client, outside of academic computing centers and high-end engineering workstations, it is not common as a workstation Operating System, ensure that you have more than one computer drawn–each workstation Operating System should be shown on a separate machine.
6. Add the quantity of each type of workstation to the bottom of the list.

   Now your workstations are quantified. If you are going to build a client/server network and will require one or more servers, add the servers in at the bottom of the diagram and list the applications and resources each server provides to the network. If you are building a WAN and have to incorporate routers and so forth to hook the LANs together, draw the routers in at the side.

   Now comes the fun part. Draw lines from each workstation type to each system to which that workstation type requires access. In other words, if an accounting PC requires file storage resources on a file server, select a colored marker, draw a line between the two systems and write the name of the resource the workstation client will use.

   If a workstation has a shared printer, ensure that other systems that have to use it are connected to it using lines of a different color than the first.

   If a router provides connectivity between the network and the workstations, but must first route data through a server, draw that full path as well in yet another color.

Drawing the Physical Network Diagram

Drawing the physical network really isn't as hard as it sounds. If you already know which clients have to be connected to specific resources and which topology you'll be using, you're halfway there,

1. Start by drawing the physical center of your network. If you're using a star configuration (such as Ethernet, Token Ring or FDDI), the center of your network is the concentrator: a hub, MAU or switch of some sort. If your network needs only one hub, draw a box and label it as the hub.
2. Draw as many boxes as you will have shared media hubs. (Keep in mind that hubs are measured by the number of ports they have; an 8-port hub supports eight workstations, 16 ports support 16 workstations, and so forth).

   For performance reasons, it's a good idea to divide the network into single hubs with no more than 16 ports per segment. Connect lines between the switch and the segments; each of these lines represents a crossover cable, or a specially made cable that can be used to connect concentrators together.
3. Draw the servers and mark them as connected directly to the switch. A server

connected directly to a switch offers compelling advantages in terms of performance at the workstation because the server has a direct connection to the port to which the workstation is connected.

This holds true even if a workstation is connected through a hub connected to a switch port; the collision domain of individual hubs are usually fairly small, so there isn't much competition for bandwidth.

4. Refer to the drawing of the logical network and do some analysis. Look at which workstations require access to which servers and try to group them together.
5. Once you analyze the relative bandwidth requirements of your users, you're ready to start figuring out which class of user has to connect to which device.

Take the time to think about this. If users don't have sufficient bandwidth initially, they will have network problems and consequently lose faith in the network. It's important to roll out systems that work for the users, otherwise the network has no credibility.

Writing Specification & Getting Other's Input

Once you've gotten this far, you have enough data to write a document that includes the following:

- ☐ The organisational purpose of the network
- ☐ The specifics of the network's use
- ☐ The quantity of both users and computers
- ☐ Whether or not the network will be centralized or decentralized
- ☐ The network topology you plan to use

You also have a pair of diagrams that portray the logical and physical connections required by network. Pat yourself on the back – you deserve it.

You've created the basis for an initial specification document, which enumerates all the preceding points and includes the diagrams.

Writing the Specification Document

Now is the time to actually write your specification for the network. The specification document should take into account all the points in the preceding section and list, quite specifically, the various users of the network. Specifications do not have to be long, but they must be complete and clear; as English teachers are prone to say, "It should be as long as it needs to be – but no longer."

Specifying Hardware

Until this point, the network-planning process has dealt entirely with use and software application issues. At this point, you should know what the network needs to do, but you haven't begun looking at hardware products ... at least, not specifically.

Selecting Hardware

Networking hardware typically comes in two configurations: the latest and greatest hub/switch/chasis that costs. If the network you are building is small and not slated to expand, the cheaper is acceptable; it will provide basic connectivity and adequate performance.

If your network is expanding, try to get as much capacity as possible because doing so buys you breathing space. Because networking technology changes so rapidly, purchasing excess capacity is often the only way to get a full, useful life span out of equipment.

It's not a terribly platable decision to make, but unfortunately it's the dirty little secret of networking hardware capacity planning.

The following list provides a baseline for the physical part of your network. This list doesn't provide specific recommendations because hardware changes so rapidly. But it does tell you the features you're like to find useful.

Network Interface Cards

For each computer, you need at least one network card. NICs can cost as little as Rs.2000 or as much as Rs.15000. Make certain that your network cards are the correct topology; even through Token-Ring cards have the same network-cable connector as Ethernet 10BASE-T cards, Ethernet cards won't work on Token-Ring networks and vice versa.

Concentrators (MAUs, hubs and switches)

Once you know how many computers will be on your network, you know how many ports you need. Once you know how many ports you require, it's a matter of determining whether they will be switched or shared media, as detailed (in the abstract) in the specification you've already created.

Wiring

If you're using a star-configuration network, you'll have to run cables from the wiring closet in which the hubs are stored to each workstation's location. Ensure that you use at least Category 5 or better twisted-pair wire; even at twice the price of the lower cable certifications such as Category 3, it's cheap because it has a longer useful life span.

If you're using a bus-configuration network, you'll have to run coaxial cable serially between workstations. If you decide to install the cable yourself, remember to handle it gently, regardless of whether it's coax or twisted pair.

Treating the wire gently (that is, not crimping or breaking it) helps ensure that you'll get a better connection.

A better solution, if your organisation has the finances, is to hire someone who runs cable for a living. Electricians are often smaller cable installers because they run so many cables through walls and other inaccessible locations.

Workstation computers

Once you have specified your network cards, hubs and cables, you're ready to spec out your computers. Refer to the specification you wrote to determine which users need powerful workstations and which ones can use lower-end systems and specify them. Because hardware changes so rapidly, it's pointless to create a fixed specification here, but as of 2001, the fastest chips are reaching 1 gigahertz speeds, so workstations in the 600 to 850 Mhz range are fine for now.

Don't consider this recommendation to be a standard; see what the market is offering. What constitutes a powerful PC changes incredibly fast, so do research to find out what's currently available in the market and that too at a reasonable price.

Server computers

By the same token, overbuild your servers. Get as much power a machine as you can afford and add as much memory as possible. No matter what your application, the power and memory you provide will be used in six months or less and will be tight in a year or so.

Figure out your server's disk-space requirements (a good minimum is 100 Mb per user; more is always better) and then double it if possible. Don't worry; the disk space will be used – probably sooner than you expect.

Management features

When you purchase your hardware, ensure that it can support the SNMP or RMON network-management standard. Even if you don't use the management features immediately, as your network grows, SNMP and RMON capability can extend the useful life of a piece of equipment by ensuring that it can be managed as part of a greater network.

Other features

Likewise, try to find working hardware that can support advanced features like VLANs. Having the capability is crucial because it ensures that you have options.

The more options your hardware has, the more it prevents your networking hardware from becoming quickly obsolete.

Building the Network

Once you've settled on the hardware; you're ready to begin building the network.

4

Network Architecture

ARCnet Specifications

ARCnet is an acronym for *Attached Resource Computer NETwork* , which was founded by the Datapoint Corporation. Novell uses the term RX-Net to denote its form of this architecture and TRX-Net for the Turbo version. ARCnet uses a *token-bus* packet passing scheme.

ARCnet operates at 2.5 Mbps throughput and can be connected using RG-62 A/U coax cable or unshielded twisted pair (UTP) wiring. Although ARCnet can support up to 255 node numbers on a single network, systems of this size are not practical.

Typical ARCnet coax cable specifications:

- RG-62 A/U, solid conductor, CL2, 90%+ braided shield, PVC jacket, nominal 93 ohm impedance, 15.5 nominal capacitance/ft.
- RG-62 A/U, solid conductor, CL2P, 90%+ braided shield, plenum jacket, nominall 93 ohm impedance, 12.5 nominal capacitance/ft.

ARCnet was one of the topologies used early on in networking and is rarely used as the topology of choice in current LAN environments. ARCnet, however, still is a solid, functional and cost-effective means of networking.

The diagram next shows the components of a typical ARCnet card. This card is configured for use with twisted pair wiring. ARCnet cards for use with coax cable have a BNC (*Bayonne Neil Councelman* also commonly called *British Naval Connector*). You will find jumpers or DIP switches for setting the following characteristics:

- Node number
- Base I/O address
- Memory address
- Interrupt
- Network timeout.

The node number and network timeout are characteristics unique to ARCnet.

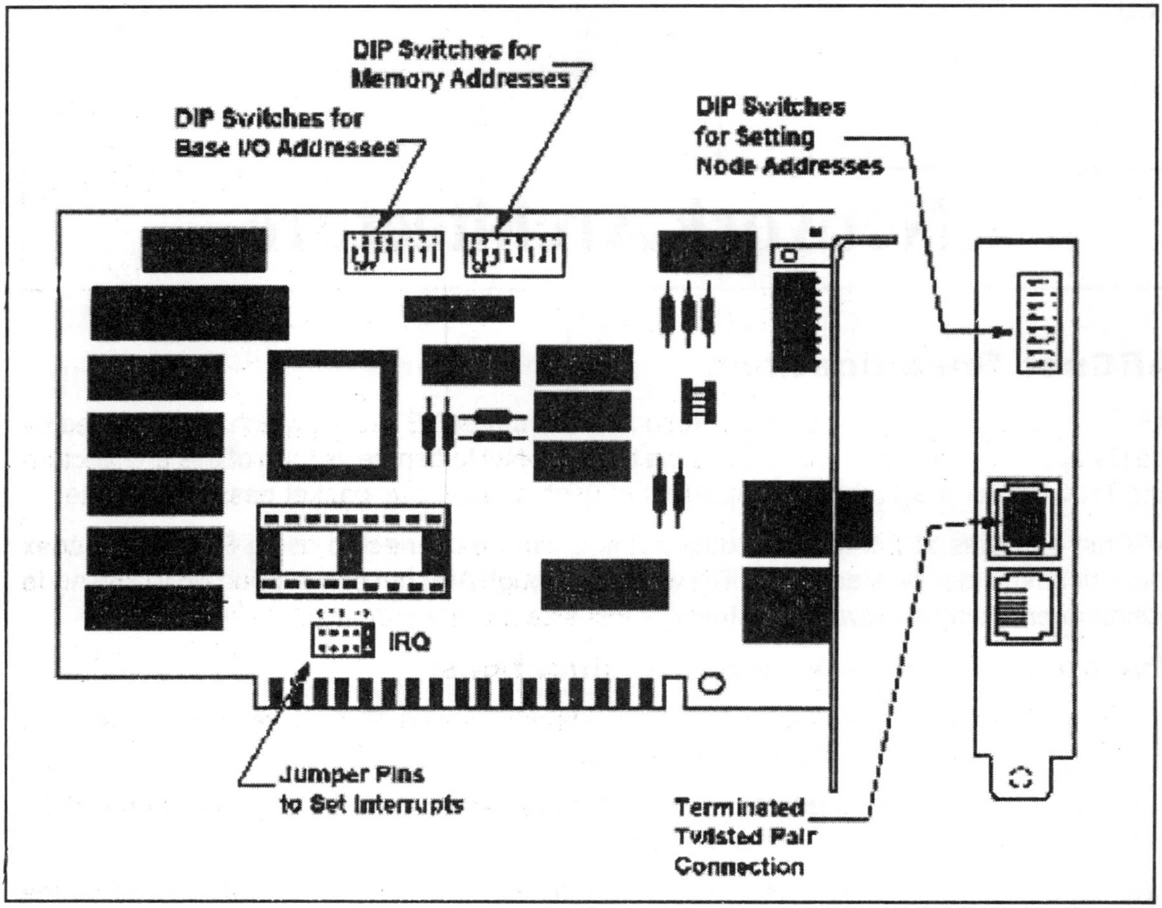

Each network interface card (NIC) on an ARCnet network is assigned a *node number.* This number must be unique on each network and in the range of 1 to 255.

ARCnet manages network access with a *token passing bus* mechanism. The token (permission to speak on the LAN) is passed from the lowest number node to higher number nodes in ascending order. Lower numbered addresses get the token before the higher numbered addresses.

Network traffic is made more efficient by assigning sequential numbers to nodes using the same order in which they are cabled. Choosing random numbers can create a situation in which a node numbered 23 can be a whole building away from the next number, 46, but in the same room as numbers 112 and 142. The token has to travel in a haphazard manner that is less effective than if you numbered the three workstations in the same office sequentially, 46, 47, and 48, and the workstation in the other building 112. With this configuration, the packet stays within the office before venturing on to other stations.

ARCnet Board Settings

Depending on the vendor design specifications of your ARCnet card, most *base I/O addresses, node addresses*, and *memory addresses* are set by DIP switches. These addresses are set using a binary mode calculation with an on or off setting in the required switch block. *Interrupt settings* are made by jumper combinations at marked locations on the network interface card (NIC). Many types and brands of ARCnet cards are on the market today. Refer to the documentation for the NIC or call the technical support group for the specific vendor of the component.

Most ARCnet cards require a *shared memory address.* Many manufacturers use the area of D000:0 to DFFF:0 as the default. Standard DOS memory is limited to the first 640 KB of a PC's memory. However, extended or expanded memory managers can be used to make memory above 640 KB available for use by DOS programs. If memory above the 640 KB line (above hex address A000:0) is used for network boards, however, the memory becomes unavailable for use by a memory manager. This makes it difficult to optimize a PC's upper memory area. If a network card requires a memory area such as D000:0-DFFF:0, the memory available for use by DOS memory managers is reduced by 64 KB. This is usually accomplished with an optional switch setting such as X=D000-DFFF to exclude the shared memory address range.

ARCnet Cabling

The ARCnet topology uses coax, twisted pair, or fiber optic cabling to connect network devices. An ARCnet network is used primarily with either coax or twisted pair cable. Most older ARCnet installations are coax and use RG-62 A/U type cable terminated with 93 Ohm terminators. Twisted pair (UTP) installations are newer and use stranded 24 or 26 gauge wire, or solid core 22, 24, or 26 gauge type cable terminated with 100 Ohm terminators. Many ARCnet networks use a mix of both coax and UTP cabling. UTP cable is simple to install and provides a reliable connection to the workstations, whereas coax provides a means to span longer distances.

Typical ARCnet installations are wired as a star. ARCnet can run off a linear bus topology using coax or twisted pair as long as the cards specifically support BUS. The most popular star-wired installations of ARCnet run off two types of hubs:

- *Passive hubs* cannot amplify signals. Each hub has four connectors. Because of the characteristics of passive hubs, unused ports must be equipped with a terminator, a connector containing a resistor that matches the ARCnet cabling characteristics. A port on a passive hub can only connect to an active device (an active hub or an NIC). Passive hubs can never be connected to passive hubs.
- *Active hubs* have active electronics that amplify signals and split them to multiple ports. The number of ports on an active hub varies with the manufacturer, but eight is typical. A port on an active hub can be connected to a port on another active device (such as another active hub or an NIC) or to a passive hub.

One of the greatest flexibilities of ARCnet is that you can integrate connections from active hubs to a linear bus connection as long as you terminate at the last connection point.

A maximum time limit of 31 microseconds is allotted for an ARCnet signal. This is also called a *time-out setting*. Signals on an ARCnet can travel up to 20,000 feet during the *31 microsecond* default time-out period. You can sometimes extend the range of an ARCnet by increasing the time out value. However, 20,000 feet is the distance at which ARCnet signals begin to seriously degrade. Extending the network beyond that distance can result in unreliable or failed communication. Therefore, the time-out parameter and cabling distance recommendations should be increased only with great caution.

The maximum cable distances between individual components in an ARCnet network are dependent on how the components are connected.

In cabling ARCnet networks with coax cable, you must follow these rules:

- Never connect a passive hub to another passive hub directly.
- Passive hubs should never be used to connect two active hubs.
- Passive hubs are only used to connect an active hub and a node.
- Unused connectors on active hubs do not need to be terminated.
- Unused connectors on passive hubs must be terminated using a 93 Ohm terminator.

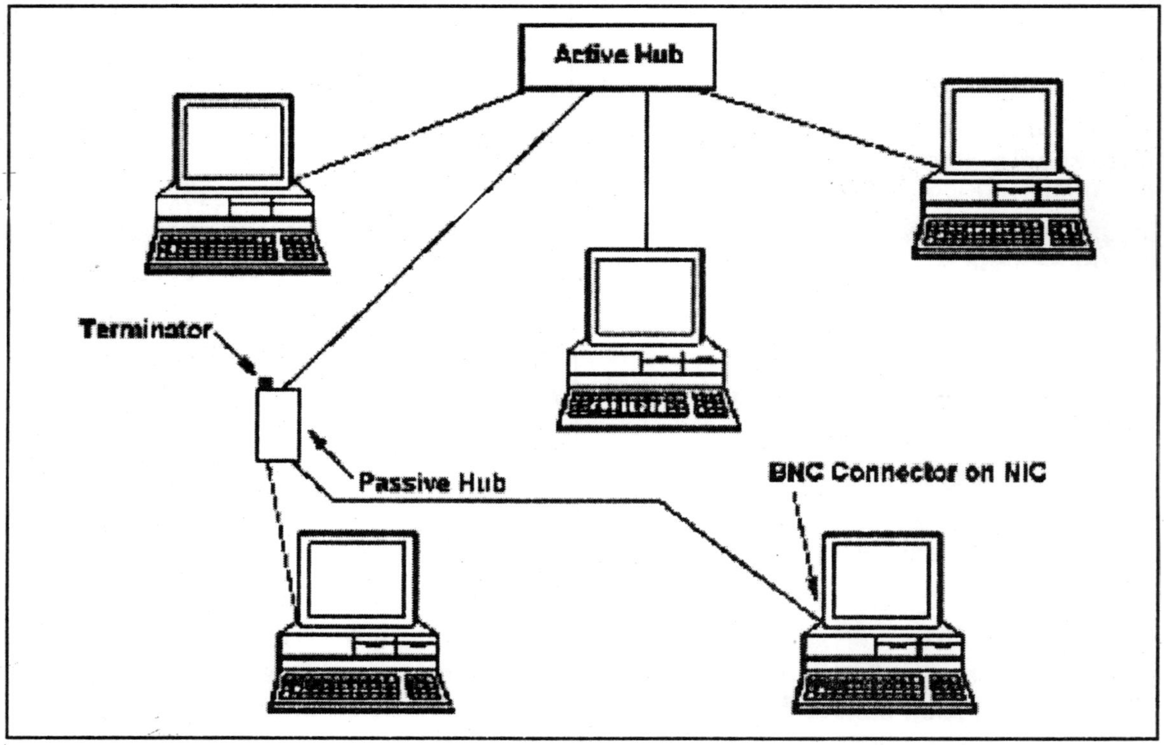

The figure above shows an ARCnet configuration using active and passive hubs. Active hubs are required to extend the network for long distances and to configure networks that have more than four nodes. Passive hubs are used as an economical means of splitting a port on an active hub to support three devices.

ARCnet Trouble shooting

Common sources of problems on ARCnet networks are as follows:

- Duplicate addresses. No more than one node can have a given node address on the same network. If two or more nodes share an address, one of the two workstations will either lose its network connection or will not be able to find a network.
- Missing terminators

Missing terminators may not present visible problems on a small network. Missing terminators cause data retransmits on smaller systems, eventually appearing as transmit time out errors or network errors.

- Using a terminator with an incorrect rating. Coax uses 93 Ohm; UTP must use 100 Ohm terminators.

A terminator's value in ohms depends on the impedance of the cable. The cable's impedance and the terminator's value should always match.

- Failed NICs
- Failed active hubs (or a port on that hub)
- Cable lengths that exceed specifications. Twisted pair, cabled in a bus rather than a star, cannot have more than ten NICs per segment. This number varies with different manufacturers.

ARCnet UTP installed in a bus configuration is generally used only in very small networks of six nodes or less. This configuration has the major drawback of halting the network if a single cable is disconnected. In an ARCnet bus configuration, the network must be brought down to make any changes or service to the ARCnet cards.

- Coax connector not built and/or crimped correctly. Twist-on connectors are responsible for more intermittent errors on a network than most other failures because of their design.

Twist-on coax connectors became popular in the IBM 3XXX systems. These systems used RG-62 coax cable and operated at 1.5 Mbps throughput. The twist-on connectors are not recommended for use on any modern LAN cable system because of the higher data rates employed.

Maximum ARCnet Cable Distances

Maximum Distance	From	To
2,000 feet	Network node	Active hub
2,000 feet	Active Hub	Active hub
100 feet	Active Hub	Passive hub
Not supported	Passive Hub	Passive hub
100 feet	Network node	Passive hub
2,000 feet	Network node	Network node
20,000 feet	Farthest node	Farthest node

The primary characteristics of ARCnet are:

- ARCnet operates at 2.5 Mbps throughput using a token-passing-bus scheme.
- ARCnet is cabled with RG-62 A/U coax with 93 Ohm terminators or the newer UTP with 100 Ohm terminators.
- The maximum time it takes for the ARCnet signal to travel the length of the network is 31 microseconds.
- The maximum distance an ARCnet signal can travel between the two nodes farthest away from each other is 20,000 feet.
- The absolute maximum number of ARCnet nodes that can occupy a given network

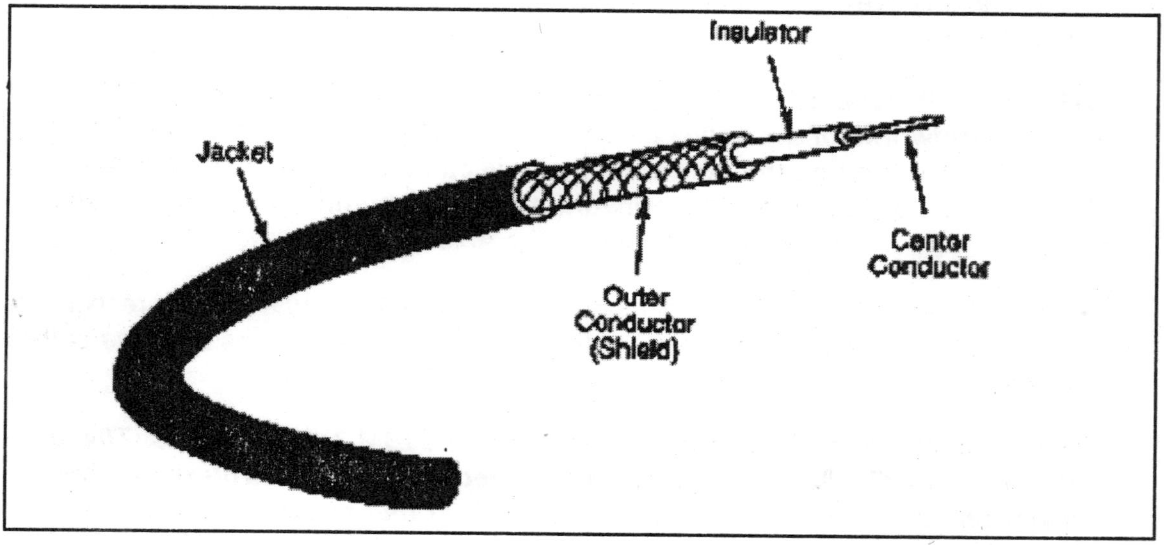

segment is 255. An ARCnet segment consists of all cabling and nodes that share a given network address.

Application:

We will be building a typical ARCnet coax cable for our hands-on lab project for this lesson.

From your LAN-Wire materials kit locate the:

- 6' length of RG-62 A/U coax cable
- RG-62 A/U crimp-on BNC connectors (Qty. 3).

Fabrication Instructions:

1. Set the Coax wire stripper to the RG-59 setting. (RG-59 & RG-62 are the same diameter)
2. The dual-set blades of the coax wire stripper will strip the end of the coax cable with a precise two-stage cut. Strip the ends of your RG-62 cable using a rotary motion with the coax stripper.
3. Crimp the center pin of the BNC connector onto the end of the center conductor.
4. Slide the crimp ferrule over the coax cable.
5. Slip the body of the BNC connector under the braided shield as far as it will go.
6. Slide the crimp ferrule over the braided shield up to the BNC body shoulder.
7. Use the ratchet crimping tool to evenly and completely crimp the ferrule to the BNC body.
8. Repeat for the other end of the cable.
9. Use a digital multimeter to test your cable for shorts. (any Ohm reading other than infinity)
10. Using a BNC butt-splice and terminating resistor, also test for a perfect 93 Ohm reading.

Ethernet Specification

Ethernet was originally developed by DIX - the Digital Corporation, the Intel Corporation, and the Xerox Corporation in the early 1970s. Ethernet is known as a *spanning tree topology* because the networks expand by branching in tree structures that do not allow redundant paths between nodes. Ethernet uses the *CSMA/CD* (Carrier Sense Multiple Access with Collision Detection) media contention access method and supports a maximum throughput of 10 or 100 Mbps. The original Ethernet and later *IEEE 802.3 protocols* are similar but not usually interchangeable.

The origins of Ethernet are commemorated in the initials *DIX*, which is a 15-pin connector used to interface Ethernet components (also called the *AUI* - Attachment Unit Interface). The acronym "DIX" is derived from the combination of leading letters of the founding Ethernet vendors — Digital, Intel, and Xerox.

The term Ethernet commonly refers to original Ethernet (now most frequently identified as *Ethernet II*) as well as the *IEEE 802.3 standards*. However, Ethernet and the IEEE 802.3 standards differ in ways significant enough to make standards incompatible in terms of packet formats. At the Physical Layer, Ethernet and IEEE 802.3 are generally compatible in terms of cables, connectors, and electronic devices.

RG 58 A/U Coax cable

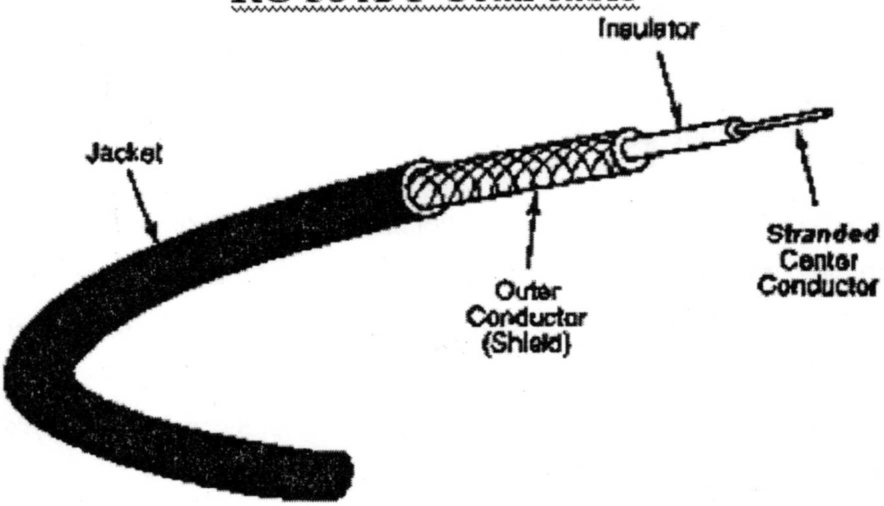

RG 58 A/U Coax cable

Ethernet is generally used on light to medium traffic networks, and performs best when a network's data traffic is sent in short bursts. Ethernet is the most popular network standard. It has become especially popular in many university and government installations.

Ethernet Board Settings

Most versions of Ethernet NICs are configured using jumpers to set *addresses* and *interrupts*. Certain models of newer type *Network Interface Cards* (NICs) can be configured using a diagnostic program that allows changing of interrupt and memory address settings stored in a special memory chip on the NIC.

An example of an Ethernet NIC is shown above. Some of the features of these cards are:

- Shared memory address selection *(most Ethernet cards do not require the use of shared memory)*

- I/O address
- Interrupt
- Connectors (DIX/AUI, BNC, RJ-45)
- Active connector selection jumpers
- Socket for a remote boot PROM.

Ethernet cards can have one, two, or possibly all three of the following *connectors*:

- DIX/AUI connectors support 10Base5 external transceivers
- BNC connectors support 10Base2 coax cabling
- RJ-45 connectors support 10Base-T/100Base-TX (UTP) cabling.

In many cases, DIP switches or blocks of jumpers are used to select the active connector. With some cards, however, the active connector can be selected with configuration software.

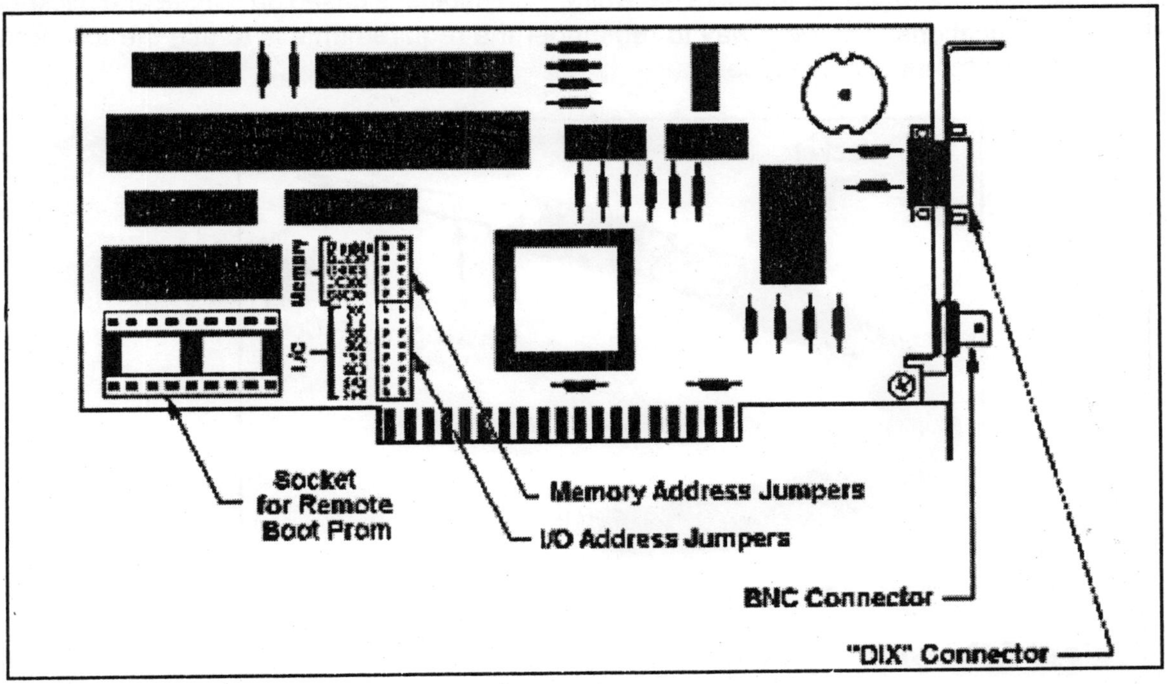

A limitation of 1,024 nodes (physical addresses) per network address exists on an Ethernet network. Addresses are assigned by IEEE to the vendor for the first three bytes of a six-byte address. The vendor is responsible for assigning the rest of the address and ensuring unique IDs. These unique addresses are called *Burned-In Addresses* (BIA).

As with the Token Ring cards, the card's manufacturer *"burns in"* a unique node address into a ROM on each NIC. Unless you override the *burned-in address* (using what are called

Locally administered Addresses - LAA), address conflicts should not occur on an Ethernet. Vendors sometimes label their cards with the node address. If the address is not visible, use the diagnostic disk supplied by the vendor.

Ethernet Cabling

A variety of cables can be used to implement Ethernet networks. Traditionally, Ethernets have been cabled with *coax cables* of several different types (similar to RG 8 for 10Base5 and RG 58 A/U for 10Base2). *Fiber optic cables* (FOIRL) Fiber Optic Inter-Repeater Link; are now frequently employed to extend the geographic range of Ethernets.

The contemporary interest in using *twisted pair wiring* (UTP) has resulted in a new scheme for cabling using unshielded twisted pair. The 10Base-T cabling standard, which uses UTP in a star topology, is described later.

Ethernet remains closely associated with coaxial cable, however. Two types of coaxial cable still used in small and large environments are *thin net* (also known as cheapernet) and *thick net*. The Ethernet networks have different limitations based on thinnet and thicknet cable specifications. The best way to remember the requirements is to use the following rule of thumb for each cable type.

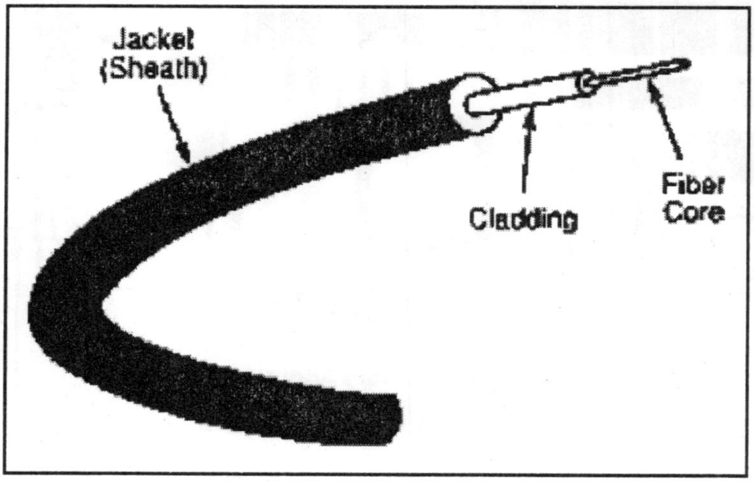

Typical Ethernet Coax Cable Specifications:

- RG-58 A/U, stranded conductor, CL2, 95%+ copper braided shield, PVC jacket, nominal 50 ohm impedance, 29.5 nominal capacitance/ft.
- RG-58 A/U, stranded conductor, CL2P, 95%+ copper braided shield, Plenum jacket, nominal 50 ohm impedance, 27.0 nominal capacitance/ft.
- RG-58/U, solid conductor, CL2, 90%+ copper braided shield, PVC jacket, nominal 50 ohm impedance. 26.0 nominal capacitance/ft.

- Thick Ethernet Yellow Trunk Cable, solid conductor, CL2, double foil and braided shield, PVC jacket, nominal 50 ohm impedance, 26.0 nominal capacitance /ft.

The 5-4-3 Rule

The 5-4-3 rule states that between any two nodes in the Ethernet network can be:

- Up to (5) five segments in a series
- Up to (4) four concentrators or repeaters
- Up to (3) three populated segments (coax only).

10Base2 (ThinNet)

The 10Base2, *thinnet* topology generally uses the *on-board transceiver* of the network interface card to translate the signals to and from the rest of the network. Thin net cabling uses RG-58 A/U coaxial type cable, 50 Ohm terminators, and BNC T-connectors that directly attach to the connector on the NIC. A *grounded terminator* must be used on only one end of the network segment. The components of a *thin net network* are shown below.

A transceiver is a device that takes the digital signal from the node and translates it to communicate on a baseband cabling system. NICs that support thinnet or 10Base-T/100Base-TX cable have built-in transceivers. External transceivers are used for 10Base5 thick Ethernet.

Several additional rules must be adhered to in 10Base2 thinnet Ethernet environments, including the following:

- The minimum cable distance between workstations must be 1.5 feet or .5 meters.
- Pig tails, also known as drop cables, from BNC T-connectors should _not_ be used to connect to the BNC connector on the NIC. The BNC T-connector on the coax must be connected directly to the NIC.
- You may not go beyond the maximum network segment limitation of 607 feet or 185 meters (not the 200 meters commonly stated).
- The entire network cabling scheme cannot exceed 3,035 feet or 925 meters.
- The maximum number of nodes per network segment is 30 (this includes workstations and repeaters).

The *IEEE 802.3 standard* for thinnet is 10Base2. This standard describes a 10 Mbps baseband network with a maximum segment length of approximately 200 meters (the actual limit, as stated above is 185 meters).

10BASE5 (ThickNet)

The 10Base5, *thicknet* topology uses an *external transceiver* to attach to the network

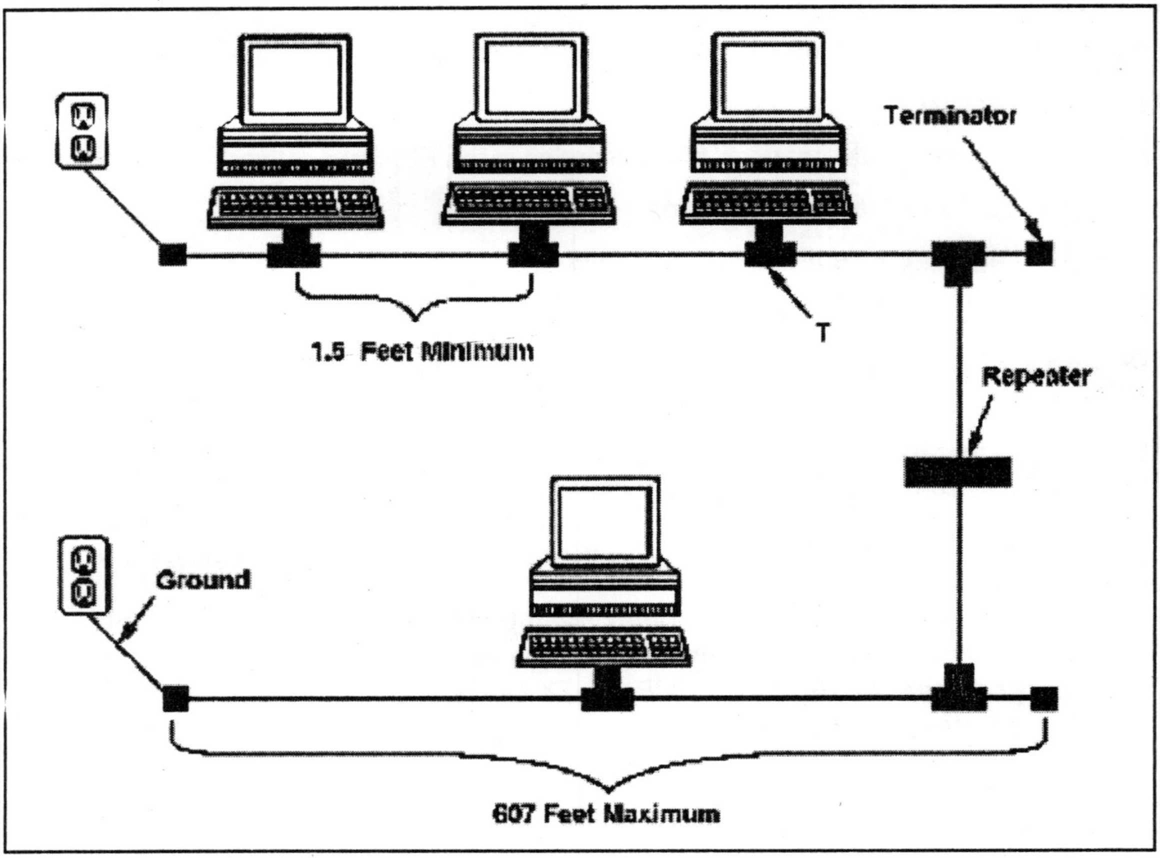

interface card. The NIC attaches to the external transceiver by an *AUI cable* to the *DIX connector* on the card. Some external transceivers clamp to the thick net cable with metal points that resemble a vampire's teeth *(vampire tap)*, others connect with standard *BNC* or *N-series barrel connectors.* As with thin net, each network segment must be terminated at both ends with one end using a grounded terminator. The components of a *thicknet network* are shown in the figure below.

Several additional guidelines along with the 5-4-3 rule must be followed in 10Base5 thicknet Ethernet networks:

- The minimum cable distance between transceivers is eight feet or 2.5 meters.
- You may not go beyond the maximum network segment length of 1,640 feet or 500 meters.
- The entire network cabling scheme cannot exceed 8,200 feet or 2,500 meters.
- One end of the terminated network segment must be grounded.
- The maximum number of nodes per network segment is 100. (This includes all repeaters.)

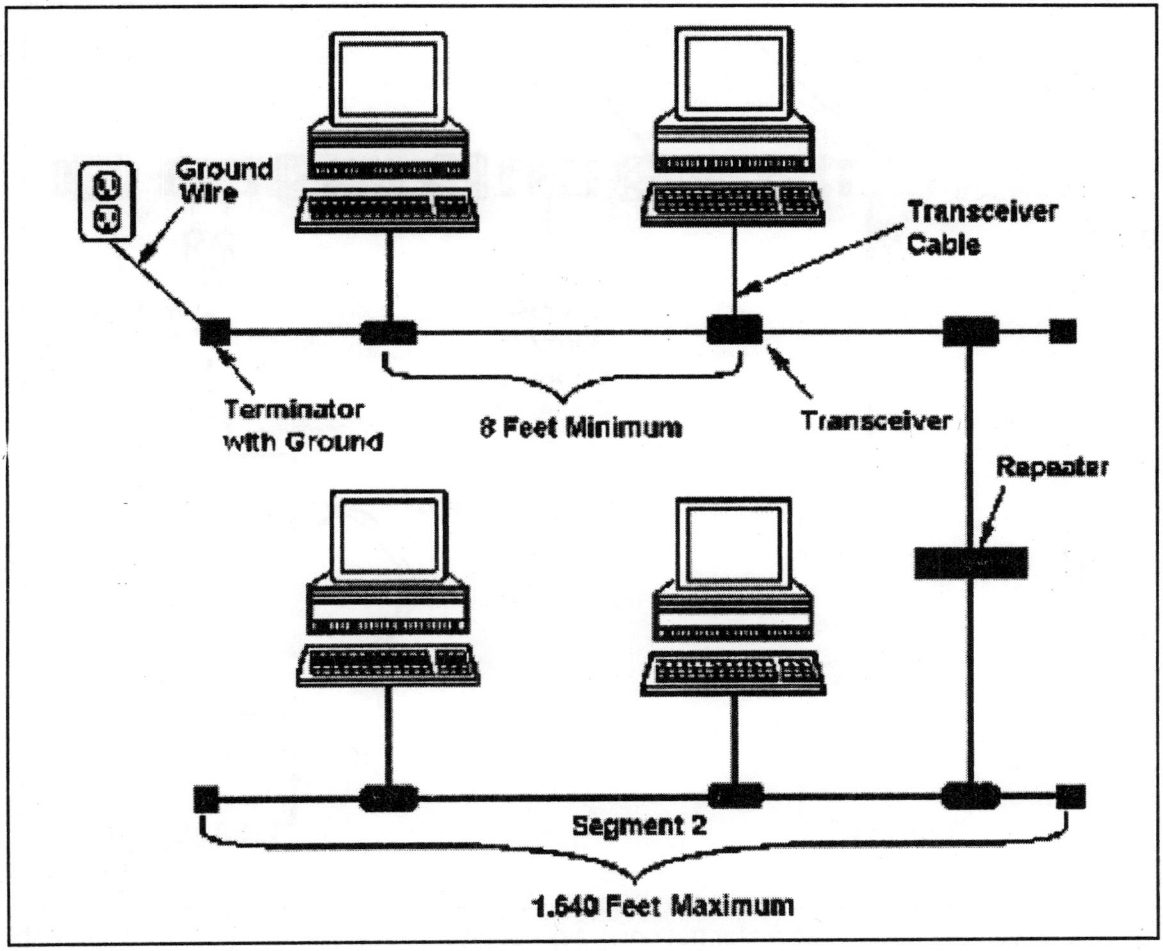

The *IEEE 802.3 standard* that describes thicknet is 10Base5. This standard describes a 10 Mbps baseband network that can have segments up to 500 meters long.

The 10Base5 cabling scheme and components are shown next.

10Base-T/100Base-TX (Twisted Pair Ethernet)

The trend in wiring Ethernet networks is to use unshielded twisted pair (UTP) cable. UTP cable has a lower cost than coax. Another significant advantage is that UTP is smaller than coax, which relieves congestion of wiring conduits. *UTP Ethernet* is wired in a star-shaped design and is referred to in the technical world as 10BaseT. The cable uses *RJ-45 connectors*, and the network interface card can have RJ-45 jacks built into the back of the cards. External transceivers attached to a DIX connector can also be used to connect standard Ethernet cards into a twisted pair topology.

The figure next shows 10Base-T Ethernet cabled using twisted pair and a concentrator.

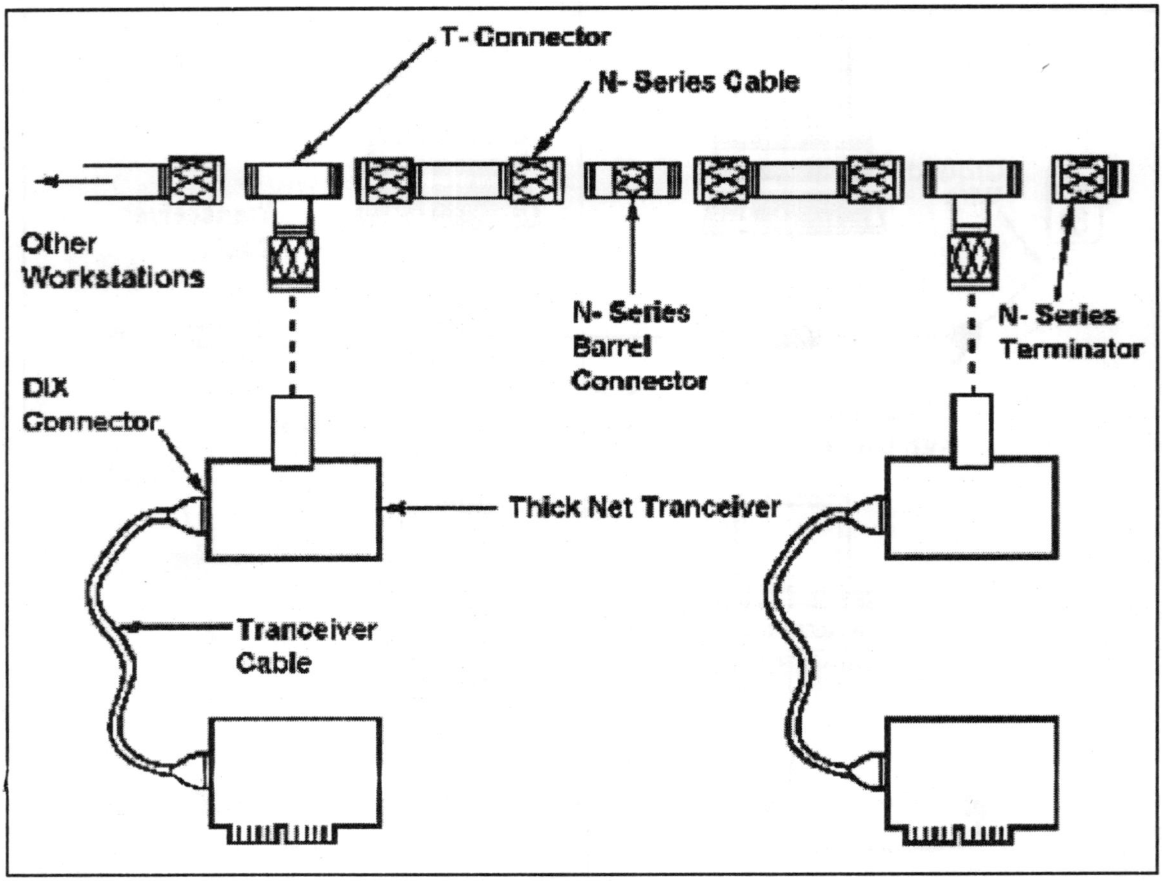

Networks with star wiring topologies can be significantly easier to trouble shoot and repair than bus wired networks. With a star network, a problem node can be isolated from the rest of the network by simply disconnecting the cable and directly connecting it to the cable hub. If the hub is considered "intelligent", management software developed for that hub type can disconnect the suspect port.

The additional rules for a 10Base-T network are as follows:

- The maximum number of network segments is 1,024.
- The maximum unshielded cable segment length is 328 feet or 100 meters.

10Base-T requires that the UTP cable system be compliant with a minimum rating of Category 3. RJ-45 connectors wired with two pairs (4 wires) on pins 1,2,3, & 6 are used with 10Base-T. Level IV is cable certified to operate at 10Base-T required throughput.

Fast Ethernet

An extension of the popular 10Base-T Ethernet standard, **Fast Ethernet** transports data at 100 Mbps. With rules defined by the **IEEE 802.3u** standard, Fast Ethernet leverages the

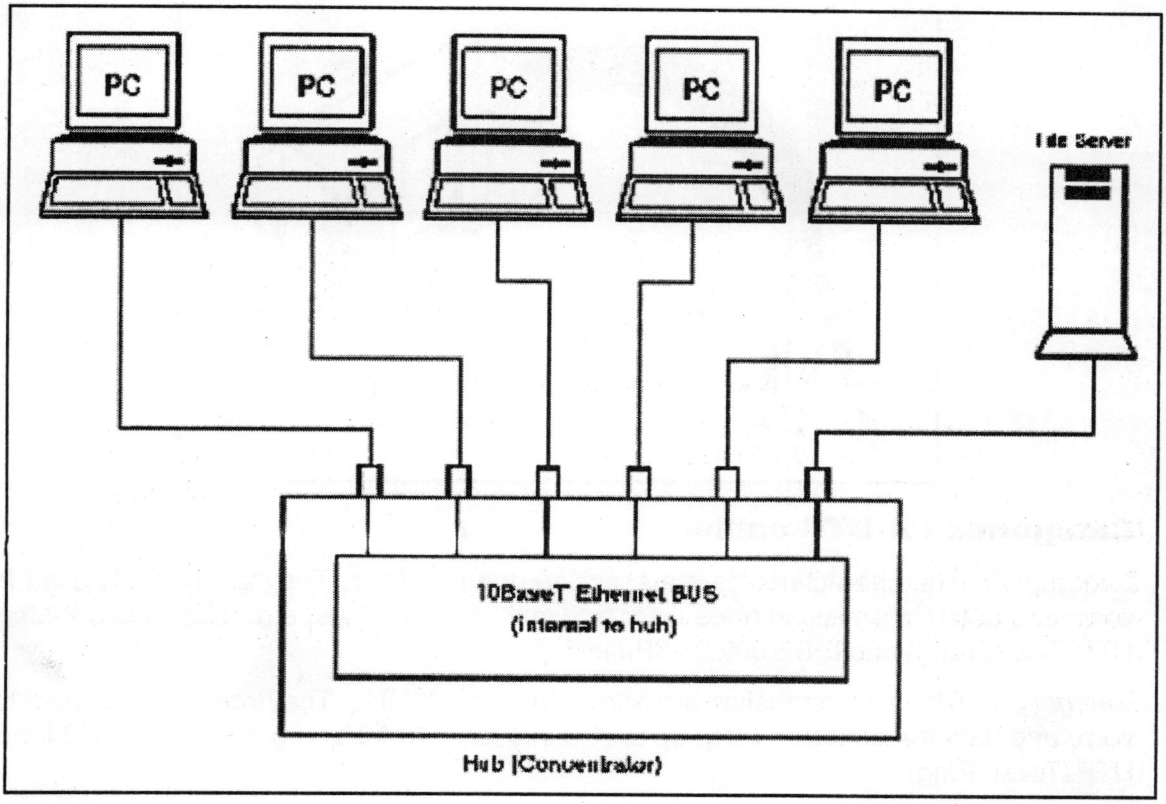

familiar Ethernet technology and retains the CSMA/CD protocol of 10 Mbps Ethernet. Three types of Fast Ethernet are available: **100Base-TX**, which runs over Category 5 UTP; **100Base-T4** which runs over existing Category 3 UTP; and **100Base-FX**, which operates over multimode fiber optic cabling.

EIA/TIA T568B Colour Codes & Pin-out for the 10Base-T & 100Base-TX RJ-45 connector

1	**2**	**3**	**4**	**5**	**6**	**7**	**8**
TD+	**TD-**	**RD+**	**N/C**	**N/C**	**RD-**	**N/C**	**N/C**

Pins 1 & 2 - Pair #1 Transmit Data

Pins 3 & 6 - Pair #2 Receive Data

Pins 4, 5, 7, & 8 - Not Connected

As specified for 10Base-T (CAT3 minimum) & 100Base-TX (CAT5 minimum), cables should be 100 Ohm unshielded or shielded twisted pair (UTP or STP) wire of AWG gauge 24, 26, or 28. Maximum length is 100 meters. IBM Type-1 cable and other 150 Ohm STP cables are not suitable.

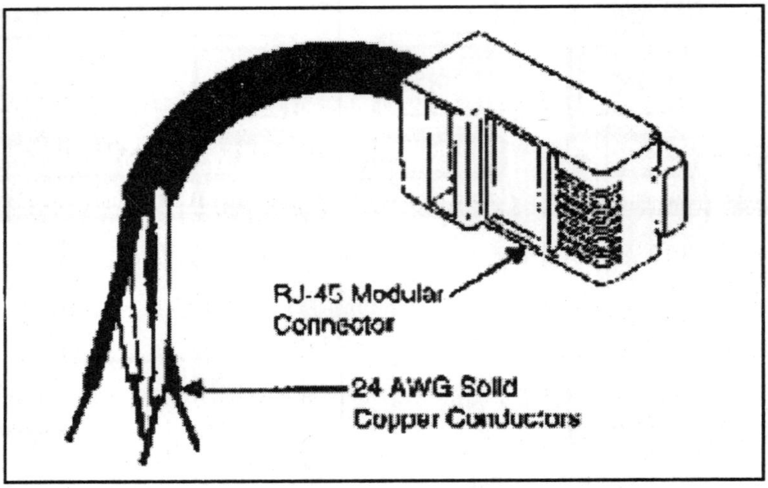

Categories for UTP cable:

Category 3 - The characteristics are specified up to 16 MHz. They are typically used for voice and data transmission rates up to and including 10 Mbps, e.g. IEEE 802.5 4-Mbps UTP (Token Ring) and IEEE 802.3 10Base-T (Ethernet).

Category 4 - The characteristics are specified up to 20MHz. They are typically used for voice and data transmission rates up to and including 16 MHz, e.g. IEEE 802.5 16-Mbps UTP (Token Ring).

Category 5 - The characteristics are specified up to 100 MHz. They are typically used for voice and data transmissions up to and including 100 Mbps e.g. the 100Base-TX Fast Ethernet, 100 Mbps Fast ARCnet, and others.

Ethernet Trouble shooting

Look for the following things when trouble shooting Ethernets:

- With 10Base-T & 100Base-TX, make sure that the cable used has the correct number of twists to meet the data grade specifications.
- Electrical interference can be caused by tying the network cable together with monitor

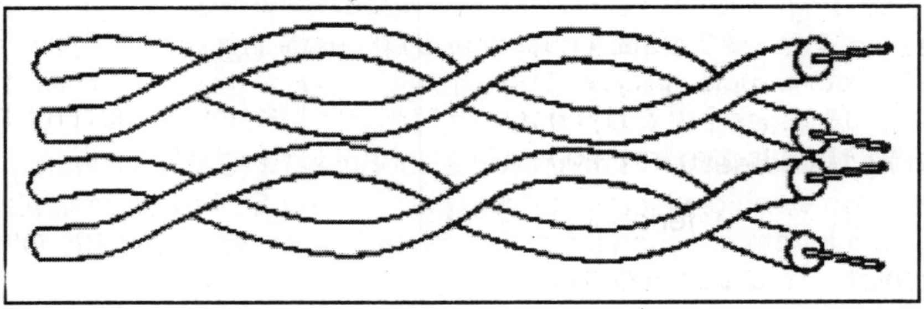

and power cords. Outside interference also can be caused by fluorescent lights, electric motors, and other electrical devices.

- Make sure that connectors are pinned properly and crimped tightly.
- Check the cable lengths to make sure that distance specifications are not exceeded.
- If excess shielding on coax cable is exposed, it may be grounding out the connector.
- Make sure that coax cables are not coiled tightly together.
- Check the grade of the cable being used. For thinnet, RG-58 A/U is required. Thick net cable must meet Ethernet specifications.
- If using a linear bus setup, make sure that the topology rules are followed.
- Check for missing terminator or terminators with improper impedance ratings.
- Make sure that all the component cables in a segment are connected together. A user who moves his workstation and removes the T-connector incorrectly can cause a broken segment.

10Base2, thinnet and 10Base5, thick net cable can be combined to extend the distance of an Ethernet network topology (spanning tree topology). The following formula can be used to define the maximum amount of thinnet cable that can be used in one network segment combination:

Maximum length of thinnet that can be used =

1,640 feet (length of new networksegment to be added)

A linear bus topology is economical to wire because it is not necessary to have a separate cable run for each workstation. However, some local problems on a linear bus have the capability of bringing the entire network down.

If a break is in the cable or a streaming (beaconing) NIC is in the channel, the entire network can go down. Streaming is more frequently referred to as a broadcast storm. This occurs when a network card fails, and the transmitter floods the cable with traffic, just like a faucet that is stuck open. At this point, the network becomes unusable.

Application Projects:

We will be building a typical coax cable for 10Base2 thinnet for our first hands-on lab project for this lesson. We will then build a typical UTP patch-cable for 10Base-T & 100Base-TX Ethernet for our second project. Then we will build a cross-cable (sometimes called a 10Base-T / 100Base-TX null-modem cable) for directly connecting two 10Base-T or 100Base-TX NICs together without the need for a concentrator.

From your LAN-Wire materials kit locate the:

- 6' length of RG-58A/U coax cable

- RG-58 A/U crimp-on BNC connectors (Qty. 3)
- Two 6' lengths of four-pair (8 wire) UTP cable
- RJ-45 crimp-on connectors (Qty. 6).

Project #1 - 10Base2 coax cable

1. Set the Coax wire stripper to the RG-58 setting. (RG-59 & RG-62 are the same diameter).
2. The dual-set blades of the coax wire stripper will strip the end of the coax cable with a precise two-stage cut. Strip the ends of your RG-58 cable using a rotary motion with the coax stripper.
3. Crimp the center pin of the BNC connector onto the end of the center conductor.
4. Slide the crimp ferrule over the coax cable.
5. Slip the body of the BNC connector under the braided shield as far as it will go.
6. Slide the crimp ferrule over the braided shield up to the BNC body shoulder.
7. Use the ratchet crimping tool to evenly and completely crimp the ferrule to the BNC body.
8. Repeat for the other end of the cable.
9. Use a digital multimeter to test your cable for shorts. (any Ohm reading other than infinity).
10. Using a BNC butt-splice and terminating resistor, also test for a perfect 50 Ohm reading.

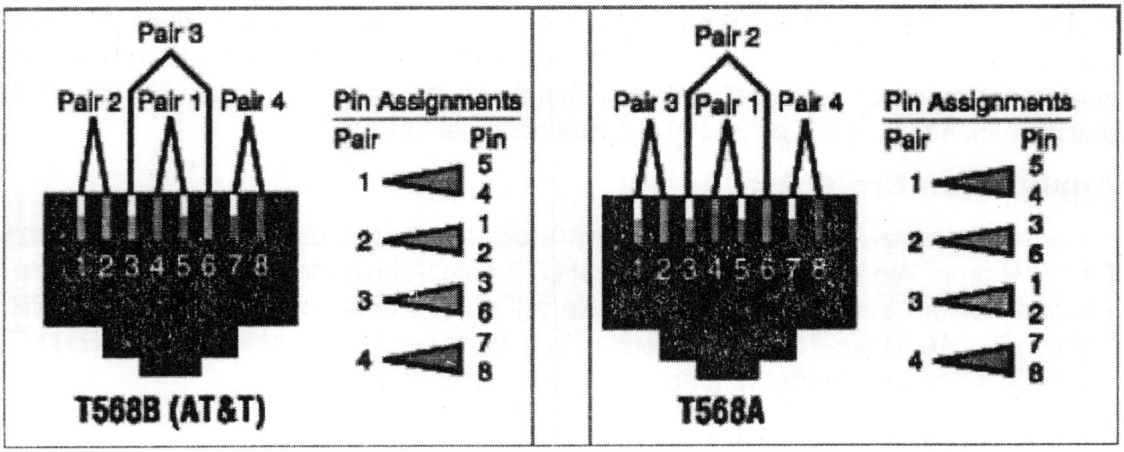

Project #2 - 10Base-T/100Base-TX patch-cable

Technically, as long as you build your 10Base-T/100Base-TX patch-cable with straight-through connections for pins 1, 2, 3, & 6 it will work. But there is a EIA/TIA 568 standard that specifies minimum recommendations for telecommunications wiring within a structure, including telecommunication outlets, and between structures in a campus environment. It specifies a wiring system with a recommended topology and distances. It specifies media by parameters which determine performance and specifies connectors and their pin assignments to ensure interconnectability.

Using the USOC/PDS wiring pair colour codes and the EIA/TIA T568B (AT&T 258A) wiring scheme assemble a *standard* 10BaseT cable with straight-through wiring using pins 1, 2, 3 & 6. Use the Paladin twisted pair tester to insure connection integrity.

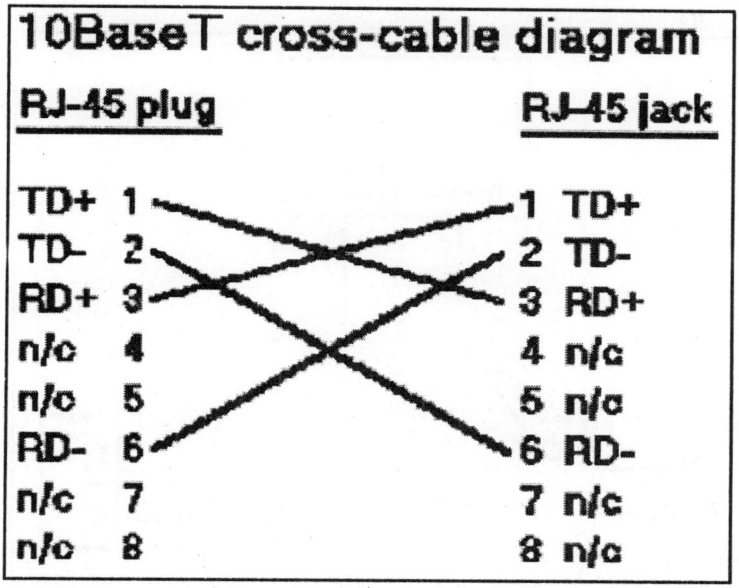

Universal Service Ordering Codes (USOC): are a series of Registered Jack (RJ) wiring configurations developed by the Bell System for connection of customer premise equipment to the public network.

Banded & Solid / Wiring Pair Colour Codes:

Pair #	ID	Pin #T568B	Bandcode	Pin #USOC	Solidcode
1	T1	5	White/Blue	5	Red
	R1	4	Blue(White)	4	Green
2	T2	1	White/Orange	6	Black
	R2	2	Orange(White)	3	Yellow

3	T3	3	White/Green	7	Orange
	R3	6	Green(White)	2	Blue
4	T4	7	White/Brown	8	Gray (or White)
	R4	8	Brown(White)	1	Brown

Project #3 - 10Base-T/100Base-TX Cross-cable

To direct-connect two 10BaseT NIC's for testing or trouble shooting you will assemble a 10Base-T/100Base-TX cross-cable (sometimes called a UTP null-modem cable or plug-to-jack cable). This cable will allow you to connect two 10Base-T or 100Base-TX nodes together without the need for a concentrator. This can create a two-node LAN. Be sure to check the wiring with the Padadin test tool.

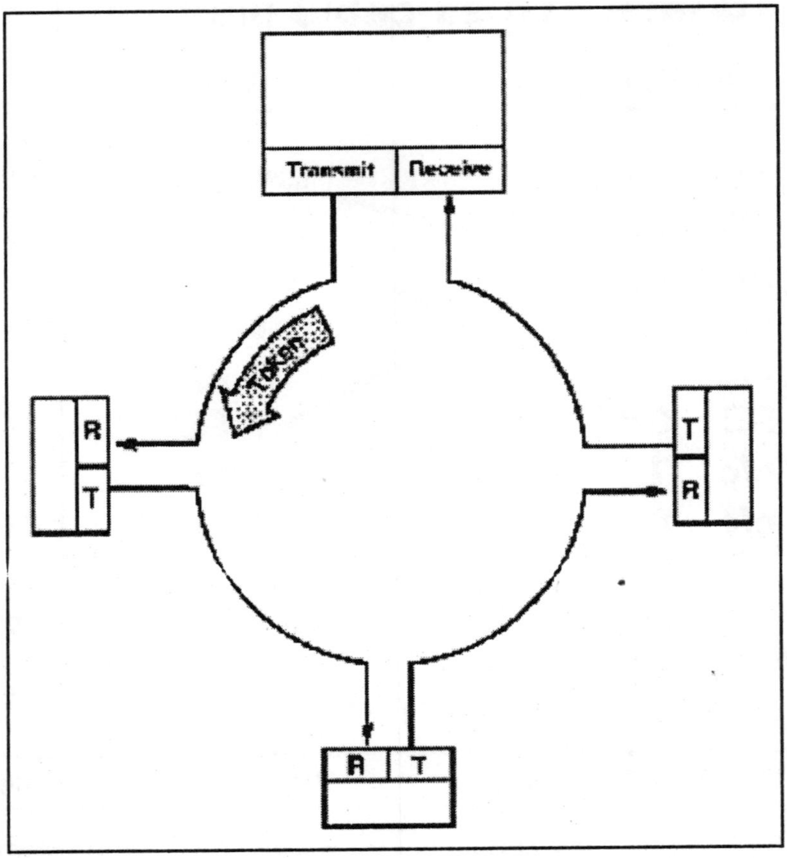

Token Ring Specifications

Token Ring uses a non-contention *token-passing* architecture that adheres to the *IEEE 802.5* standard. The topology is physically a star, but logically uses a ring to pass the token from station to station. Each node must be attached to a hub/concentrator called a *multistation access unit* (MAU or MSAU).

Token Ring network interface cards (NICs) can run at *4 Mbps or 16 Mbps.* 4 Mbps cards can run only at that data rate. However, 16 Mbps cards can be configured to run at 4 or 16 Mbps. All cards on a given network ring must be running at the same rate.

As shown below, each node acts as a *repeater* that receives token and data frames from its *nearest active upstream neighbour* (NAUN). After a frame is processed by the node, the frame is passed (rebroadcast) downstream to the next attached node. Each token makes at least one trip around the entire ring. It then returns to the originating node. Workstations that indicate problems send a *"beacon"* to identify an address of the potential failure.

On a Novell LAN, to find out if any beacon messages have been sent on your Token Ring network, review your System Error Log found in SYSCON through Supervisor Options.

Token Ring Board Settings

As with the Ethernet cards, the node address on each NIC is *"burned in"* (BIA) at the manufacturer and is unique to each card. The node address in some cases can be overridden by vendor specified software instructions *(this is called a Locally Administered Address - LAA)*. A maximum of two Token Ring cards can be installed in any node, with each card being defined as the primary or alternate Token Ring card in the machine. A typical Token Ring card is shown below.

The common features of a Token Ring NIC are:

- Interrupt (IRQ)
- I/O address (Primary or Secondary)
- Shared RAM address
- Shared RAM size
- Data Rate (4Mbps or 16Mbps)
- DMA channel
- 9-pin female connector
- (optional RJ-45 connector)
- Remote boot PROM socket.

The *interrupt* (IRQ), *I/O address*, and *shared memory address* on each Token Ring NIC must be set to avoid conflicts with all other components. The *DMA channel* may or may not be sharable depending on your system.

Each Token Ring card comes with a diagnostic disk that provides testing for the adapter. Refer to the appropriate documentation for your card for more detailed instructions.

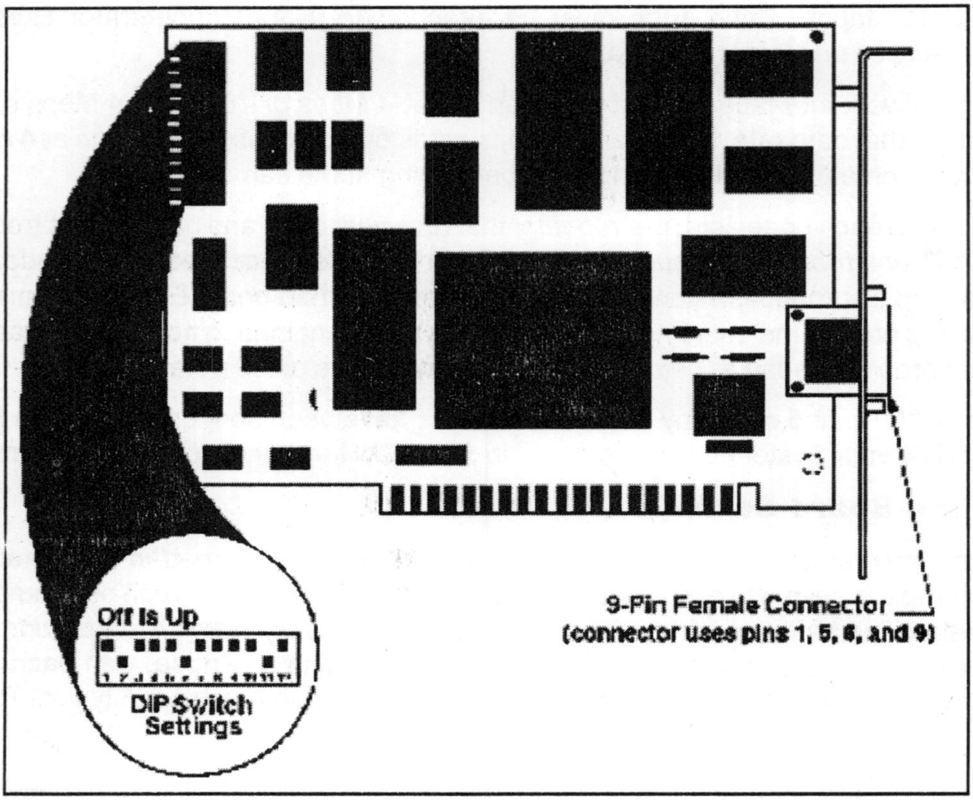

Token Ring Cabling

IBM defines Token Ring cabling in terms of two types of systems:

- Small movable
- Large non-movable.

The *small movable system* supports up to 96 workstations and file servers and 12 MAUs. It uses *Type 6* cable to attach workstations and servers to IBM Model *8228 MAUs*. Type 6 cable is a *shielded twisted pair* (STP) cable with *stranded conductors*. This cable is flexible, but has limited distance capabilities. The characteristics of this cable make it suitable for small networks and for *patch cords* (wiring closet jumpers).

The *large non-movable system* supports up to 260 workstations and file servers, with up to 33 MAUs. This network configuration uses IBM *Type 1* or *Type 2* cable. These are shielded twisted pair cables with *solid-wire conductors* suitable for carrying signals greater distances than are possible with *Type 6*. The large non-movable system also involves other wiring needs such as punch panels or distribution panels, equipment racks for MAUs, and wiring closets to contain the previously listed components.

The *Multistation Access Unit* (MAU) is the central cabling component for IBM Token Ring networks. The *8228 MAU* was the original wiring hub developed by IBM for Token Ring networks. The figure above shows an example of a network cabling several workstations and 8228 MAUs. The distances noted in the figure are based on the rules for the small, movable cabling system. Each 8228 has *ten connectors*, eight of which accept cables to workstations or servers. The other connectors are labeled *RI* (ring in) and *RO* (ring out). The RI and RO connectors are used to connect multiple 8228s to form larger networks.

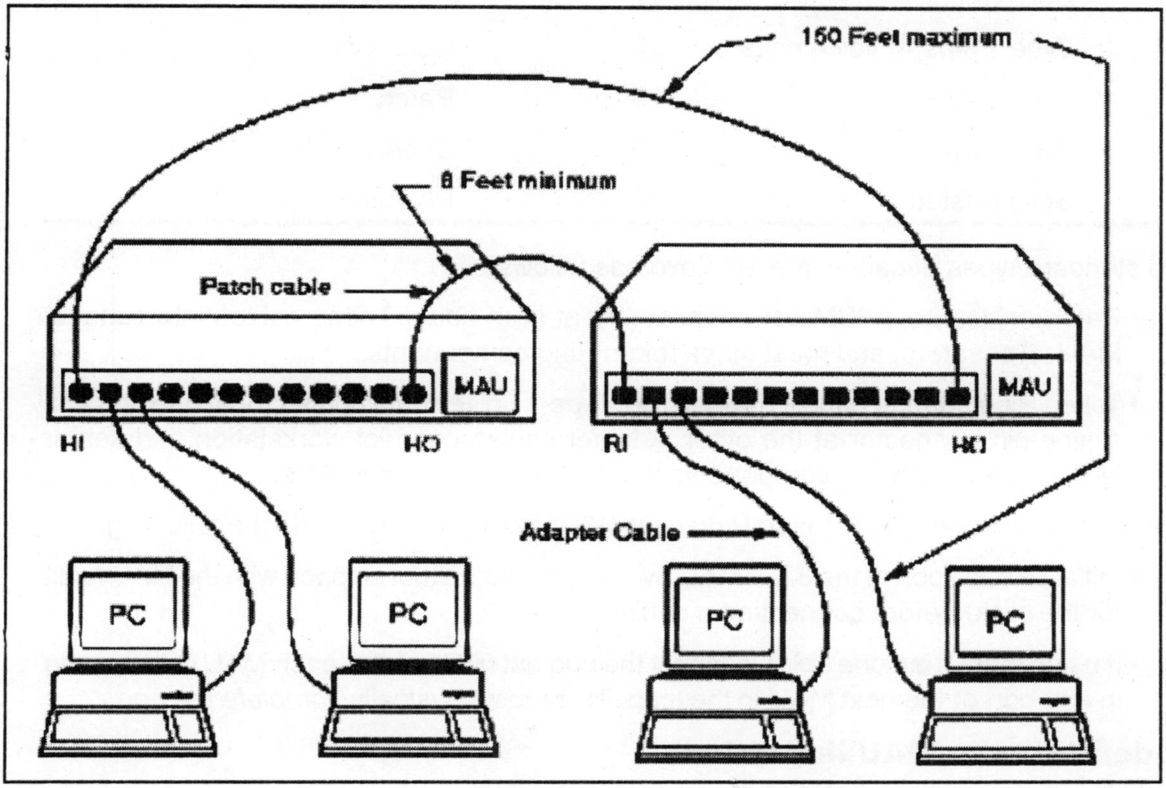

MAUs are mechanical devices that consist of relays and connectors. Their purpose is to *switch* workstations in and out of the network. Each port is controlled by a *relay* powered by a voltage sent to the MAU from the NIC. When an 8228 is first set up, each of these relays must be initialized with a *setup tool* (sometimes referred to as a phaser) shipped with the unit. The setup tool is inserted into each port and held there until a light indicates that the port is properly initialized (charged).

Remember that when talking about Token Ring; MAU and MSAU both refer to Multistation Access Units.

IBM Token Ring networks use two (or three) types of connectors. NICs are equipped with a female *(DB-9)* nine-pin connector (only four pins are used) and/or an RJ-45 connector. MAUs, repeaters, and most other equipment use a special *IBM Type-1 unisex data connector*. (Newer Token Ring cards and MAUs use *RJ-45 connectors* and CAT5 UTP cabling).

IBM STP Cable

TYPE	PAIRS	AWG	USE
1	Solid twisted	22	Data
2	Type 1 *plus*(4) voice pairs	22	Data &Voice
6	Stranded twisted	26	Patch
8	Solid parallel	26	Undercarpet
9	Solid twisted	26	Plenum

Two standard types of cables are employed as follows:

- Patch cables have IBM data connectors at both ends. These cables interconnect MAUs, repeaters, and most other Token Ring components.
- Token Ring adapter cables have an IBM Type-1 unisex data connector at one end and a nine-pin connector at the other. Adapter cables connect workstation and server NICs to other network components that use IBM data connectors.

When you are connecting a Token Ring network, make sure that you do the following:

- Initialize each port in the 8228 MAU by using the setup tool shipped with the MAU (wait for the click) before connecting a cable.
- If using more than one MAU, connect the ring out (RO) port of each MAU with the ring in (RI) port of the next MAU in the loop. This must physically *complete the ring*.

Node/Distance/MAU limitations

A variety of rules must be observed when configuring a Token Ring LAN. The following rules apply to Token Ring networks:

- The minimum patch cable distance between two MAUs is eight feet.
- The maximum patch cable distance between two MAUs is 150 feet. Patch cables come in standard lengths of 8, 30, 75, and 150 for Type 6.
- The maximum patch cable distance connecting all MAUs is 400 feet.
- The maximum patch cable distance between a MAU and a node is 150 feet.

These additional configuration rules apply to a small movable Token-Ring cable system:

- Maximum 96 nodes

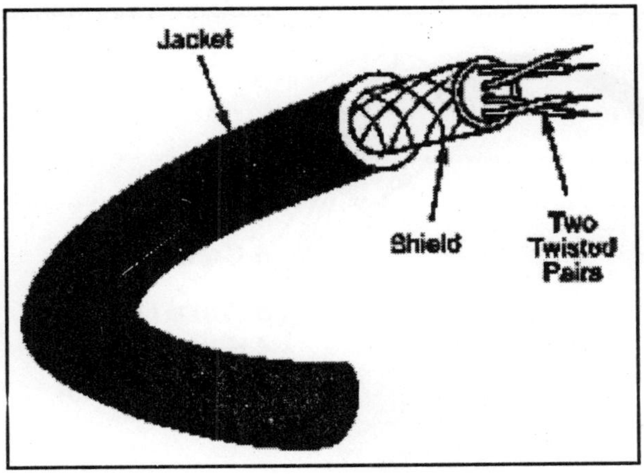

- Maximum 12 MAUs
- Uses Type 6 cable.

A large non-movable Token-Ring cable system is subject to the following rules:

- Maximum 260 nodes
- Maximum 33 MAUs
- Uses Type 1 or Type 2 cable.

Token Ring networks also can be cabled using UTP (CAT5) cable. The IEEE 802.5 standard describes 4 Mbps Token Ring using IBM Type 3 UTP cable (equivalent to CAT3). However, CAT4 or CAT5 cable must be used for 16 Mbps Token Ring.

When using UTP wiring with older non-UTP cards, a *media filter* must be installed between the NIC and the UTP cable. Some newer Token Ring NICs have built-in media filters and RJ-45 jacks ready to interface with UTP wiring.

Token-Ring Trouble Shooting

When trouble shooting Token Ring networks, look for the following:

- Any base I/O, DMA shared memory, or Interrupt conflicts with other boards.
- The version of the workstation or server software driver to make sure that its revision level is compatible with your NIC. Drivers are different for file servers and workstations.
- Make sure that the MAUs are connected properly, with ring out ports connecting to ring in ports throughout the ring.
- Some MAUs other than the 8228 are active and require a power supply. These MAUs fail if they have a blown fuse or a bad power source.
- Check that patch cables are correctly attached to the adapter cable. Patch cables

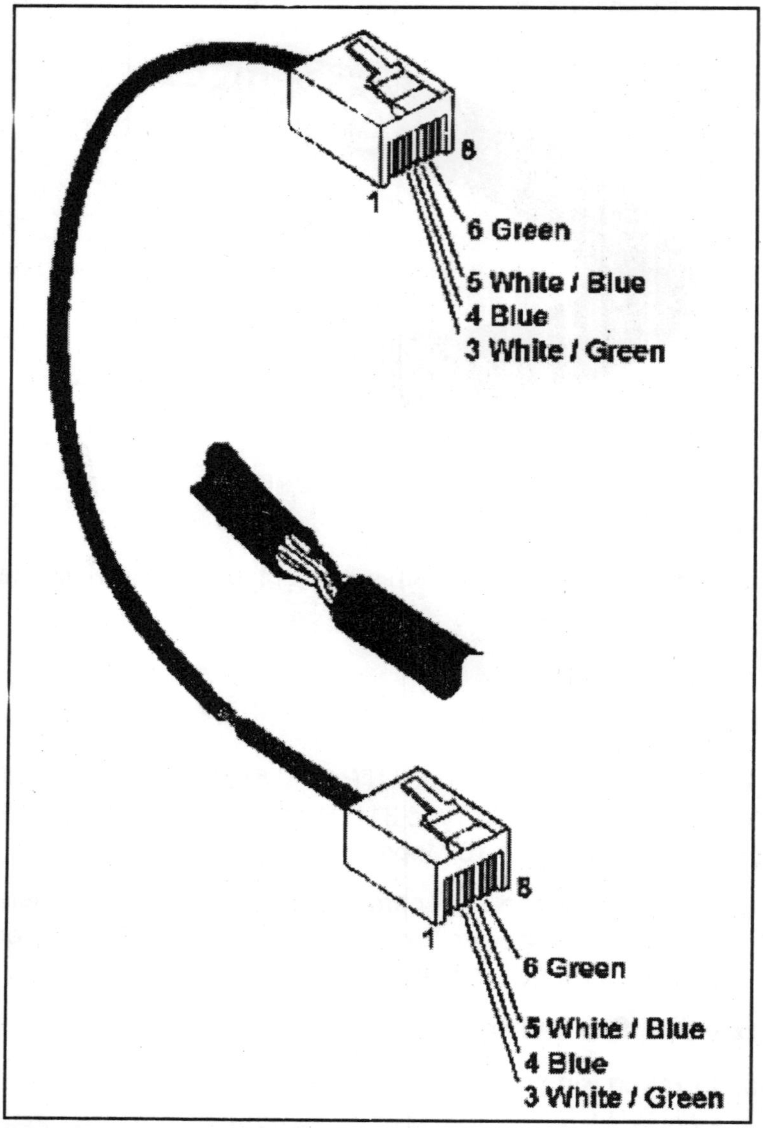

connect MAUs together. Another type of connecting cable is called an adapter cable which connects the NIC to the MAU.

- You may have a failed NIC. Try substituting another one known to work properly.
- Determine if the MAU or the MAU port is bad. Ports may need to be reinitialized with the setup tool.
- Check to see if a 16 Mbps card is inserted into a 4 Mbps ring or vice versa. Neither situation is correct.
- Determine if the wrong type of cable for speed of network is used.

- Examine the pins on the adapter cable to see if they are bent or broken.
- If you are overriding the burned-in network addresses, it is possible that duplicate node addresses may be set.
- If connecting to a 4 Mbps twisted pair network, check the Type 3 media filter.

Application Project:

We will be building a typical Token Ring adapter cable for this lesson project.

From your LAN-Wire materials kit locate the:

- 6' length of IBM Type 6 cable
- 1 IBM unisex data connector
- 1 DB-9 male (pin) connector
- 1 DB-9 hood
- 4 (or more) DB male pins
- 1 DB Insertion/Extraction tool.

The unisex IBM Type-1 data connector is on both sides of a patch cable or on one side of an adapter cable. This unique IBM connector is *unisex* in that two of the same connector will attach to each other. You will find these connectors on the standard IBM 8228 MAU, in patch panels, and in the walls of most pre-wired token-ring installations. Installing the unisex IBM data connector is a learning experience even for the most ardent cable installer.

Some data connector kits come with 45, 90, and 180 degree cable exit strain reliefs. You will only use one. This snap-together kit looks easy to assemble at first, and <u>is</u> easy after you develop a little finesse. Do make sure that the cable colour coded wire pairs for the "Christmas Pair" (receive) and "Halloween Pair" (transmit) are correctly inserted into the built-in punch-down block (use the punch-down block slide as a colour code guide).

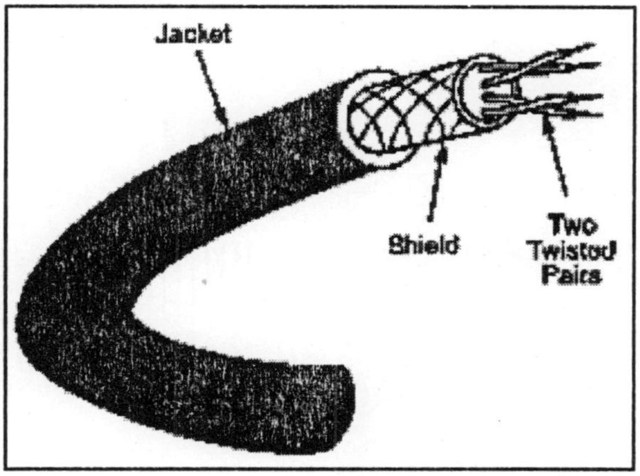

A common mistake is to leave out the metal ferrule strain relief or the strain relief collar. You may have to assemble/disassemble this data connector several times. When done properly the snap-together unit looks clean and is very rigid. Two pieces in the kit can be ignored until after assembly, the dust cover (with attachment loop) and the installation lock (usually beige in colour).

The node side of the Token Ring adapter cable is a standard DB-9 male connector using only pins 1, 5, 6, & 9 (the outside narrow edge pins). Assembling this end of the cable is the same as installing any DB type connector. Make sure you follow the wiring diagram and connect the "Christmas Pair" (Red & Green) to pins 1 & 6 respectively and the "Halloween Pair" (**Black** & Orange) to pins 5 & 9 respectively.

You will need to use a pin crimp tool to install the male pins. Be sure to crimp the rear fingers of the pin around the insulation of the stripped wire for strain relief and crimp the front fingers around the conductor for a positive connection. After all four pins have been crimped on and inspected, use the Insertion/Extraction tool to insert the pins into the DB-9 connector as per the colour code diagram. Be sure to inspect and re-inspect the colour coding at the data connector end and the DB-9 end. After the pins have been inserted and inspected, attach the DB-9 hood. Be sure to secure the strain relief of the hood.

We will test the Token Ring adapter cable two ways. First, you will use the digital multimeter to test for continuity and correct wiring. Second, you will disconnect one of the adapter cables from one of the nodes on the Token-Ring LAN, reconnect *your* cable, power up the workstation, and log on to the file server.

5

Network Connectivity

Network Connectivity Devices

Network connection devices connect the various segments of network media that make up a network or internetwork. A segment is one section of network transmission media that is assigned a specific network address; it provides servers and clients on the network with access to network resources.

A network interface board attaches a device, such as a computer, to a transmission medium. Network interface cards (NICs) are circuit boards that provide the means to change a computer's electric signals to those used by the transmission medium.

The transceiver is the basic component of a NIC, this is what enables the NIC to send and receive data.

Hubs

A hub is a wiring concentrator for a LAN or WAN that provides a central attachment point for network cabling. Coaxial cable doesn't use hubs.

An active hub can regenerate or amplify a signal, it connects multiple media segments, extends cable length and thereby increases transmission length.

A passive hub connects multiple media segments together, it does not regenerate or amplify a signal.

Switches - Data Link - Switching hubs (Switches)

These are intelligent hubs which contain circuitry that very quickly routes signals between ports on the hub. This method reduced bandwidth waste because only the device which needs to receive the packet does rather than the entire network segment.

Switch filters traffic through MAC addresses. A switch receives a transmission and retransmits it using only that port through which the intended receiver can be reached.

Repeater - Physical

Regenerates signals for retransmission. Moves packets from one physical media to another.

Will pass broadcast storms. Cannot connect different network topologies or access methods.

Repeaters work in the Physical layer of the OSI model to provide fast signal regeneration. In digital computer networks, repeaters aren't simply amplifiers; repeaters deal with attenuation by receiving and evaluating the data then immediately re-transmitting a clean copy of the signal on to the next segment of the network cable.

Bridge - Data Link (MAC Sublayer)

Bridges are used to segment networks. They forward packets based on address of destination node. Uses RAM to build a routing table based on hardware addresses. Will connect dissimilar network topologies. Will forward all protocols. Regenerates the signal at the packet level.

A bridge, like a repeater, extends a network's transmission distance, however, a bridge is used to connect segments on different networks.

Bridges are used to segment networks. They forward packets based on address of destination node. Uses RAM to build a routing table based on hardware addresses. Some bridge types are capable of connecting dissimilar network topologies. Will forward all protocols. A hub is a single point where media segments can connect.

Remote Bridge - Data Link (MAC Sublayer)

Same as bridge, but used for telephone communications. Uses STA (Spanning Tree Algorithm).

Router - Network

Routes packets across multiple networks. Uses RAM to build a routing table based on network addresses (i.e. TCP address). Shares status and routing information to other routers to provide better traffic management and bypass slow connections. Will not pass broadcast traffic. Are slower than bridges due to complex functions. Strips off Data Link Layer source and destination addresses and then recreates them for packets. Routers can accommodate multiple active paths between LAN segments. Will not pass unroutable protocols.

Routers, operating in the Network layer, use network address information to move data through the best path to its destination. To connect different networks, routers must be aware of network addresses. Because routers can determine network addresses, they can be "intelligent" about routing data through a complex internetwork involving multiple networks.

Multiplexers

Multiplexers (mux) enable several devices to simultaneously share a high-bandwidth line.

half-duplexing - each device in the configuration can send and receive information, but only one at a time; while sending the device cannot receive, very much like walkie-talkies.

full-duplexing - each device in the configuration can send and receive simultaneously. The best example of this is the telephone.

Brouter - Data Link and Network

Will act as a router for specified protocols and as a bridge for other specified protocols. Brouters are a hybrid of routers and bridges. Brouters function like routers, relaying data transmissions between networks, but when they encounter a data unit that uses a protocol with which they are unfamiliar, they work like a bridge and forward the data to the next segment by using a physical address. Because of this ability, you can use brouters for networks on which there is mixed-protocol traffic and for networks that use protocols that do not support routing.

Channel Service Unit/Digital Service Unit (CSU/DSU)

The units are designed to shield network users from electric voltages as well as electrical interference. They also ready data for transmission by adhering to any network rules.

Both units are parts of a data communications equipment (DCE) device and are collectively referred to as a CSU/DSU. A CSU/DSU operates like a modem; however, it is a digital-to-digital device rather than digital-to-analog. It readies digital signals and guarantees that they have sufficient strength and the proper format to be transmitted over digital WAN links.

Gateway - Transport, Session, Presentation and Application. Used for communications between different NOS's. Takes the packet, strips off the old protocol and repackages it for the receiving network. A gateway basically grants a workstation a direct connection to the host computer and acts as a messenger between the two systems. Gateways operate between the OSI Transport layer through the Application Layer.

Transmission Media Adapter - - Adapter used to connect dissimilar NIC and cable connections (i.e. RJ-45 to RS-232 adapter).

MAUs - (Multistation Access Unit) an access device used to connect the main cabling structure to devices in use on a Token Ring network. This device adds fault tolerance to the network so that a single failure doesn't stop the whole network.

Broadband and Baseband

Baseband transmissions use the entire medium's capacity for a single channel over digital signaling. Since only one signal at a time can occupy a channel, the use of a MUX will allow multiple devices to send multiple signals using a single transmission medium. Provide excellent throughput because the digital signal occupies the entire channel.

Broadband transmissions share the medium's bandwidth over multiple analog channels unidirectionally. This is performed using different frequencies and a process known as FDM (frequency division multiplexing). Since these transmission work very well over long distances, WAN communications take advantage of this technology.

NICs

A **network card**, **network adapter** or **NIC** (network interface card) is a piece of computer hardware designed to allow computers to communicate over a computer network. It is both an OSI layer 1 (physical layer) and layer 2 (data link layer) device, as it provides physical access to a networking medium and provides a low-level addressing system through the use of MAC addresses. It allows users to connect to each other either by using cables or wirelessly.

Although other network technologies exist, Ethernet has achieved near-ubiquity since the mid-1990s. Every Ethernet network card has a unique 48-bit serial number called a MAC address, which is stored in ROM carried on the card. Every computer on an Ethernet network must have a card with a unique MAC address.

No two cards ever manufactured share the same address.

This is accomplished by the Institute of Electrical and Electronics Engineers (IEEE), which is responsible for assigning unique MAC addresses to the vendors of network interface controllers.

Whereas network cards used to be expansion cards that plug into a computer bus, the low cost and ubiquity of the Ethernet standard means that most newer computers have a network interface built into the motherboard. These motherboards either have Ethernet capabilities integrated into the motherboard chipset, or implemented via a low cost dedicated Ethernet chip, connected through the PCI (or the newer PCI express bus). A separate network card is not required unless multiple interfaces are needed or some other type of network is used. Newer motherboards may even have dual network (Ethernet) interfaces built-in.

The card implements the electronic circuitry required to communicate using a specific physical layer and data link layer standard such as Ethernet or token ring. This provides a base for a full network protocol stack, allowing communication among small groups of computers on the same LAN and large-scale network communications through routable protocols, such as IP. There are four techniques used to transfer data, the NIC may use one or more of these techniques.

- Polling is where the microprocessor examines the status of the peripheral under program control.
- Programmed I/O is where the microprocessor alerts the designated peripheral by applying its address to the system's address bus.
- Interrupt-driven I/O is where the peripheral alerts the microprocessor that it's ready to transfer data.
- DMA is where the intelligent peripheral assumes control of the system bus to access memory directly. This removes load from the CPU but requires a separate processor on the card.

A network card typically has a twisted pair, BNC, or AUI socket where the network cable is connected, and a few LEDs to inform the user of whether the network is active, and whether or not there is data being transmitted on it. The Network Cards are typically available in 10/100/1000 Mbit/s(Mbit/s). This means they can support a transfer rate of 10 or 100 or 1000 Megabits per second.

Notable manufacturers

- 3Com
- AMD
- Belkin
- Cisco
- Intel
- National Semiconductor
- Novell
- VIA Networking.
- AEI Intelligent Technologies
- ASIX Electronics
- Broadcom
- Digital Equipment Corporation (DEC)
- Marvell Technology Group
- Netgear
- Realtek

Hubs

An **Ethernet hub** or **concentrator** is a device for connecting multiple twisted pair or fiber optic Ethernet devices together, making them act as a single segment. Hubs work at the physical layer (layer 1) of the OSI model. The device is thus a form of multiport repeater. Ethernet hubs are also responsible for forwarding a jam signal to all ports if it detects a collision.

Hubs also often come with a BNC and/or AUI connector to allow connection to legacy 10BASE2 or 10BASE5 network segments. The availability of low-priced Ethernet switches has largely rendered hubs obsolete but they are still seen in older installations and more specialist applications.

Technical information

A hubbed Ethernet network behaves like a shared-medium, that is, only one device can successfully transmit at a time and each host remains responsible for collision detection and retransmission. With 10BASE-T and 100BASE-T links (which generally account for most or all of the ports on a hub) there are separate pairs for transmit and receive but they are used in half duplex mode in which they still effectively behave like shared medium links. An Ethernet hub, or repeater, is a fairly unsophisticated broadcast device. Hubs do not manage any of the traffic that comes through them, and any packet entering any port is broadcast out on every other port (every port other than the port of entry). Since every packet is being sent out through every other port, packet collisions result—which greatly impedes the smooth flow of traffic.

The need for hosts to be able to detect collisions limits the number of hubs and the total size of the network. For 10 Mbit/s networks, up to 5 segments (4 hubs) are allowed between any two end stations. For 100 Mbit/s networks, the limit is reduced to 3 segments (2 hubs) between any two end stations, and even that is only allowed if the hubs are of the low delay variety.

Some hubs have special (and generally manufacturer specific) stack ports allowing them to be combined in a way that allows more hubs than simple chaining through Ethernet cables, but even so a large Fast Ethernet network is likely to require switches to avoid the chaining limits of hubs.

Most hubs detect typical problems, such as excessive collisions on individual ports, and *partition* the port, disconnecting it from the shared medium. Thus, hub-based Ethernet is generally more robust than coaxial cable-based Ethernet, where a misbehaving device can disable the entire segment. Even if not partitioned automatically, a hub makes troubleshooting easier because status lights can indicate the possible problem source or, as a last resort, devices can be disconnected from a hub one at a time much more easily than a coaxial cable. They also remove the need to troubleshoot faults on a huge cable with multiple taps.

Hub-based Ethernet is generally more robust than coaxial cable-based Ethernet

Dual speed hubs

In the early days of Fast Ethernet, Fast Ethernet switches were relatively expensive devices. However, hubs suffered from the problem that as simple repeaters they could only support a single speed. Whilst normal PCs with expansion slots could be easily upgraded to Fast Ethernet with a new network card, computers with less common expansion mechanisms, or no expansion bus at all, and other equipment, such as printers, could be expensive or impossible to upgrade.

Therefore, a compromise between a hub and a switch appeared known as a dual speed hub. These split the network into two segments, each acting like a hubbed network at its respective speed with a two-port switch between them. Therefore, they allowed mixing of the two speeds without the cost of a Fast Ethernet switch.

Usefulness

Historically, the main reason for purchasing hubs rather than switches was price. This has largely been eliminated by reductions in the price of switches, but hubs can still be useful in special circumstances:

- A protocol analyzer connected to a switch does not always receive all the desired packets since the switch separates the ports into different segments. Connecting the protocol analyzer to a hub allows it to see all the traffic on the segment. (Expensive switches can be configured to allow one port to listen in on traffic on another port. However, these cost much more than a hub.)

- Some computer clusters require each member computer to receive all of the traffic going to the cluster. A hub will do this naturally; using a switch requires implementing special tricks.
- When a switch is accessible for end users to make connections, for example, in a conference room, an inexperienced or careless user (or saboteur) can bring down the network by connecting two ports together, causing a loop. This can be prevented by using a hub, where a loop will break other users on the hub, but not the rest of the network. (It can also be prevented by buying switches that can detect and deal with loops, for example by implementing the Spanning Tree Protocol.)
- A cheap hub with a 10BASE2 port is probably the cheapest and easiest way to connect devices that only support 10BASE2 to a modern network (cheap switches don't tend to come with 10BASE2 ports). The same goes for linking in an old thicknet network segment using an AUI port on a hub (individual devices that were intended for thicknet can be linked to modern Ethernet by using an AUI-10BASE-T transceiver).

Repeaters

A **repeater** is an electronic device that receives a weak or low-level signal and retransmits it at a higher level or higher power, so that the signal can cover longer distances without degradation.

The term "repeater" originated with telegraphy and referred to an electromechanical device used to regenerate telegraph signals.

Use of the term has continued in telephony and data communications.In telecommunication, the term **repeater** has the following standardized meanings:

1. An analog device that amplifies an input signal regardless of its nature (analog or digital).
2. A digital device that amplifies, reshapes, retimes, or performs a combination of any of these functions on a digital input signal for retransmission.

Because repeaters work with the actual physical signal, and do not attempt to interpret the data being transmitted, they operate on the Physical layer, the first layer of the OSI model.

A digipeater is a blend meaning "digital repeater", particularly used in amateur radio. Digipeaters generally receive a transmission and then retransmit it on the same frequency, unlike repeaters that receive on one and transmit on another frequency.

Repeaters are often used in trans-continental and trans-oceanic cables, because the attenuation (signal loss) over such distances would be completely unacceptable without them. Repeaters are used in both copper-wire cables carrying electrical signals, and in fibre optics carrying light.

Repeaters are used in radio communication services. Radio repeaters often transmit and receive on different frequencies. A special subgroup of those repeaters is those used in amateur radio.

Repeaters are also used extensively in broadcasting, where they are known as translators or boosters.

When providing a point-to-point telecom link using radio beyond line of sight, one uses repeaters in a microwave radio relay. A reflector, often on a mountain top, that relays such signals around an obstacle, is called a **passive repeater.**

In optical communications the term **repeater** is used to describe a piece of equipment that receives an optical signal, converts that signal into an electrical one, regenerates it, and then retransmits an optical signal. Since such a device converts the optical signal into an electrical one, and then back to an optical signal, they are often known as Optical-Electrical-Optical (OEO) repeaters.

Before the invention of electronic amplifiers, mechanically coupled carbon microphones were used as amplifiers in telephone repeaters. The invention of the audion tube made transcontinental telephony practical. In the 1930s vacuum tube repeaters using hybrid coils became common place, allowing the use of thinner wires.

In the 1950s negative impedance gain devices were more popular, and a transistorized version called the E6 repeater was the final major type used in the Bell System before the low cost of digital transmission made all voice band repeaters obsolete.

Multiplexers

A **multiplexer** or **mux** (*occasionally the term* ***muldex*** *is also found, for a combination multiplexer-demultiplexer*) is a device that selects one of many data-sources and outputs that source into a single channel.

A demultiplexer (or demux) is a device taking a single input that selects one of many data-output-lines and connects the single input to the selected output line. A multiplexer is often used with a complementary demultiplexer on the receiving end.

In electronics, multiplexers function as multiple-input, single-output switches. A multiplexer has multiple inputs and a selector that connects a specific input to the single output. The schematic symbol for a multiplexer is an isosceles trapezoid with the longer parallel side containing the input pins and the short parallel side containing the output pin. The schematic on the right shows a 2-to-1 multiplexer on the left and an equivalent switch on the right. The *sel* wire connects the desired input to the output.

In digital signal processing (DSP), the multiplexer takes several separate digital data streams and combines them together into one data stream of a higher data rate. This allows multiple data streams to be carried from one place to another over one physical link, which saves cost.

Modes and Routers

Router is a computer networking device that buffers and forwards data packets across an internetwork toward their destinations, through a process known as routing. Routing occurs at layer 3 (the Network layer e.g. IP) of the OSI seven-layer protocol stack.

Router acts as a junction between two or more networks to buffer and transfer data packets among them. A router is different from a switch and a hub: a router is working on layer 3 of OSI model, a switch on layer 2 and a hub on layer 1. This makes them work for different situations: a switch connects devices to form a Local area network (LAN) (which might, in turn, be connected to *another* network via a router).

One easy illustration for the different functions of routers and switches is to think of switches as neighbourhood streets, and the router as the intersections with the street signs. Each house on the street has an address within a range on the block. In the same way, a switch connects various devices each with their own IP address(es) on a LAN. However, the switch knows nothing about IP addresses except its own management address. Routers connect networks together the way that on-ramps or major intersections connect streets to both highways and freeways, etc. The street signs at the intersection (routing table) show which way the packets need to flow.

So for example, a router at home connects the Internet Service Provider's (ISP) network (usually on an Internet address) together with the LAN in the home (typically using a range of private IP addresses, see network address translation) and a single broadcast domain. The switch connects devices together to form the LAN. Sometimes the switch and the router are combined together in one single package sold as a multiple port router.

In order to route packets, a router communicates with other routers using routing protocols and using this information creates and maintains a routing table. The routing table stores the best routes to certain network destinations, the "routing metrics" associated with those routes, and the path to the next hop router. See the routing article for a more detailed discussion of how this works.

Routing is most commonly associated with the Internet Protocol, although other less-popular routed protocols are in use.

History

The first Internet router was developed at BBN as part of their contract to build out the original Arpanet. The first multiprotocol router was created at Stanford University by a staff researcher named William Yeage in January of 1980. His boss at the time told him that he was the "network guy" and to find a way to connect the computers in the computer science department, medical center and department of electrical engineering. He first wrote a network operating system and routing code to run on a DEC PDP11/05. He used Alan Snyder's Portable C compiler but it generated too much code so he modified the compiler to improve the code generators.That still wasn't good enough so he wrote an optimizer for PDP11/05 assembler that reduced the code size further.

Types of routers

In the origin era of routing (from the mid-1970s through the 1980s), general-purpose mini-computers served as routers. Although general-purpose computers can perform routing, modern high-speed routers are highly specialized computers, generally with extra hardware added to accelerate both common routing functions such as packet forwarding and specialised functions such as IPsec encryption.

Other changes also improve reliability, such as using DC power rather than line power (which can be provided from batteries in data centers), and using solid-state rather than magnetic storage for program loading.

Large modern routers have thus come to resemble telephone switches, with whose technology they are currently converging and may eventually replace, whilst small routers have become a common household item.

A router that connects clients to the Internet is called an *edge router*. A router that serves solely to transmit data between other routers, e.g. inside the network of an Internet service provider, is called a *core router*.

A router is normally used to connect at least two networks, but a special variety of router is the one-armed router, used to route packets in a virtual LAN environment. In the case of a one-armed router, the multiple attachments to different networks are all over the same physical link.

In mobile ad-hoc networks every host performs routing and forwarding by itself, while in wired networks there is usually just one router for a whole broadcast domain.

6

Network Administration Security

Server Chief Technology and Server Management

Server (also called a server application) is "an application program that accepts connections in order to service requests by sending back responses." (RFC 2616 (Hypertext Transfer Protocol — HTTP/1.1)) A server application can run on the same computer as the client application using it, or they can connect through a computer network. Examples include file server, database server, backup server, print server, mail server, web server, FTP server, application server, VPN server, DHCP server, DNS server, WINS server, logon server, security server, domain controller, backup domain controller, proxy server, firewall, etc.

Server is an adjective in the term server operating system.

A server operating system is intended, enabled, or better able to run server applications. The differences between the server version and the "workstation" version of an operating system vary. Sometimes (as in the case of Windows 2000 and Windows 2000 Server), the primary difference is the removal of arbitrary license-dependent limits on the number of network file share connections accepted. Some server editions include additional server applications bundled with the operating system. Some server applications (e.g. Microsoft IIS) impose arbitrary limits on the number of HTTP connections they will accept, depending on whether they are running under a server operating system or not.

A server computer (often called server for short) is a computer system that has been designated for running a specific server application or applications.

A computer that is designated for only one server application is often named for that application. For example, when Apache HTTP Server (software) is a company's web server, the computer running it is also called the web server. Server applications can be divided among server computers over an extreme range, depending upon the workload. Under light loading, every server application can run concurrently on a single computer. Under heavy loading, multiple server computers may be required for each application. Under medium loading, it is common to use one server computer per server application, in order to limit the amount of damage caused by failure of any single server computer or security breach of any single server application. Any server computer can also be used as a workstation, but it is avoided in practice, again to contain risk.

Server or server computer is also a designation for computer models intended for use running server applications, often under heavy workloads, unattended, for extended time. While any "workstation" computer can run server operating systems and server applications, a server computer usually has special features intended to make it more suitable. Distinctions often include faster processor and memory, more RAM, larger hard drives, higher reliability, redundant power supplies, redundant hard drives (RAID), compact size and shape, modular design (e.g., blade servers often used in server farms), rack or cabinet mountability, serial console redirection, etc.

The name server or server appliance also applies to network-connected computer appliances or "appliance hardware" that provides specific services onto the network. Though the appliance is a server computer, loaded with a server operating system and a server application, the user need not configure any of it. It is a black box that does a specific job. The simplest servers are most often sold as appliances, for example switches, routers, gateways, print servers, net modems.

Server Hardware

Although servers can be built from commodity computer components—particularly for low-load and/or non-critical applications—dedicated, high-load, mission-critical servers use specialized hardware that is optimized for the needs of servers.

For example, servers may incorporate "industrial-strength" mechanical components such as disk drives and fans that provide very high reliability and performance at a correspondingly high price. Aesthetic considerations are ignored, since most servers operate in unattended computer rooms and are only visited for maintenance or repair purposes. Although servers usually require large amounts of disk space, smaller disk drives may still be used in a trade-off of capacity vs. reliability.

CPU speeds are far less critical for many servers than they are for many desktops. Not only are typical server tasks likely to be delayed more by I/O requests than processor requirements, but the lack of any graphical user interface (GUI) in many servers frees up very large amounts of processing power for other tasks, making the overall processor power requirement lower. If a great deal of processing power is required in a server, there is a tendency to add more CPUs rather than increase the speed of a single CPU, again for reasons of reliability and redundancy.

The lack of a GUI in a server (or the rare need to use it) makes it unnecessary to install expensive video adapters. Similarly, elaborate audio interfaces, joystick connections, USB peripherals, and the like are usually unnecessary.

Because servers must operate continuously and reliably, noisy but efficient and trustworthy fans may be used for ventilation instead of inexpensive and quiet fans; and in some cases, centralized air-conditioning may be used to keep servers cool, instead of or in addition to fans. Special uninterruptible power supplies may be used to ensure that the servers continue to run in the event of a power failure.

Typical servers include heavy-duty network connections in order to allow them to handle the large amounts of traffic that they typically receive and generate as they receive and reply to client requests.

The major difference between servers and desktop computers is not in the hardware but in the software. Servers often run operating systems that are designed specifically for use in servers. They also run special applications that are designed specifically to carry out server tasks.

Servers have a unique property where the more powerful and complex the system, the longer it takes for the hardware to turn on and begin loading the operating system. Servers often do extensive pre-boot memory testing and verification, along with starting up remote management services The hard drive controllers then start up banks of drives in sequence so as not to overload the power supply with the sudden surge of everything turning on at once, then followed by RAID system prechecks for correct operation of redundancy. It is not uncommon for all these preboot hardware checks to take several minutes, but then for the machine to run continuously for months at a time.

Server Operating Systems

The Microsoft Windows operating system is predominant among desktop computers, but in the world of servers, the most popular operating systems—such as FreeBSD, Solaris, and GNU/Linux—are derived from or similar to the UNIX operating system. UNIX was originally a minicomputer operating system, and as servers gradually replaced traditional minicomputers, UNIX was a logical and efficient choice of operating system for the servers.

Server-oriented operating systems tend to have certain features in common that make them more suitable for the server environment, such as the absence of a GUI (or an optional GUI); the ability to be reconfigured (in both hardware and software) to at least some extent without stopping the system; advanced backup facilities to permit online backups of critical data at regular and frequent intervals; facilities to enable the movement of data between different volumes or devices in such a way that is transparent to the end user; flexible and advanced networking capabilities; features (such as daemons in UNIX or services in Windows) that make unattended execution of programs more reliable; tight system security, with advanced user, resource, data, and memory protection, and so on.

Server-oriented operating systems in many cases can interact with hardware sensors to detect conditions such as overheating, processor and disk failure, and either alert an operator, take remedial action, or both, depending on the configuration.

Because the requirements of servers are, in some cases, almost diametrically opposed to those of desktop computers, it is extremely difficult to design an operating system that handles both environments well; thus, operating systems that are well suited to the desktop may not be ideal for servers and vice versa. Nevertheless, certain versions of Windows are also used on a minority of servers as are recent versions of the popular Mac OS X (which is Unix-based, and gives users complete access to the Unix operating system) family of desktop operating systems and even some proprietary mainframe operating systems (such as z/OS); but the dominant operating systems among servers continues to be UNIX versions or clones. Even in the case of GNU/Linux, a popular UNIX-like operating system frequently used on servers, configurations that are ideal for servers may be unsatisfactory for desktop use, and configurations that perform well on the desktop may leave much to be desired on servers.

The rise of the microprocessor-based server was facilitated by the development of several versions of the Unix operating system to run on the Intel x86 microprocessor architecture, including Solaris, GNU/Linux and FreeBSD. The Microsoft Windows family of operating systems also runs on Intel hardware, and versions beginning with Windows NT have incorporated features making them suitable for use on servers.

Whilst the role of server and desktop operating systems remains distinct, improvements in both hardware performance and reliability and operating system reliability have blurred the distinction between these two classes of system, which at one point remained largely separate in terms of code base, hardware and vendor providers. Today, many desktop and server operating systems share the same code base, and differ chiefly in terms of configuration. Furthermore, the rationalisation of many corporate applications towards web-based and middleware platforms has lessened the demand for specialist application servers.

Servers on the Internet

Almost the entire structure of the Internet is based upon a client-server model. Many millions of servers are connected to the Internet and run continuously throughout the world.

Among the many services provided by Internet servers are: the Web; the Domain Name System; electronic mail; file transfer; instant messaging; streaming audio and video, online gaming, and countless others. Virtually every action taken by an ordinary Internet user requires one or more interactions with one or more servers.

There are also technologies that operate on an inter-server level.

Servers in Daily Life

Remember that any computer or device serving out applications or services can technically be called a server. In an office or enterprise environment, the network server is easy to identify. However, if you are reading this, you probably have a server in your home. Your DSL/Cable router is a server as it provides your computer with application services such as assigning an IP address via Dynamic Host Configuration Protocol, DHCP), and Network Address Translation (NAT) services which is the firewall that protects your computer from the internet.

Your iTunes software on your computer acts as your music server for your iPod. When you share your printer or a folder on your computer, your computer suddenly becomes a server. It is these instances, often, that can cause security problems in homes. Your wireless access point, if not secured properly, can also serve out your network connection to your neighbour who then can see the folder you shared out to your wife's computer with all the financial information she needs to do your taxes. Hence why securing home networks has become so important.

Raid Management and Mirroring

In computing, specifically computer storage, a Redundant Array of Independent Drives (or Disks), also known as Redundant Array of Inexpensive Drives (or Disks) (RAID) is an umbrella term for data storage schemes that divide and/or replicate data among multiple hard drives. They offer, depending on the scheme, increased data reliability and/or I/O performance.

Most schemes are numbered and referred to as levels. RAID began as a collection of five such levels but has since grown to include many more, notably several nested levels and many non-standard levels (mostly proprietary).

Basic Functions

Fundamentally, RAID combines multiple hard disks into a single logical unit. There are two ways this can be done: in hardware and in software. Hardware combines the drives into a logical unit in dedicated hardware which then presents the drives as a single drive to the operating system. Software does this within the operating system and presents the drives as a single drive to the users of the system.

RAID is typically used on servers but can be used on workstations. This is especially true in storage-intensive computers such as those used for video and audio editing.

History

Norman Ken Ouchi at IBM was awarded a 1978 U.S. patent 4,092.732 titled "System for recovering data stored in failed memory unit." The claims for this patent describe what would later be termed RAID 5 with full stripe writes. This 1978 patent also mentions that disk mirroring or duplexing (what would later be termed RAID 1) and protection with dedicated parity (that would later be termed RAID 4) were prior art at that time.

The term RAID was first defined by David A. Patterson, Garth A. Gibson and Randy Katz at the University of California, Berkeley in 1987. They studied the possibility of using two or more drives to appear as a single device to the host system and published a paper: "A Case for Redundant Arrays of Inexpensive Disks (RAID)" in June 1988 at the SIGMOD conference.

This specification suggested a number of prototype "RAID levels", or combinations of drives.

Each had theoretical advantages and disadvantages. Over the years, different implementations of the RAID concept have appeared. Most differ substantially from the original idealized RAID levels, but the numbered names have remained. This can be confusing, since one implementation of RAID 5, for example, can differ substantially from another. RAID 3 and RAID 4 are often confused and even used interchangeably.

Their paper formally defined RAID levels 1 through 5 in sections 7 to 11:

- "First Level RAID: Mirrored drives"
- "Second Level RAID: Hamming Code for Error Correction"
- "Third Level RAID: Single Check Disk Per Group"
- "Fourth Level RAID: Independent Reads and Writes"
- "Fifth Level RAID: Spread data/parity over all drives (no single check disk)"

RAID levels have been recently standarized by SNIA.

Standard RAID levels

A quick summary of the most commonly used RAID levels (N.B This summary assumes you have your system partition on another disk i.e. Raid 5 Requires 3 Disks Min for RAID + 1 for System Partiton):

- RAID 0: Striped Set (2 disks minimum) without parity. Provides improved performance and additional storage but no fault tolerance from disk errors or disk failure. Any disk failure destroys the array, which becomes more likely with more disks in the array. The reason a single disk failure destroys the entire array is because when data is written to a RAID 0 drive, the data is broken into "fragments". The number of fragments is dictated by the number of disks in the drive. Each of these fragments are written to their respective disks simultaneously on the same sector. This allows the entire chunk of data to be read off the drive in parallel, giving this type of arrangement huge bandwidth. When one sector on one of the disks fails though, the corresponding sector on every other disk is rendered useless because part of the data is now corrupted. RAID 0 does not implement error checking so any error is unrecoverable. More disks in the drive means higher bandwidth, but greater risk of data loss.
- RAID 1: Mirrored Set (2 disks minimum) without parity. Provides fault tolerance from disk errors and single disk failure. Increased read performance occurs when using a multi-threaded operating system that supports split seeks, very small performance reduction when writing. Array continues to operate so long as at least one drive is functioning.
- RAID 3 and RAID 4: Striped Set (3 disks minimum) with Dedicated Parity, the parity bits represent a memory location each, they have a value of 0 or 1, whether the given memory location is empty or full, thus enhancing the speed of read and write. Provides

improved performance and fault tolerance similar to RAID 5, but with a dedicated parity disk rather than rotated parity stripes. The single disk is a bottle-neck for writing since every write requires updating the parity data. One minor benefit is that the dedicated parity disk allows the parity drive to fail and operation will continue without parity or performance penalty.

- RAID 5: Striped Set (3 disks minimum) with Distributed Parity. Distributed parity requires all but one drive to be present to operate; drive failure requires replacement, but the array is not destroyed by a single drive failure. Upon drive failure, any subsequent reads can be calculated from the distributed parity such that the drive failure is masked from the end user. The array will have data loss in the event of a second drive failure and is vulnerable until the data that was on the failed drive is rebuilt onto a replacement drive.
- RAID 6: Striped Set (4 disks minimum) with Dual Distributed Parity. Provides fault tolerance from two drive failures; array continues to operate with up to two failed drives. This makes larger RAID groups more practical. This is becoming a popular choice for SATA drives as they approach 1 Terabyte in size. This is because the single parity RAID levels are vulnerable to data loss until the failed drive is rebuilt. The larger the drive, the longer the rebuild will take. With dual parity, it gives the array time to rebuild onto a large drive with the ability to sustain another drive failure.

Nested RAID levels

Many storage controllers allow RAID levels to be nested. That is, one RAID can use another as its basic element, instead of using physical drives. It is instructive to think of these arrays as layered on top of each other, with physical drives at the bottom.

Nested RAIDs are usually signified by joining the numbers indicating the RAID levels into a single number, sometimes with a '+' in between. For example, RAID 10 (or RAID 1+0) conceptually consists of multiple level 1 arrays stored on physical drives with a level 0 array on top, striped over the level 1 arrays. In the case of RAID 0+1, it is most often called RAID 0+1 as opposed to RAID 01 to avoid confusion with RAID 1. However, when the top array is a RAID 0 (such as in RAID 10 and RAID 50), most vendors choose to omit the '+', though RAID 5+0 is more informative.

Common nested RAID levels

- RAID 0+1: Striped Set + Mirrored Set (4 disks minimum; Even number of disks) provides fault tolerance and improved performance but increases complexity. The key difference from RAID 1+0 is that RAID 0+1 creates a second striped set to mirror a primary striped set. The Array continues to operate with one or more drives failed in the same mirror set, but if two or more drives fail on different sides of the mirroring, the data on the RAID system is lost.
- RAID 1+0: Mirrored Set + Striped Set (4 disks minimum; Even number of disks)

provides fault tolerance and improved performance but increases complexity. The key difference from RAID 0+1 is that RAID 1+0 creates a striped set from a series of mirrored drives. The array can sustain multiple drive losses as long as no two drives lost comprise a single pair of one mirror.

- RAID 5+0: A stripe across distributed parity RAID systems.
- RAID 5+1: A mirror striped set with distributed parity (some manufacturers label this as RAID 53).

Non-standard RAID levels

Given the large amount of custom configurations available with a RAID array, many companies, organizations, and groups have created their own non-standard configurations, typically designed to meet at least one but usually very small niche groups of arrays. Most of these non-standard RAID levels are proprietary.

Some of the more prominent modifications are:

- ATTO Technology's DVRAID™ adds parity RAID protection to systems which demand performance for 4K film, 2K film, high-definition audio and video.
- The Storage Computer Corporation uses RAID 7, which adds caching to RAID 3 and RAID 4 to improve performance.
- EMC Corporation offers RAID S as an alternative to RAID 5 on their Symmetrix systems.
- RAID-Z in the zfs file system of Open Solaris solves the "write hole" problem of RAID-5.

RAID Implementations

Hardware and/or software RAID based solutions: The distribution of data across multiple drives can be managed either by dedicated hardware or by software. Additionally, there are hybrid RAIDs that are partially software and hardware-based solutions.

Software RAID

Software implementations are provided by most operating systems. A software layer sits above the (generally block based) disk device drivers and provides an abstraction layer between the logical drives (RAID arrays) and physical drives. Software RAID is typically limited to RAID 0 (striping across multiple drives for increased space and performance), RAID 1 (mirroring two drives) and RAID 5 (data striping with parity).

In a multi-threaded operating system (such as Linux, FreeBSD, Mac OS X, Windows NT/2000/XP/Vista and Novell NetWare) the operating system can perform overlapped I/O, allowing multiple read or write requests to be initiated without waiting for completion on each request. This is the capability that makes RAID 0/1 possible in an operating system.

However, most operating systems do not support RAID 0/1 striping or mirroring with parity, due to the substantial processing demands of calculating parity.

Software implementations require some very small amount of processing time, which is provided by the main CPU in the host system. Since SCSI, PATA, and SATA drives all support asynchronous read/write, any multi-threaded operating system can support non-parity RAID on multiple hard drives with only a one percent increase in CPU overhead.

Software implementations can exceed the performance levels of hardware-based RAID due to the high-performance of modern CPUs[citation needed]. Since the software must run on a host server attached to storage, the processor (as mentioned above) on that host must dedicate processing time to run the RAID software. Like hardware-based RAID, if the server experiences a hardware failure, the attached storage could be inaccessible for a period of time.

Software implementations can allow RAID arrays to be created from partitions rather than entire physical drives.

Hardware RAID

A hardware implementation of RAID requires at a minimum a special-purpose RAID controller. On a desktop system, this may be a PCI expansion card, or might be a capability built in to the motherboard. In industrial applications the controller and drives are provided as a stand alone enclosure. The drives may be IDE/ATA, SATA, SCSI, SSA, Fibre Channel, or any combination thereof. The using system can be directly attached to the controller or, more commonly, connected via a SAN. The controller hardware handles the management of the drives, and performs any parity calculations required by the chosen RAID level.

Most hardware implementations provide a non-volatile read/write cache which, depending on the I/O workload, will improve performance. Cached RAID controllers are most commonly used in industrial applications.

Hardware implementations provide guaranteed performance, add no overhead to the local CPU complex and can support many operating systems, as the controller simply presents a logical disk to the operating system.

Hardware implementations also typically support hot swapping, allowing failed drives to be replaced while the system is running.

Hybrid RAID

Hybrid RAID implementations have become very popular with the introduction of inexpensive RAID controllers, implemented using a standard disk controller and then implementing the RAID in the controllers BIOS extension (for early boot-up/real mode operation) and the operating system driver (for after the system switches to protected mode). Since these controllers actually do all calculations typically proprietary to a given RAID controller manufacturer and typically cannot span multiple controllers. The only advantages over software RAID are that the BIOS can boot from them, and the tighter integration with the device driver may offer better error handling.

Both hardware and software implementations may support the use of hot spare drives, a pre-installed drive which is used to immediately (and almost always automatically) replace a drive that has failed. This reduces the mean time to repair period during which a second drive failure in the same RAID redundancy group can result in loss of data. It also prevents data loss when multiple drives fail in a short period of time, as is common when all drives in an array have undergone very similar use patterns, and experience wear-out failures.

Reliability of RAID configurations

Failure Rate

The mean time to failure (MTTF) or the mean time between failure (MTBF) of a given RAID may be lower or higher than those of its constituent hard drives, depending on what type of RAID is employed.

Mean Time to Data Loss (MTTDL)

In this context, the average time before a loss of data in a given array.

Mean Time to Recovery (MTTR)

In arrays that include redundancy for reliability, this is the time following a failure to restore an array to its normal failure-tolerant mode of operation. This includes time to replace a failed disk mechanism as well as time to re-build the array (i.e. to replicate data for redundancy).

Unrecoverable Bit Error Rate (UBE)

This is the rate at which a disk drive will be unable to recover data after application of cyclic redundancy check (CRC) codes and multiple retries. This failure will present as a sector read failure. Some RAID implementations protect against this failure mode by remapping the bad sector, using the redundant data to retrieve a good copy of the data, and rewriting that good data to the newly mapped replacement sector. The UBE rate is typically specified at 1 bit in 1015 for enterprise class disk drives (SCSI, FC, SAS) , and 1 bit in 1014 for desktop class disk drives (IDE, ATA, SATA). Increasing disk capacities and large RAID 5 redundancy groups have led to an increasing inability to successfully rebuild a RAID group after a disk failure because an unrecoverable sector is found on the remaining drives. Double protection schemes such as RAID 6 are attempting to address this issue, but suffer from a very high write penalty.

Atomic Write Failure

Also known by various terms such as torn writes, torn pages, incomplete writes, interrupted writes, non-transactional, etc. This is a little understood and rarely mentioned failure mode for redundant storage systems that do not utilize transactional features. Database researcher Jim Gray wrote "Update in Place is a Poison Apple" during the early days of relational database commercialization. However, this warning largely went unheeded and fell by the wayside upon the advent of RAID, which many software engineers mistook as solving all data storage integrity and reliability problems. Many software programs update a storage object "in-place"; that is, they write a new version of the object on to the same disk addresses as the old version of the object. While the software may also log some delta information elsewhere, it expects the storage to present "atomic write semantics," meaning that the write of the data either occurred in its entirety or did not occur at all.

However, very few storage systems provide support for atomic writes, and even fewer specify their rate of failure in providing this semantic. Note that during the act of writing an object, a RAID storage device will usually be writing all redundant copies of the object in parallel, although overlapped or staggered writes are more common when a single RAID processor is responsible for multiple drives. Hence an error that occurs during the process of writing may leave the redundant copies in different states, and furthermore may leave the copies in neither the old nor the new state. The little known failure mode is that delta logging relies on the original data being either in the old or the new state so as to enable backing out the logical change, yet few storage systems provide an atomic write semantic on a RAID disk.

Since transactional support is not universally present in hardware RAID, many operating systems include transactional support to protect against data loss during an interrupted write.

Novell Netware, starting with version 3.x, included a transaction tracking system. Microsoft introduced transaction tracking via the journalling feature in NTFS.

To mitigate this problem, some high-end RAID cards use a battery-backed write cache. If an "atomic" write only partially completes because of power failure, the controller flushed the unwritten data to disk when the power is restored. Some provide the capability of testing the battery periodically (however, this leaves the system without a fully charged battery for several hours). This solution still has potential failure cases: the battery may have worn out, the power may be off for too long, the disks could be moved to another controller, the controller itself could fail in the middle of a write, etc. However, on a well-maintained machine it probably prevents corruption in most incidents.

Hauffman Code and Cryptography

Cryptography is the study of message secrecy. In modern times, cryptography is considered to be a branch of both mathematics and computer science, and is affiliated closely with information theory, computer security, and engineering. Cryptography is used in many applications encountered in everyday life; examples include the security of ATM cards, computer passwords, and electronic commerce, all of which depend on cryptography.

Terminology

Until modern times, cryptography referred almost exclusively to encryption, the process of converting ordinary information (plaintext) into unintelligible gibberish (ie, ciphertext). Decryption is the reverse, moving from unintelligible ciphertext to plaintext. A cipher (or cypher) is a pair of algorithms which perform this encryption and the reversing decryption. The detailed operation of a cipher is controlled both by the algorithm and, in each instance, by a key. This is a secret parameter (known only to the communicants) for a specific message exchange context. Keys are important as ciphers without variable keys are trivially breakable and so rather less than useful for most purposes. Historically, ciphers were often used directly for encryption or decryption, without additional procedures such as authentication or integrity checks.

In colloquial use, the term "code" is often used to mean any method of encryption or concealment of meaning. However, in cryptography, code has a more specific meaning; it means the replacement of a unit of plaintext (i.e., a meaningful word or phrase) with a code word (for example, apple pie replaces attack at dawn). Codes are no longer used in serious cryptography—except incidentally for such things as unit designations (eg, 'Bronco Flight' or Operation Overlord) — since properly chosen ciphers are both more practical and more secure than even the best codes, and better adapted to computers as well.

Some use the English terms cryptography and cryptology interchangeably, while others use cryptography to refer to the use and practice of cryptographic techniques, and cryptology to refer to the subject as a field of study. In this respect, English usage is more tolerant of overlapping meanings and word origins than are several European languages in which meanings of cognate words are more restricted.

History of Cryptography and Cryptanalysis

The Ancient Greek scytale probably much like this modern reconstruction, may have been one of the earliest devices used to implement a cipher.

Before the modern era, cryptography was concerned solely with message confidentiality (i.e., encryption) — conversion of messages from a comprehensible form into an incomprehensible one, and back again at the other end, rendering it unreadable by interceptors or eavesdroppers without secret knowledge (namely, the key needed for decryption of that message). In recent decades, the field has expanded beyond confidentiality concerns to include techniques for message integrity checking, sender/receiver identity authentication, digital signatures, interactive proofs, and secure computation, amongst others.

The earliest forms of secret writing required little more than local pen and paper analogs, as most people could not read. More literacy, or opponent literacy, required actual cryptography. The main classical cipher types are transposition ciphers, which rearrange the order of letters in a message (e.g. 'help me' becomes 'ehpl em' in a trivially simple rearrangement scheme), and substitution ciphers, which systematically replace letters or groups of letters with other letters or groups of letters (e.g., 'fly at once' becomes 'gmz bu podf' by replacing each letter with the one following it in the alphabet). Simple versions of either offered little confidentiality from enterprising opponents, and still don't.

The Enigma machine, used in several variants by the German military between the late 1920s and the end of World War II, implemented a complex electro-mechanical polyalphabetic cipher to protect sensitive communications. Breaking the Enigma cipher at the Biuro Szyfrów, and the subsequent large-scale decryption of Enigma traffic at Bletchley Park, was an important factor contributing to the Allied victory in WWII.

Although frequency analysis is a powerful and general technique, encryption was still often effective in practice; many a would-be cryptanalyst was unaware of the technique. Breaking a message without frequency analysis essentially required knowledge of the cipher used, thus encouraging espionage, bribery, burglary, defection, etc. to discover it. It was finally recognized in the 19th century that secrecy of a cipher's algorithm is not a sensible or practical safeguard; in fact, any adequate cryptographic scheme (including ciphers) should remain secure even if the adversary knows the cipher algorithm itself. Secrecy of the key should alone be sufficient for confidentiality when under attack — for good ciphers. This fundamental principle was first explicitly stated in 1883 by Auguste Kerckhoffs and is generally called Kerckhoffs' principle; alternatively and more bluntly, it was restated by Claude Shannon as Shannon's Maxim — 'the enemy knows the system'.

Various physical devices and aids have been used to assist with ciphers. One of the earliest may have been the scytale of ancient Greece, a rod supposedly used by the Spartans as an aid for a transposition cipher. In medieval times, other aids were invented such as the cipher grille, also used for a kind of steganography. With the invention of polyalphabetic ciphers came more sophisticated aids such as Alberti's own cipher disk, Johannes Trithemius' tabula recta scheme, and Thomas Jefferson's multi-cylinder (invented independently by Bazeries around 1900). Early in the 20th century, several mechanical encryption/decryption devices were invented, and many patented, including rotor machines — most famously the Enigma machine used by Germany in World War II. The ciphers implemented by better quality examples of these designs brought about a substantial increase in cryptanalytic difficulty after WWI.

The development of digital computers and electronics after WWII made possible much more complex ciphers.

Furthermore, computers allowed for the encryption of any kind of data that is represented by computers in any binary format, unlike classical ciphers which only encrypted written language texts, dissolving the utility of a linguistic approach to cryptanalysis in many cases. Many computer ciphers can be characterized by their operation on binary bit sequences (sometimes in groups or blocks), unlike classical and mechanical schemes, which generally manipulate traditional characters (i.e., letters and digits) directly.

However, computers have also assisted cryptanalysis, which has compensated to some extent for increased cipher complexity. Nonetheless, good modern ciphers have stayed ahead of cryptanalysis; it is usually the case that use of a quality cipher is very efficient (i.e., fast and requiring few resources), while breaking it requires an effort many orders of magnitude larger, making cryptanalysis so inefficient and impractical as to be effectively impossible. A credit card with smart card capabilities. The 3 by 5 mm chip embedded in the card is shown enlarged in the insert. Smart cards attempt to combine portability with the power to compute modern cryptographic algorithms.

Extensive open academic research into cryptography is relatively recent — it began only in the mid-1970s with the public specification of DES (the Data Encryption Standard) by the NBS, the Diffie-Hellman paper, and the public release of the RSA algorithm. Since then, cryptography has become a widely used tool in communications, computer networks, and computer security generally. The present security level of many modern cryptographic techniques is based on the difficulty of certain computational problems, such as the integer factorisation problem or the discrete logarithm problem. In many cases, there are proofs that cryptographic techniques are secure if a certain computational problem cannot be solved efficiently.With one notable exception—the one-time pad—these proofs are contingent, and thus not definitive, but are currently the best available for cryptographic algorithms and protocols.

As well as being aware of cryptographic history, cryptographic algorithm and system designers must also sensibly consider probable future developments in their designs. For instance, the continued improvements in computer processing power have increased the scope of brute-force attacks when specifying key lengths. The potential effects of quantum computing are already being considered by some cryptographic system designers; the announced imminence of small implementations of these machines is making the need for this pre-emptive caution fully explicit.

Essentially, prior to the early 20th century, cryptography was chiefly concerned with linguistic patterns. Since then the emphasis has shifted, and cryptography now makes extensive use of mathematics, including aspects of information theory, computational complexity, statistics, combinatorics, abstract algebra, and number theory. Cryptography is also a branch of engineering, but an unusual one as it deals with active, intelligent, and malevolent opposition most other kinds of engineering need deal only with neutral natural forces. There is also active research examining the relationship between cryptographic problems and quantum physics.

Modern Cryptography

The modern field of cryptography can be divided into several areas of study. The chief ones are discussed here;

Symmetric-key Cryptography

Symmetric-key cryptography refers to encryption methods in which both the sender and receiver share the same key (or, less commonly, in which their keys are different, but related in an easily computable way). This was the only kind of encryption publicly known until 1976.

One round (out of 8.5) of the patented IDEA cipher, used in some versions of PGP for high-speed encryption of, for instance, e-mail.

The modern study of symmetric-key ciphers relates mainly to the study of block ciphers and stream ciphers and to their applications. A block cipher is, in a sense, a modern embodiment of Alberti's polyalphabetic cipher: block ciphers take as input a block of plaintext and a key, and output a block of ciphertext of the same size. Since messages are almost always longer than a single block, some method of knitting together successive blocks is required. Several have been developed, some with better security in one aspect or another than others. They are the mode of operations and must be carefully considered when using a block cipher in a cryptosystem.

The Data Encryption Standard (DES) and the Advanced Encryption Standard (AES) are block cipher designs which have been designated cryptography standards by the US government (though DES's designation was finally withdrawn after the AES was adopted). Despite its deprecation as an official standard, DES (especially its still-approved and much more secure triple-DES variant) remains quite popular; it is used across a wide range of applications, from ATM encryption to e-mail privacy and secure remote access. Many other block ciphers have been designed and released, with considerable variation in quality. Many have been thoroughly broken.

Stream ciphers, in contrast to the 'block' type, create an arbitrarily long stream of key material, which is combined with the plaintext bit-by-bit or character-by-character, somewhat like the one-time pad. In a stream cipher, the output stream is created based on an internal state which changes as the cipher operates. That state's change is controlled by the key, and, in some stream ciphers, by the plaintext stream as well. RC4 is an example of a well-known stream cipher.

Cryptographic hash functions (often called message digest functions) do not use keys, but are a related and important class of cryptographic algorithms. They take input data (often an entire message), and output a short, fixed length hash, and do so as a one-way function. For good ones, collisions (two plaintexts which produce the same hash) are extremely difficult to find.

Message authentication codes (MACs) are much like cryptographic hash functions, except that a secret key is used to authenticate the hash value on receipt.

Public-key Cryptography

Symmetric-key cryptosystems typically use the same key for encryption and decryption, though this message or group of messages may have a different key than others. A significant disadvantage of symmetric ciphers is the key management necessary to use them securely. Each distinct pair of communicating parties must, ideally, share a different key, and perhaps each ciphertext exchanged as well. The number of keys required increases as the square of the number of network members, which very quickly requires complex key management schemes to keep them all straight and secret. The difficulty of establishing a secret key between two communicating parties, when a secure channel doesn't already exist between them, also presents a chicken-and-egg problem which is a considerable practical obstacle for cryptography users in the real world.

In addition to encryption, public-key cryptography can be used to implement digital signature schemes.

A digital signature is reminiscent of an ordinary signature; they both have the characteristic that they are easy for a user to produce, but difficult for anyone else to forge. Digital signatures can also be permanently tied to the content of the message being signed; they cannot be 'moved' from one document to another, for any attempt will be detectable. In digital signature schemes, there are two algorithms: one for signing, in which a secret key is used to process the message (or a hash of the message, or both), and one for verification, in which the matching public key is used with the message to check the validity of the signature. RSA and DSA are two of the most popular digital signature schemes. Digital signatures are central to the operation of public key infrastructures and many network security schemes (SSL/TLS, many VPNs, etc).

Public-key algorithms are most often based on the computational complexity of "hard" problems, often from number theory. For example, the hardness of RSA is related to the integer factorization problem, while Diffie-Hellman and DSA are related to the discrete logarithm problem. More recently, elliptic curve cryptography has developed in which security is based on number of theoretic problems involving elliptic curves. Because of the difficulty of the underlying problems, most public-key algorithms involve operations such as modular multiplication and exponentiation, which are much more computationally expensive than the techniques used in most block ciphers, especially with typical key sizes.

As a result, public-key cryptosystems are commonly hybrid cryptosystems, in which a fast high-quality symmetric-key encryption algorithm is used for the message itself, while the relevant symmetric key is sent with the message, but encrypted using a public-key algorithm. Similarly, hybrid signature schemes are often used, in which a cryptographic hash function is computed, and only the resulting hash is digitally signed.

Cryptanalysis

The goal of cryptanalysis is to find some weakness or insecurity in a cryptographic scheme, thus permitting its subversion or evasion. Cryptanalysis might be undertaken by a malicious attacker, attempting to subvert a system, or by the system's designer (or others) attempting to evaluate whether a system has vulnerabilities, and so it is not inherently a hostile act. In modern practice, however, cryptographic algorithms and protocols must be carefully examined and tested to offer any assurance of the system's security (at least, under clear — and hopefully reasonable — assumptions).

There are a wide variety of cryptanalytic attacks, and they can be classified in any of several ways. A common distinction turns on what an attacker knows and what capabilities are available. In a ciphertext-only attack, the cryptanalyst has access only to the ciphertext (good modern cryptosystems are usually effectively immune to ciphertext-only attacks). In a known-plaintext attack, the cryptanalyst has access to a ciphertext and its corresponding plaintext (or to many such pairs). In a chosen-plaintext attack, the cryptanalyst may choose a plaintext and learn its corresponding ciphertext (perhaps many times); an example is gardening, used by the British during WWII. Finally, in a chosen-ciphertext attack, the cryptanalyst may choose ciphertexts and learn their corresponding plaintexts. Also important, often overwhelmingly so, are mistakes (generally in the design or use of one of the protocols) involved;

Cryptanalysis of symmetric-key ciphers typically involves looking for attacks against the block ciphers or stream ciphers that are more efficient than any attack that could be against a perfect cipher. For example, a simple brute force attack against DES requires one known plaintext and 255 decryptions, trying approximately half of the possible keys, to reach a point at which chances are better than even the key sought will have been found. But this may not be enough assurance; a linear cryptanalysis attack against DES requires 243 known plaintexts and approximately 243 DES operations. This is a considerable improvement on brute force attacks.

Public-key algorithms are based on the computational difficulty of various problems. The most famous of these is integer factorization (eg, the RSA algorithm is based on a problem related to factoring), but the discrete logarithm problem is also important. Much public-key cryptanalysis concerns numerical algorithms for solving these computational problems, or some of them, efficiently. For instance, the best known algorithms for solving the elliptic curve-based version of discrete logarithm are much more time-consuming than the best known algorithms for factoring, at least for problems of more or less equivalent size. Thus, other things being equal, to achieve an equivalent strength of attack resistance, factoring-based encryption techniques must use larger keys than elliptic curve techniques. For this reason, public-key cryptosystems based on elliptic curves have become popular since their invention in the mid-1990s.

While pure cryptanalysis uses weaknesses in the algorithms themselves, other attacks on cryptosystems are based on actual use of the algorithms in real devices, and are called side-channel attacks. If a cryptanalyst has access to, say, the amount of time the device took to encrypt a number of plaintexts or report an error in a password or PIN character, he may be able to use a timing attack to break a cipher that is otherwise resistant to analysis. An attacker might also study the pattern and length of messages to derive valuable information; this is known as traffic analysis,and can be quite useful to an alert adversary. And, of course, social engineering, and other attacks against the personnel who work with cryptosystems or the messages they handle (e.g., bribery, extortion, blackmail, espionage, ...) may be the most productive attacks of all.

Cryptographic Primitives

Unsolved problems in computer science: One-way functions are functions that are easy to compute but hard to invert. Can one-way functions be proved to exist?

Much of the theoretical work in cryptography concerns cryptographic primitives — algorithms with basic cryptographic properties — and their relationship to other cryptographic problems. For example, a one-way function is a function intended to be easy to compute but hard to invert. In a very general sense, for any cryptographic application to be secure (if based on such computational feasibility assumptions), one-way functions must exist. However, if one-way functions exist, this implies that $P \neq NP$. Since the P versus NP problem is currently unsolved, we don't know if one-way functions really do exist. For instance, if one-way functions exist, then secure pseudorandom generators and secure pseudorandom functions exist.

Currently known cryptographic primitives provide only basic functionality. These are usually noted as confidentiality, message integrity, authentication, and non-repudiation. Any other functionality in a cryptosystem must be built in using combinations of these algorithms and assorted protocols. Such combinations are called cryptosystems and it is they which users will encounter. Examples include PGP and its variants, SSH, SSL/TLS, all PKIs, digital signatures, etc. Other cryptographic primitives include the encryption algorithms themselves, one-way permutations, trapdoor permutations, etc.

Cryptographic Protocols

In many cases, cryptographic techniques involve back and forth communication among two or more parties in space (eg, between the home office and a branch office) or across time (e.g., cryptographically protected backup data). The term cryptographic protocol captures this general idea.

Cryptographic protocols have been developed for a wide range of problems, including relatively simple ones like interactive proofs, secret sharing, and zero-knowledge, and much more complex ones like electronic cash and secure multiparty computation.

When the security of a good cryptographic system fails, it is rare that the vulnerability leading to the breach will have been in a quality cryptographic primitive. Instead, weaknesses are often mistakes in the protocol design (often due to inadequate design procedures, or less than thoroughly informed designers), in the implementation (e.g., a software bug), in a failure of the assumptions on which the design was based (e.g., proper training of those who will be using the system), or some other human error. Many cryptographic protocols have been designed and analyzed using ad hoc methods, but they rarely have any proof of security. Methods for formally analyzing the security of protocols, based on techniques from mathematical logic and more recently from concrete security principles, have been the subject of research for the past few decades. Unfortunately, to date these tools have been cumbersome and are not widely used for complex designs. The study of how best to implement and integrate cryptography in applications is itself a distinct field.

7

Wireless Networking

Basics of Wireless LAN

A wireless LAN or WLAN is a wireless local area network, which is the linking of two or more computers without using wires. WLAN utilizes spread-spectrum or OFDM (802.11a) modulation technology based on radio waves to enable communication between devices in a limited area, also known as the basic service set. This gives users the mobility to move around within a broad coverage area and still be connected to the network.

For the home user, wireless has become popular due to ease of installation, and location freedom with the gaining popularity of laptops. Public businesses such as coffee shops or malls have begun to offer wireless access to their customers; some are even provided as a free service. Large wireless network projects are being put up in many major cities. Google is even providing a free service to Mountain View, California and has entered a bid to do the same for San Francisco. New York City has also begun a pilot program to cover all five boroughs of the city with wireless Internet access.

History

In 1970 University of Hawaii, under the leadership of Norman Abramson, developed the world's first computer communication network using low-cost ham-like radios, named ALOHAnet.

The bi-directional star topology of the system included seven computers deployed over four islands to communicate with the central computer on the Oahu Island without using phone lines.

"In 1979, F.R. Gfeller and U. Bapst published a paper in the IEEE Proceedings reporting an experimental wireless local area network using diffused infrared communications. Shortly thereafter, in 1980, P. Ferrert reported on an experimental application of a single code spread spectrum radio for wireless terminal communications in the IEEE National Telecommunications Conference. In 1984, a comparison between Infrared and CDMA spread spectrum communications for wireless office information networks was published by Kaveh Pahlavan in IEEE Computer Networking Symposium which appeared later in the IEEE Communication Society Magazine. In May 1985, the efforts of Marcus led the FCC to announce experimental ISM bands for commercial application of spread spectrum technology.

Later on, M. Kavehrad reported on an experimental wireless PBX system using code division multiple access. These efforts prompted significant industrial activities in the development of a new generation of wireless local area networks and it updated several old discussion in the portable and mobile radio industry.

The first generation of wireless data modems was developed in the early 1980's by amateur communication groups. They added a voice band data communication modem, with data rates below 9600 bit/s, to an existing short distance radio system such as a walkie talkie. The second generation of wireless modems was developed immediately after the FCC announcement in the experimental bands for non-military use of the spread spectrum technology. These modems provided data rates on the order of hundreds of kbit/s. The third generation of wireless modem then aimed at compatibility with the existing LANs with data rates on the order of Mbit/s. Several companies developed the third generation products with data rates above 1 Mbit/s and a couple of products had already been announced by the time of the first IEEE Workshop on Wireless LANs."

The first of the IEEE Workshops on Wireless LAN was held in 1991. At that time early wireless LAN products had just appeared in the market and the IEEE 802.11 committee had just started its activities to develop a standard for wireless LANs. The focus of that first workshop was evaluation of the alternative technologies. By 1996, the technology was relatively mature, a variety of applications had been identified and addressed and technologies that enable these applications were well understood. Chip sets aimed at wireless LAN implementations and applications, a key enabling technology for rapid market growth, were emerging in the market. Wireless LANs were being used in hospitals, stock exchanges, and other in building and campus settings for nomadic access, point-to-point LAN bridges, ad-hoc networking, and even larger applications through internetworking. The IEEE 802.11 standard and variants and alternatives, such as the wireless LAN interoperability forum and the European HIPERLAN specification had made rapid progress, and the unlicensed PCS [Unlicensed Personal Communications Services] and the proposed SUPERNet [,later on renamed as UNII,] bands also presented new opportunities."

On July 21, 1999, AirPort debuted at the Macworld Expo in New York City with Steve Jobs picking up an iBook supposedly to give the cameraman a better shot as he surfed the Web. Applause quickly built as people realized there were no wires. This was the first time Wireless LAN became publicly available at consumer pricing and easily available for home use. Before the release of the Airport, Wireless LAN was too expensive for consumer use and used exclusively in large corporate settings.

Originally WLAN hardware was so expensive that it was only used as an alternative to cabled LAN in places where cabling was difficult or impossible.

Early development included industry-specific solutions and proprietary protocols, but at the end of the 1990s these were replaced by standards, primarily the various versions of IEEE

802.11 (Wi-Fi). An alternative ATM-like 5 GHz standardized technology, HIPERLAN, has so far not succeeded in the market, and with the release of the faster 54 Mbit/s 802.11a (5 GHz) and 802.11g (2.4 GHz) standards, almost certainly never will.

In November 2006, the Australian Commonwealth Scientific and Industrial Research Organisation (CSIRO) won a legal battle in the US federal court of Texas against Buffalo Technology which found the US manufacturer had failed to pay royalties on a US WLAN patent CSIRO had filed in 1996. CSIRO are currently engaged in legal cases with computer companies including Microsoft, Intel, Dell, Hewlett-Packard and Netgear which argue that the patent is invalid and should negate any royalties paid to CSIRO for WLAN-based products.

Benefits

The popularity of wireless LANs is a testament primarily to their convenience, cost efficiency, and ease of integration with other networks and network components. The majority of computers sold to consumers today come pre-equipped with all necessary wireless LAN technology. The benefits of wireless LANs include:

- **Convenience**: The wireless nature of such networks allows users to access network resources from nearly any convenient location within their primary networking environment (home or office). With the increasing saturation of laptop-style computers, this is particularly relevant.
- **Mobility**: With the emergence of public wireless networks, users can access the internet even outside their normal work environment. Most chain coffee shops, for example, offer their customers a wireless connection to the internet at little or no cost.
- **Productivity**: Users connected to a wireless network can maintain a nearly constant affiliation with their desired network as they move from place to place. For a business, this implies that an employee can potentially be more productive as his or her work can be accomplished from any convenient location.
- **Deployment**: Initial setup of an infrastructure-based wireless network requires little more than a single access point. Wired networks, on the other hand, have the additional cost and complexity of actual physical cables being run to numerous locations (which can even be impossible for hard-to-reach locations within a building).
- **Expandability**: Wireless networks can serve a suddenly-increased number of clients with the existing equipment. In a wired network, additional clients would require additional wiring.
- **Cost**: Wireless networking hardware is at worst a modest increase from wired counterparts. This potentially increased cost is almost always more than outweighed by the savings in cost and labour associated to running physical cables.

Disadvantages

Wireless LAN technology, while replete with the conveniences and advantages described above, has its share of downfalls. For a given networking situation, wireless LANs may not be desirable for a number of reasons. Most of these have to do with the inherent limitations of the technology.

- **Security**: Wireless LAN transceivers are designed to serve computers throughout a structure with uninterrupted service using radio frequencies. Because of space and cost, the antennas typically present on wireless networking cards in the end computers are generally relatively poor. In order to properly receive signals using such limited antennas throughout even a modest area, the wireless LAN transceiver utilizes a fairly considerable amount of power. What this means is that not only can the wireless packets be intercepted by a nearby adversary's poorly-equipped computer, but more importantly, a user willing to spend a small amount of money on a good quality antenna can pick up packets at a remarkable distance; perhaps hundreds of times the radius as the typical user. In fact, there are even computer users dedicated to locating and sometimes even hacking into wireless networks, known as wardrivers. On a wired network, any adversary would first have to overcome the physical limitation of tapping into the actual wires, but this is not an issue with wireless packets. To combat this consideration, wireless networks users usually choose to utilize various encryption technologies available such as Wi-Fi Protected Access (WPA). Some of the more older encryption methods, such as WEP are known to have weaknesses that a dedicated adversary can compromise.

- **Range**: The typical range of a common 802.11g network with standard equipment is on the order of tens of meters. While sufficient for a typical home, it will be insufficient in a larger structure. To obtain additional range, repeaters or additional access points will have to be purchased. Costs for these items can add up quickly. Other technologies are in the development phase, however, which feature increased range, hoping to render this disadvantage irrelevant.

- **Reliability**: Like any radio frequency transmission, wireless networking signals are subject to a wide variety of interference, as well as complex propagation effects (such as multipath, or especially in this case Rician fading) that are beyond the control of the network administrator. In the case of typical networks, modulation is achieved by complicated forms of phase-shift keying (PSK) or quadrature amplitude modulation (QAM), making interference and propagation effects all the more disturbing. As a result, important network resources such as servers are rarely connected wirelessly.

- **Speed**: The speed on most wireless networks (typically 1-108 Mbit/s) is reasonably slow compared to the slowest common wired networks (100 Mbit/s up to several Gbit/s). There are also performance issues caused by TCP and its built-in congestion avoidance. For most users, however, this observation is irrelevant since the speed bottleneck is not in the wireless routing but rather in the outside network connectivity itself. For example, the maximum ADSL throughput (usually 8 Mbit/s or less) offered by telecommunications companies to general-purpose customers is already far slower than the slowest wireless network to which it is typically connected. That is to say, in most environments, a wireless network running at its slowest speed is still faster than the internet connection serving it in the first place. However, in specialized environments, the throughput of a wired network might be necessary. Newer standards such as 802.11n are addressing this limitation and will support peak throughputs in the range of 100-200 Mbit/s.

Architecture

Stations

All components that can connect into a wireless medium in a network are referred to as stations. All stations are equipped with wireless network interface cards (WNICs). Wireless stations fall into one of two categories: access points and clients.

- **Access points:** Access points (APs) are base stations for the wireless network. They transmit and receive radio frequencies for wireless enabled devices to communicate with.
- **Clients:** Wireless clients can be mobile devices such as laptops, personal digital assistants, IP phones, or fixed devices such as desktops and workstations that are equipped with a wireless network interface.

Basic service set

The basic service set (BSS) is a set of all stations that can communicate with each other. There are two types of BSS: independent BSS and infrastructure BSS. Every BSS has an identification (ID) called the BSSID, which is the MAC address of the access point servicing the BSS.

- Independent basic service set

  An independent BSS is an ad-hoc network that contains no access points, which means they can not connect to any other basic service set.

- Infrastructure basic service set

  An infrastructure BSS can communicate with other stations not in the same basic service set by communicating through access points.

Extended service set

An extended service set (ESS) is a set of connected BSSes. Access points in an ESS are connected by a distribution system. Each ESS has an ID called the SSID which is a 32-byte (maximum) character string. For example, "linksys" is the default SSID for Linksys routers.

Distribution system

A distribution system connects access points in an extended service set.

Types of wireless LANs

Peer-to-Peer or ad-hoc wireless LAN

A peer-to-peer (P2P) allows wireless devices to directly communicate with each other. Wireless devices within range of each other can discover and communicate directly without involving central access points. This method is typically used by two computers so that they can connect to each other to form a network.

If a signal strength meter is used in this situation, it may not read the strength accurately and can be misleading, because it registers the strength of the strongest signal, which may be the closest computer.

802.11 specs define the physical layer (PHY) and MAC (Media Access Control) layers. However, unlike most other IEEE specs, 802.11 includes three alternative PHY standards: diffuse infrared operating at 1 Mbit/s in; frequency-hopping spread spectrum operating at 1 Mbit/s or 2 Mbit/s; and direct-sequence spread spectrum operating at 1 Mbit/s or 2 Mbit/s. A single 802.11 MAC standard is based on CSMA/CA (Carrier Sense Multiple Access with Collision Avoidance).

The 802.11 specification includes provisions designed to minimize collisions. Because two mobile units may both be in range of a common access point, but not in range of each other. The 802.11 has two basic modes of operation: Ad hoc mode enables peer-to-peer transmission between mobile units. Infrastructure mode in which mobile units communicate through an access point that serves as a bridge to a wired network infrastructure is the more common wireless LAN application the one being covered. Since wireless communication uses a more open medium for communication in comparison to wired LANs, the 802.11 designers also included a shared-key encryption mechanism, called wired equivalent privacy (WEP), or Wi-Fi Protected Access, (WPA, WPA2) to secure wireless computer networks.

Bridge

A bridge can be used to connect networks, typically of different types. A wireless Ethernet bridge allows the connection of devices on a wired ethernet network to a wireless network. The bridge acts as the connection point to the Wireless LAN.

Wireless distribution system

When it is difficult to connect all of the access points in a network by wires, it is also possible to put up access points as repeaters.

Bluetooth

Bluetooth is an industrial specification for wireless Personal Area Networks (PANs). Bluetooth provides a way to connect and exchange information between devices such as mobile phones, laptops, PCs, printers, digital cameras, and video game consoles over a secure, globally unlicensed short-range radio frequency.

The Bluetooth specifications are developed and licensed by the Bluetooth Special Interest Group.

Uses

Bluetooth is a radio standard and communications protocol primarily designed for low power consumption, with a short range (power-class-dependent: 1 meter, 10 meters, 100 m) based on low-cost transceiver microchips in each device.

Bluetooth lets these devices communicate with each other when they are in range. The devices use a radio communications system, so they do not have to be in line of sight of each other, and can even be in other rooms, as long as the received transmission is powerful enough.

Class	Maximum Permitted	Power Range (mW/dBm) (approximate)
Class 1	100 mW (20 dBm)	~100 meters
Class 2	2.5 mW (4 dBm)	~10 meters
Class 3	1 mW (0 dBm)	~1 meter

Bluetooth profiles

In order to use Bluetooth, a device must be compatible with certain Bluetooth profiles. These define the possible applications and uses.

List of applications

More prevalent applications of Bluetooth include:

- Wireless control of and communication between a cell phone and a hands-free headset or car kit. This was one of the earliest applications to become popular.
- Wireless networking between PCs in a confined space and where little bandwidth is required.
- Wireless communications with PC input and output devices, the most common being the mouse, keyboard and printer.
- Transfer of files between devices with OBEX.
- Transfer of contact details, calendar appointments, and reminders between devices with OBEX.
- Replacement of traditional wired serial communications in test equipment, GPS receivers, medical equipment and traffic control devices.

- For controls where infrared was traditionally used.
- Sending small advertisements from Bluetooth enabled advertising hoardings to other, discoverable, Bluetooth devices.
- Seventh-generation game consoles—Nintendo Wii, Sony PlayStation 3—use Bluetooth for their respective wireless controllers.

Bluetooth vs. Wi-Fi in networking

Bluetooth and Wi-Fi both have their places in today's offices, homes, and on the move: setting up networks, printing, or transferring presentations and files from PDAs to computers.

Bluetooth

Bluetooth is implemented in a variety of new products such as phones, printers, modems, and headsets. Bluetooth is acceptable for situations when two or more devices are in proximity to each other and don't require high bandwidth. Bluetooth is most commonly used with phones and hand-held computing devices, either using a Bluetooth headset or transferring files from phones/PDAs to computers.

Bluetooth also simplifies the discovery and setup of services. Bluetooth devices advertise all services they provide. This makes the utility of the service that much more accessible, without the need to worry about network addresses, permissions and all the other considerations that go with typical networks.

Wi-Fi

Wi-Fi is more analogous to the traditional Ethernet network and requires configuration to set up shared resources, transmit files, set up audio links (for example, headsets and hands-free devices). It uses the same radio frequencies as Bluetooth, but with higher power output resulting in a stronger connection. Wi-Fi is sometimes called "wireless Ethernet." Although this description is inaccurate, it provides an indication of its relative strengths and weaknesses. Wi-Fi requires more setup, but is better suited for operating full-scale networks because it enables a faster connection, better range from the base station, and better security than Bluetooth.

One method for comparing the efficiency of wireless transmission protocols such as Bluetooth and Wi-Fi is spatial capacity, or bits per second per square meter.

Computer Requirements

A personal computer must have a Bluetooth adapter in order to be able to communicate with other Bluetooth devices (such as mobile phones, mice and keyboards).While some portable computers and fewer desktop computers already contain an internal Bluetooth dongle, most PCs require an external USB Bluetooth dongle. Most Macs come with built-in Bluetooth adapters.

Unlike its predecessor, IrDA, in which each device requires a separate dongle, multiple Bluetooth devices can communicate with a computer over a single dongle.

Operating system support

Linux provides two Bluetooth stacks, with the BlueZ stack included with most Linux kernels. It was originally developed by Qualcomm and Affix. BlueZ supports all core Bluetooth protocols and layers.

Only Microsoft Windows XP Service Pack 2 and later versions of Windows have native support for Bluetooth. Previous versions required the users to install their Bluetooth adapter's own drivers, which was not directly supported by Microsoft. Microsoft's own Bluetooth dongles (that are packaged with their Bluetooth computer devices) have no external drivers and thus require at least Windows XP Service Pack 2. Mac OS X has supported Bluetooth since version 10.2 released in 2002.

Specifications and features

The Bluetooth specification was developed in 1994 by Sven Mattisson and Jaap Haartsen, who were working for Ericsson Mobile Platforms in Lund, Sweden. The specifications were formalized by the Bluetooth Special Interest Group (SIG). The SIG was formally announced on May 20, 1998. Today it has over 7000 companies worldwide. It was established by Ericsson, Sony Ericsson, IBM, Intel, Toshiba, and Nokia, and later joined by many other companies. Bluetooth is also known as IEEE 802.15.1.

Bluetooth 1.0 and 1.0B

Versions 1.0 and 1.0B had many problems, and manufacturers had difficulties making their products interoperable. Versions 1.0 and 1.0B also had mandatory Bluetooth hardware device address (BD_ADDR) transmission in the Connecting process, rendering anonymity impossible at a protocol level, which was a major setback for services planned to be used in Bluetooth environments, such as Consumerium.

Bluetooth 1.1

- Many errors found in the 1.0B specifications were fixed.
- Added support for non-encrypted channels.
- Received Signal Strength Indicator (RSSI).

Bluetooth 1.2

This version is backward-compatible with 1.1 and the major enhancements include the following:

- Faster Connection and Discovery.
- Adaptive frequency-hopping spread spectrum (AFH), which improves resistance to

radio frequency interference by avoiding the use of crowded frequencies in the hopping sequence.

- Higher transmission speeds in practice, up to 721 kbit/s, as in 1.1.
- Extended Synchronous Connections (eSCO), which improve voice quality of audio links by allowing retransmissions of corrupted packets.
- Host Controller Interface (HCI) support for three-wire UART.

Bluetooth 2.0

This version, specified in November 2004, is backward-compatible with 1.1. The main enhancement is the introduction of an enhanced data rate (EDR) of 3.0 Mbit/s. This has the following effects:

- Three times faster transmission speed—up to 10 times in certain cases (up to 2.1 Mbit/s).
- Lower power consumption through a reduced duty cycle.
- Simplification of multi-link scenarios due to more available bandwidth.
- Further improved (bit error rate) performance.

Bluetooth 2.1

Bluetooth Core Specification Version 2.1 + EDR, is fully backward-compatible with 1.1, and will be adopted by the Bluetooth SIG once interoperability testing has completed. This specification includes the following features:

- **Extended inquiry response**: provides more information during the inquiry procedure to allow better filtering of devices before connection. This information includes the name of the device, a list of services the device supports, as well as other information like the time of day, and pairing information.
- **Sniff subrating**: reduces the power consumption when devices are in the sniff low-power mode, especially on links with asymmetric data flows. Human interface devices (HID) are expected to benefit the most, with mouse and keyboard devices increasing the battery life from 3 to 10 times those currently used.
- **Encryption Pause Resume**: enables an encryption key to be refreshed, enabling much stronger encryption for connections that stay up for longer than 24 hours.
- **Secure Simple Pairing**: radically improves the pairing experience for Bluetooth devices, while increasing the use and strength of security. It is expected that this feature will significantly increase the use of Bluetooth.
- **NFC cooperation**: automatic creation of secure Bluetooth connections when NFC radio interface is also available. For example, a headset should be paired with a Bluetooth 2.1 phone including NFC just by bringing the two devices close to each

other (a few centimeters). Another example is automatic uploading of photos from a mobile phone or camera to a digital picture frame just by bringing the phone or camera close to the frame.

Future of Bluetooth

- **Broadcast Channel: enables** Bluetooth information points. This will drive the adoption of Bluetooth into cell phones, and enable advertising models based around users pulling information from the information points, and not based around the object push model that is used in a limited way today.
- **Topology Management**: enables the automatic configuration of the piconet topologies especially in scatternet situations that are becoming more common today. This should all be invisible to the users of the technology, while also making the technology just work.
- **Alternate MAC PHY**: enables the use of alternative MAC and PHY's for transporting Bluetooth profile data. The Bluetooth Radio will still be used for device discovery, initial connection and profile configuration, however, when lots of data needs to be sent, the high speed alternate MAC PHY's will be used to transport the data. This means that the proven low power connection models of Bluetooth are used when the system is idle, and the low power per bit radios are used when lots of data needs to be sent.
- **QoS improvements**: enable audio and video data to be transmitted at a higher quality, especially when best effort traffic is being transmitted in the same piconet.

Bluetooth technology already plays a part in the rising Voice over IP (VOIP) scene, with Bluetooth headsets being used as wireless extensions to the PC audio system. As VOIP becomes more popular, and more suitable for general home or office users than wired phone lines, Bluetooth may be used in cordless handsets, with a base station connected to the Internet link.

Bluetooth 3.0

The next version of Bluetooth after v2.1, code-named Seattle, that will be called Bluetooth 3.0, has many of the same features, but is most notable for plans to adopt ultra-wideband (UWB) radio technology. This will allow Bluetooth use over UWB radio, enabling very fast data transfers of up to 480 Mbit/s, while building on the very low-power idle modes of Bluetooth.

High Speed Bluetooth

On 28 March 2006, the Bluetooth Special Interest Group announced its selection of the WiMedia Alliance Multi-Band Orthogonal Frequency Division Multiplexing (MB-OFDM) version of UWB for integration with current Bluetooth wireless technology.

UWB integration will create a version of Bluetooth wireless technology with a high-speed/

high-data-rate option. This new version of Bluetooth technology will meet the high-speed demands of synchronizing and transferring large amounts of data, as well as enabling high-quality video and audio applications for portable devices, multi-media projectors and television sets, and wireless VOIP. At the same time, Bluetooth technology will continue catering to the needs of very low power applications such as mice, keyboards, and mono headsets, enabling devices to select the most appropriate physical radio for the application requirements, thereby offering the best of both worlds.

Ultra Low Power Bluetooth

On 12 June 2007, Nokia and Bluetooth SIG announced that Wibree will be a part of the Bluetooth specification as an ultra low power Bluetooth technology. Expected user cases includes watches displaying Caller ID information, sports sensors monitoring your heart rate during exercise, as well as medical devices. The Medical Devices Working Group is also creating a medical devices profile and associated protocols to enable this market.

The main contributer to the development of the Wibree standard is the world known Norwegian company Nordic Semiconductor.

Technical information

Communication and Connection

A master Bluetooth device can communicate with up to seven devices. This network group of up to eight devices is called a piconet. A piconet is an ad-hoc computer network, using Bluetooth technology protocols to allow one master device to interconnect with up to seven active devices. Up to 255 further devices can be inactive, or parked, which the master device can bring into active status at any time.

At any given time, data can be transferred between the master and one other device. However, the master switches rapidly from device to another in a round-robin fashion. (Simultaneous transmission from the master to multiple other devices is possible, but not used much.) Either device can switch roles and become the master at any time.

Bluetooth specification allows connecting two or more piconets together to form a scatternet, with some devices acting as a bridge by simultaneously playing the master role and the slave role in one piconet. These devices are planned for 2007.

Setting up Connections

Any Bluetooth device will transmit the following sets of information on demand:

- Device name.
- Device class.
- List of services.
- Technical information, for example, device features, manufacturer, Bluetooth specification, clock offset.

Any device may perform an inquiry to find other devices to which to connect, and any device can be configured to respond to such inquiries. However, if the device trying to connect knows the address of the device, it always responds to direct connection requests and transmits the information shown in the list above if requested. Use of device services may require pairing or acceptance by its owner, but the connection itself can be started by any device and held until it goes out of range.

Some devices can be connected to only one device at a time, and connecting to them prevents them from connecting to other devices and appearing in inquiries until they disconnect from the other device.

Every device has a unique 48-bit address. However, these addresses are generally not shown in inquiries. Instead, friendly Bluetooth names are used, which can be set by the user. This name appears when another user scans for devices and in lists of paired devices.

Most phones have the Bluetooth name set to the manufacturer and model of the phone by default. Most phones and laptops show only the Bluetooth names and special programs that are required to get additional information about remote devices. This can be confusing as, for example, there could be several phones in range named T610 .

Pairing

Pairs of devices may establish a trusted relationship by learning (by user input) a shared secret known as a passkey. A device that wants to communicate only with a trusted device can cryptographically authenticate the identity of the other device. Trusted devices may also encrypt the data that they exchange over the air so that no one can listen in. The encryption can, however, be turned off, and passkeys are stored on the device file system, not on the Bluetooth chip itself. Since the Bluetooth address is permanent, a pairing is preserved, even if the Bluetooth name is changed.

Pairs can be deleted at any time by either device. Devices generally require pairing or prompt the owner before they allow a remote device to use any or most of their services. Some devices, such as Sony Ericsson phones, usually accept OBEX business cards and notes without any pairing or prompts.

Certain printers and access points allow any device to use its services by default, much like unsecured Wi-Fi networks. Pairing algorithms are sometimes manufacturer-specific for transmitters and receivers used in applications such as music and entertainment.

Air interface

The protocol operates in the license-free ISM band at 2.45 GHz. To avoid interfering with other protocols that use the 2.45 GHz band, the Bluetooth protocol divides the band into 79 channels (each 1 MHz wide) and changes channels up to 1600 times per second. Implementations with versions 1.1 and 1.2 reach speeds of 723.1 kbit/s. Version 2.0 implementations feature Bluetooth Enhanced Data Rate (EDR) and reach 2.1 Mbit/s.

Technically, version 2.0 devices have a higher power consumption, but the three times faster rate reduces the transmission times, effectively reducing power consumption to half that of 1.x devices (assuming equal traffic load).

Bluetooth differs from Wi-Fi in that the latter provides higher throughput and covers greater distances, but requires more expensive hardware and higher power consumption. They use the same frequency range, but employ different multiplexing schemes. Bluetooth is often thought of as wireless USB, whereas Wi-Fi is wireless Ethernet, both operating at much lower bandwidth than the cable systems they are trying to replace. However, this analogy is not entirely accurate since any Bluetooth device can, in theory, host any other Bluetooth device—something that is not universal to USB devices.

While Bluetooth is a cable replacement for a variety of applications, Wi-Fi is a cable replacement only for local area network access.

Many USB Bluetooth adapters are available, some of which also include an IrDA adapter. Older (pre-2003) Bluetooth adapters, however, have limited services, offering only the Bluetooth Enumerator and a less-powerful Bluetooth Radio incarnation.

Such devices can link computers with Bluetooth, but they do not offer much in the way of services that modern adapters do.

Security

Bluetooth implements authentication and key derivation with custom algorithms based on the SAFER+ block cipher. The initialization key and master key are generated with the E22 algorithm.

The E0 stream cipher is used for encrypting packets. This makes eavesdropping on Bluetooth-enabled devices more difficult.

Social Concerns

2003:

In November 2003, Ben and Adam Laurie from A.L. Digital Ltd. discovered that serious flaws in Bluetooth security may lead to disclosure of personal data. It should be noted, however, that the reported security problems concerned some poor implementations of Bluetooth, rather than the protocol itself.

In a subsequent experiment, Martin Herfurt from the trifinite.group was able to do a field-trial at the CeBIT fairgrounds, showing the importance of the problem to the world. A new attack called BlueBug was used for this experiment.

2004:

In April 2004, security consultant firm @stake (now Symantec) revealed a security flaw that makes it possible to crack conversations on Bluetooth based wireless headsets by reverse engineering the PIN. This is one of a number of concerns that have been raised over the security of Bluetooth communications. In 2004 the first purported virus using Bluetooth to spread itself among mobile phones appeared on the Symbian OS. The virus was first described by Kaspersky Lab and requires users to confirm the installation of unknown software before it can propagate.

The virus was written as a proof-of-concept by a group of virus writers known as 29A and sent to anti-virus groups. Thus, it should be regarded as a potential (but not real) security threat to Bluetooth or Symbian OS since the virus has never spread in the wild.

In August 2004, a world-record-setting experiment showed that the range of Class 2 Bluetooth radios could be extended to 1.78 km (1.08 mile) with directional antennas. This poses a potential security threat because it enables attackers to access vulnerable Bluetooth-devices from a distance beyond expectation. However, such experiments do not work with signal amplifiers. The attacker must also be able to receive information from the victim to set up a connection. No attack can be made against a Bluetooth device unless the attacker knows its Bluetooth address and which channels to transmit on.

2005:

In April 2005, Cambridge University security researchers published results of their actual implementation of passive attacks against the PIN-based pairing between commercial Bluetooth devices, confirming the attacks to be practicably fast and the Bluetooth symmetric key establishment method to be vulnerable. To rectify this vulnerability, they carried out an implementation which showed that stronger, asymmetric key establishment is feasible for certain classes of devices, such as handphones.

In June 2005, Yaniv Shaked and Avishai Wool published the paper "Cracking the Bluetooth PIN1," which shows both passive and active methods for obtaining the PIN for a Bluetooth link. The passive attack allows a suitably equipped attacker to eavesdrop on communications and spoof if they were present at the time of initial pairing. The active method makes use of a specially constructed message that must be inserted at a specific point in the protocol, to make the master and slave repeat the pairing process. After that, the first method can be used to crack the PIN. This attack's major weakness is that it requires the user of the devices under attack to re-enter the PIN during the attack when the device prompts them to. Also, this active attack probably requires custom hardware, since most commercially available Bluetooth devices are not capable of the timing necessary.

In August 2005, police in Cambridgeshire, England, issued warnings about thieves using Bluetooth-enabled phones to track other devices left in cars. Police are advising users to ensure that any mobile networking connections are de-activated if laptops and other devices are left in this way.

2006:

In April 2006, researchers from Secure Network and F-Secure published a report that warns of the large number of devices left in a visible state, and issued statistics on the spread of various Bluetooth services and the ease of spread of an eventual Bluetooth worm.

In October 2006, at the Luxemburgish Hack.lu Security Conference, Kevin Finistere and Thierry Zoller demonstrated and released a remote root shell over Bluetooth on Mac OSX 10.3.9 and 10.4. They also demonstrated the first Bluetooth PIN and Link-keys cracker, which is based on the research of Wool and Shaked.

Health concerns

Bluetooth uses the microwave radio frequency spectrum in the 2.4 GHz to 2.4835 GHz range. Maximum power output from a Bluetooth radio is 1mW, 2.5mW, and 100mW for Class 3, Class 2, and Class 1 devices respectively, which puts Class 1 at roughly the same level as cell phones, and the other two classes much lower. Accordingly, Class 2 and Class 3 Bluetooth devices are considered less of a potential hazard than cell phones, and Class 1 may be comparable to that of cell phones, which are of little concern.

Origin of the name and the logo

Bluetooth was named after a late tenth century king, Harald Bluetooth King of Denmark and Norway. He is known for his unification of previously warring tribes from Denmark (including Scania, present-day Sweden, where the Bluetooth technology was invented), and Norway.

Bluetooth likewise was intended to unify different technologies, such as computers and mobile phones.

The name may have been inspired less by the historical Harald than the loose interpretation of him in The Long Ships by Frans Gunnar Bengtsson, a Swedish Viking-inspired novel.

The Bluetooth logo merges the Nordic runes analogous to the modern Latin H and B: (haglaz) and (berkanan) forming a bind rune.

Bluetooth Consortium

In 1998, Ericsson, IBM, Intel, and Nokia, formed a consortium and adopted the code name Bluetooth for their proposed open specification. In December 1999, 3Com, Lucent Technologies, Microsoft, and Motorola joined the initial founders as the promoter group. Since that time, Lucent Technologies transferred their membership to their spinoff Agere Systems, and 3Com has left the promoter group.

8

Client Server Computing

Introduction

There has been lot of talks about Client/Server computing. But, before we go further at seeing what it does, let us first understand what this Client Server Computing is.

Client/Server

What is Client/Server? Frankly even I do not have a definite definition for it. It is not that I do not have one definition, in fact, there is no definite definition of Client Server. Maximum you can say is that this type of computing allows you to serve clients. This can be said in terms of networking that clients and servers are separate logical entities that work together over a network to accomplish a task. In any case client/server systems have the following distinguishing characteristics:

Asymmetrical protocols

There is many-to one relationship between clients and server. Clients always initiate the dialog by requesting a service. Servers are passively awaiting request from the clients.

Encapsulation of services

The server is a "specialist." A message tells a server what services are requested; it is then unto the server to determine how to get the job done.

Services can be upgraded without affecting the clients as long as the published message interface is not changed.

Integrity

The server code and server data is centrally maintained. Which results in cheaper maintenance and the guarding of shared data integrity? At the same time, the clients remain personal and independent.

Message-based-Exchanges

Clients and servers are loosely coupled systems that interact though a message-passing mechanism. The message is the delivery mechanism for the service requests and replies.

Mix-and-match

The idea client/server software is independent of hardware or operating system software platforms. You should be able to mix-and-match client and server platforms.

Scalability

Client/server systems can be scaled horizontally or vertically. Horizontally scaling means adding or removing client workstations with only a slight performance impact. Vertical scaling means migrating to a larger and faster server machine or multiservers.

Service

Client/server is primarily a relationship between processes running on separate machines. The server is a provider of services. The client is a consumer of services. In essence, client/ server a clean separation of function based on the idea of service.

Shared resources

A server can service many clients at the same time and regulate their access to shared resources.

Transparency of location

The server is a process that can reside on the same machine as the client or on a different machine across a network. Client/server software usually masks the location of the server from the client by redirecting the service calls when needed. A program can be a client, a server, or both.

The client/server characteristics described here allow intelligence to be easily distributed across a network. These features also provide a framework for the design of loosely coupled, network based applications.

What is real Client/Server?

As mentioned above that there is fixed definition of Client Server. Similarly there is fixed configuration for a client server computer system. Vendors often use client/server as if the term can only be applied to their specific packages. For example, file server vendors swear they first invented the term and databases server vendor is known in some circles solely as the client/server vendors.

The idea of splitting an application along client/server lines has been used over the last ten years to create various forms of Local Area Network (LAN) software solutions. Typically, these solutions sell as shrink-wrapped software packages and many are sold by more than one vendor.

Each of these solutions, however, is distinguished by the nature of the service it provides to its clients, as shown in the following sections.

File Servers

Computers which allow the files to be shared across the network are called file servers. They provide controlled access to files and usually have some method of determining which user have access to which files and other system resources. But, how it is done. Well, the main source for this is software.

The particular machine that is used for a file server might be a standard PC of any type, a minicomputer, or specialized proprietary computer designed specifically as a file server. In any case, it is the software running in that machine that defines it as a file server. The primary purpose of the file server software is to synchronize access to shared resources. This means the server software in cooperation with applications programs, makes sure that users have simultaneous file access where appropriate, while preventing simultaneous access where it is inappropriate. File server can also provide various levels of security and access control, allowing a system manager to designate who has access to what resources.

In this area there are vast differences in capabilities among various file server systems, the efficiency and sophistication of a file server's data management and retrieval vary widely from one network operating system to another. High-speed disk access techniques use a disk caching (keeping recently requested data blocks in server memory) and use of proprietary disk file structures are among the methods used to increase data retrieval speed.

Servers can be divided into the following categories:

Dedicated Servers

They function strictly as servers and are not available as user workstations. Dedicated servers generally provide better performance and system integrity than non-dedicated servers.

Generic Servers

These are usually industry standard mini or microcomputers. For PC LANs, 80386 and 80486 based personal computers are commonly used as file servers. Generic servers often offer greater flexibility than proprietary servers.

Non-Dedicated Servers

They function as user workstations as well as file servers. Although most manufacturers provide for non-dedicated servers, performance and system integrity issues can make this a risky approach. Users and application can easily lock up a non-dedicated server. Non-dedicated servers can sometimes provide hardware cost savings, but these savings are often quickly offset by the increased requires to resolve problems. Non-dedicated servers almost always compromise system reliability.

Proprietary Servers

These machines are designed specifically to be used as network severs for particular vendor's LAN system. They often provide high performance than generic servers because of features tailored to a server's needs.

To their disadvantage, they usually operate only with a specific vendor's LAN hardware and operating system and are usually more expensive than their generic counterparts. Novell, Banyan and 3 Com have provided proprietary servers in the past, but have move towards generic platforms.

Super Servers

They are computers designed specifically to be network servers, but which are not specific one vendor's LAN operating system. Super servers usually provide certain enhancements, such as multiple processors, fault-tolerant or high-performance disk systems. Compaq, NetFrame, Dell, Tricord and Evered, among others, all provide machines that fall into this category.

Various File Servers

File Service can be provided as task running under another operating system. Microsoft takes this approach with LAN Manager, which runs as a task under OS/2 and Novell takes this approach with NetWare VMS for DEC VAXes and portable NetWare for Unix computers.

With this approach performance is generally sacrificed to obtain the benefits of connectivity between dissimilar systems.

Batch-Processing Servers

Batch processing servers allow time consuming tasks, such as reports to be off-loaded from a user's machine to an idle LAN workstations, allowing the user to continue working while the batch processing handles the off loaded tasks. Third- party products, such as Campbell Software's Bobware Job Server provide this capability.

Central File-Server Systems

Most high-end LAN systems use a central file server approach. One or more computers on the LAN are specifically designed as file servers and generally run operating systems specifically designed or the file service tasks. Although hardware costs for central-server systems are usually higher than peer-to-peer systems, the added performance, security, system integrity and ease of maintenance more than make up for the increased cost, especially in larger systems.

Communication Servers

These provide connection between client computers on a LAN and off-LAN services or provide access to LAN resources from off-LAN systems. For example, communication servers provide LAN users with terminal emulation and access to time-sharing computers, connections to remote systems, or dial-in access from remote PCs.

Like file and print servers, communication servers can be dedicated or non-dedicated, depending on the particular communication server product. Communications service can also be a task on a network file server (again, depending on the particular product). Although communications services can be integrated into the file server operating system (Banyan VINES uses this approach), usually they are not.

Communication servers include the following:

- Host Gateways allow multiple LAN clients to access a time-sharing computer via a single connection to the LAN.

- Asynchronous communication servers allows multiple LAN users to share a pool of dial-out modems or asynchronous connection to host computers.
- Remote access servers allow remote PCs or terminals to access LAN resources via dial up phone lines or leased lines.

Database Servers

These can be divided into 3 primary components: Development tools, User interface and Database engine. The database engine does all the selecting, sorting and updating. Currently, most DBMS combine the interface software to run on each user's PC (the client) and running the database engine in a separate machine (the database server) shared by all users. This approach can increase databases performances as well as overall LAN performance because only selected records are transmitted to the user's PC, not large blocks of files.

However, because the database engine must handle multiple requests, the database server itself can become a bottleneck when a larger number of requests are pending. Database servers offer real potential for remote database access and distributed databases. Because the database server only returns selected database record(s) to the client machine (instead of large blocks of data), remote access over relatively slow telephone lines can provide acceptable performance. In addition, a client computer can make requests of multiple servers regardless of physical location.

Facsimile Servers

FAX servers (or gateways) give multiple LAN workstations the ability to send and receive FAXes through a single network connection. The FAX server can be workstation with an installed FAX board and special software or a specialized device designed for fax service.

Groupware Servers

Groupware addresses the management of semi-structured information such as text, image, mail, bulletin boards and the flow of work. These client/server systems place people in direct contact with other people. Lotus Notes is the leading example of such a system, although a number of other applications-including document management, imaging multiparty applications and workflow-are addressing some of the same needs.

Specialized groupware software can be built on top of the vendor's canned set of client/ server APIs. In most cases, applications are created using a scripting language and form-based interfaces provided by the vendor. The communication middleware between the client and the server is vendor-specific. Eventually, the Internet will become the middle ware of choice for GroupWare.

Object Server

With an object server, the client/server application is written as a set of communicating object. Client object communicates with server objects using an Object Request Broker (ORB). The client invokes a method on a remote object. The ORB locates an instance of that object server class, invokes the requested method, and returns the result to the client object. Server objects must provide support for concurrency and sharing. The ORB brings it all together. After years of incubation, some "real life" commercial ORBs are now in production. Examples of commercial ORBs that comply with the Object Management Group's CORBA standard include Digital's ObjectBroker, IBM's SOM 3.0, Sun's NEO, HP's ORB plus, Expersoft's PowerBroker, Iona's Orbix, and PostModern's BlackWidow.

Peer- to-Peer LANs

An alternative to the central server approach is the peer-to-peer approach. In a peer-to-peer LAN each user can offer his or her disks, printers and other resources for use by others. This means that any workstations can become a server. Because a special server machine is not required, peer to peer LANs can be more cost effective, but central server LANs provide for easier manageability, easier backup and greater security.

In addition, peer-to-peer LANs usually rely on the workstation operating systems to provide network services and this usually means lower performance than central-servers LANs.

Print-Servers

These provide shared access to printers. Most LAN operating systems provide print service. Print service can run on a file server or on one or more separate print server machines. Non-file server print servers can be dedicated to the task of print service, or they can be non-dedicated workstations. These disadvantages of using workstations, as print servers are similar to the disadvantages of using file servers as workstations.

The workstation may run a little slower when print services are being used, a user could shut down the server without warning, or an application could lock up the server. The consequences of a lock-up or shut-down on a print server, however, are usually less severe than the consequences of locking up a file server. The time involved in dealing with these problems, however, can be costly.

Transaction Servers

With transaction servers, the client invokes remote procedures that reside on the server with an SQL database engine. These remote procedures on the server execute a group of SQL statements. The network exchange consists of a single request/reply message (as opposed to the database server's approach of one request/reply message for each SQL statement in a transaction).

The SQL statement either all succeed or fail as a unit. These grouped SQL statements are called transactions. With a transaction server, you create the client/server application by writing the code for both the client and server components. The client component usually includes a Graphical User Interface (GUI). The server components usually consists of SQL transactions against a database.

This application called online transaction processing or OLTP. They tend to be mission–critical application that requires a 1-3 second response time 100% of the time. OLTP applications also require tight controls over the security and integrity of the databases. Two forms of OLTP are there: TP lite, based on the stored procedures provided by database vendors; and TP Heavy, based on the TP monitors provided by OLTP vendors.

Web Servers

The World Wide Web is the first truly intergalactic client/server application. This new model of client/server consists of thin, portable, "universal" clients that talk to superfat servers. In its simplest incarnation, a Web server returns documents when clients ask for them by name.

The clients and severs communicate using an RPC-like protocol called HTTP. This protocol defines a simple set of commands: parameters are passed as strings, with no provision for typed data. The Web is being extended to provide more interactive forms of client/server computing. In addition, the Web and distributed objects are starting to come together. Java is the first manifestation of this new Object Web.

Fat Servers

Client/server applications can also be differentiated by how the distributed application is split between the client and the server. The fat server model places more function on the server. The fat client model does the reverse. Groupware, transaction and web servers are examples of fat servers; database and file servers are example of fat clients. Distributed objects can be either. Fat clients are the more traditional forms of client/server. The bulk of the application runs on the client side of the equation. In both the file server and database server models, the clients know how the data is organized and stored on the server side.

Fat clients are used for decision support and personal software. They provide flexibility and opportunities for creating front-end tools that let end users create their own applications. Fat server application is easier to manage and deploy on the network because most of the code runs on the servers. Fat servers try to minimize network interchange by creating more abstract levels of service. Transaction and object servers, for example, encapsulate the database. Instead of exporting raw data, they export the procedures (or method in object-oriented terminology) that operates on that data.

The client in the fat server model provides the GUI and interacts with the server through remote procedures calls (or methods invocations). Each client/server model has its uses. In many cases, the models complement each other, and it is not unusual to have them coexist in one application. For example, a GroupWare imaging application could require an "all-in-one" server that combines file, database, and transaction and object services. Fat servers, used for mission critical application, represents the new growth area for PC based client/server computing.

2 Tier Versus Vs 3 Tier

Fat clients and Fat servers are also called 2 Tier and 3 Tier client/server architectures. It's all about how you split the client/server application into functional units that you can then assign to either the client or to one or more servers. The most typical functional units are the user interface, the business logic and the more servers. The most typical functional units are the user interface, the business logic and the shared data. There many possible variations of multi-tier architectures depending on how you split the application and the middleware you use to communicate between the tiers. In 2-tier client/server systems, the application logic is either buried inside the user interface on the client or within the database on the server (or both).

In 3-tier client/server systems, the application logic (or process) lives in the middle-tier; it is separated from the data and user interface. Processes become first-class citizens; they can be managed and deployed separately from the GUI and the database. In theory, 3-tier client/server systems are more scalable, robust and flexible. In addition, they can integrate data from multiple sources. Examples of 3-tier client/server systems are TP Monitors, distributed objects and the web. Examples of 2-tier client/server systems are file servers and database server with stored procedures.

Futuristic Client/Server

Client/server applications are on a threshold to be brought in by:

1. The exponential increase of low-cost bandwidth on Wide Area Network-for example, the internet and CompuServe; and
2. A new generation of network enabled, multi-threaded desktop operating systems-for example, OS/2 Warp Connect and Windows 95.

This new threshold marks the beginning of a transition from Ethernet client/server to intergalactic client/server that will result in the irrelevance of proximity. The center of gravity is shifting from single-server, 2- tier, LAN-based departmental client/server to a post-scarcity form of client/server where every machine on the global "information highway " can be both a client and a server. The following table contrasts these two eras of client/server computing.

Table Web client/server Versus Traditional Client/Server

Application characteristics	*Intergalactic Era Client/Server*	*Ethernet era Client/Server*
Number of clients per application	Millions	Less than 1000
Number of servers per application	100,000+	1 or 2
Geography	Global	Campus based
Server-to server interactions	Yes	No
Middleware	ORBs on top of Internet	SQL and stored procedures
Client/server architecture	3-tier (or n-tier)	2 tier
Transactional updates	pervasive	very infrequent

Multi media content	High	Low
Mobile agents	Yes	No
Client front-ends	OOUIs, compound documents, and shippable places	GUI
Time-frame	1997-2000	1985 till present

What do we need?

Some key technologies are needed at the client/server application level to make all this happen, including:

Intelligent Middleware

The distributed environment must provide the semblence of a single system-image across potentially millions of hybrid client/server machines. The middle ware must create this Houdini-sized illusion by making all servers on the global network appear to behave like a single computer system. Users and programs should be able to dynamically joint and leave the network and then discover each other. You should be able to use the same naming conventions to locate any resource on the network.

Intelligent Self-managing Entities

With the introduction of new multithread, high volume, network ready desktop operating systems, we anticipate a world where millions of machines can be both client and servers. However, we can't afford to ship a system administrator with every operating system. To avoid doing this, we need distributed software that knows how to manage and configure itself and protect itself against threats.

Rich Data Management

This includes active multimedia compound documents that you can move, store, view and edit in-place anywhere on the network. Again, most nodes on the network should provide compound document technology-for example, OLE or OpenDoc-for doing mobile document management. Of course, this environment must also be able to support existing record-based structured data including SQL databases.

Rich Transaction Processing

In addition to supporting the venerable flat transaction, the new environment requires nested transactions that can span across multiple servers, long lived transaction that execute over long periods of time as they travel from server to server and queued transaction that can be used in secure business dealings. Most nodes on the network should be able to participate in a secured transaction; superserver nodes will handle the massive transaction loads.

Roaming Agents

The new environment will be populated with electronic agents of all types. Consumers will have personal agents that look after their interests: businesses will deploy agents to sell their wares on the network; and sniffer agents will be sitting on the network, at all the times, collecting information to do system management or simply looking for trends. Agent technology includes cross-platform scripting engines, workflow and Java-like mobile code environment that allow agents to live on any machine on the network.

Which Server Goes Where?

You have a lot of flexibility in determining where server functions provide. File service, for example, can be handled by a dedicated machine, buy a non-dedicated workstations, or by a task running under an operating system such as UNIX or DEC's VMS. Print services, database services and other services can all is handled in similar fashion. How do you determine which service goes there? Here are some factors to consider:

CPU load factor and resource requirement

Consider the CPU usage, RAM (random access memory) requirements etc. that services require. Putting multiple services on one machine may have adverse performance consequences. Also, even with single services, you must make sure that the server machine is adequate to the task. An old AT-286 might be fine as a print server, for example, but it will probably be inadequate as a mainframe gateway or a communications server.

Connectivity

Using a Unix-based computers or a DEC VAX as a NetWare file server is not going to provide the highest performance, but can provide PC users with easy, transparent access to minicomputer resources.

Cost

When making cost decisions consider the cost of lower performance, down time and troubleshooting should problems occur with multiple service that are installed on a single server.

Reliability

Consider the reliability of a service (and related hardware) if you are planning to add that service to an existing server. An unreliable service can cause another service to crash, or require the server to be shut down so a problem can be fixed. If a communications service needs to be shut down for resetting, for example, it would affect any other services running in the same machine. It is, at the very least, inconvenient to have to power down a file server that everyone relies on to reset a service used by a few.

9

LAN Databases

What is a LAN Database?

Not too many years ago, the only Database Management System (DBMSs) that existed ran large mainframe computers. In that environment, needs were usually thoroughly assessed before any software was purchased or code was written. In today's PC environment, however, users often do the bulk of database designing and programming themselves. This approach, while perhaps workable on a stand-along PC, can be a problem in the LAN environment, where different levels of users may need access to a same data. LANs have extended the usefulness of database software by allowing a whole department or company to have access to a same data concurrently.

However, a DBMS designed to be used by an occasional users for simple list management would probably be completely unusable for someone trying to create a complex inventory and invoicing application. Similarly, a DBMS optimized for free-form query of data stored in table form may not be the best program for some entry and transaction processing systems. Before deciding what database system will fit your needs, you need to examine what your needs really are and in what direction they are likely to go. You should realize that the system you design includes the computer system, but must be designed in the context of the larger system that constitutes the office. System design identifies the work that an office as a whole must accomplish, the people who will participate and what each will do and the tools trey will use and the precise steps to be taken by whom, when where and with what. The system you design will change the work flow in your department or company, so the stakes can be high. For example, you will be choosing the degree of centralization for your system.

Some advantages of a more centralized system are that it can be easier for all users to access all data (the "big picture") and it can be easier for you to enforce data standards and security and the hardware costs can be less. On the other hand, a more distributed system encourages people to manage the information relevant to their jobs themselves. This helps avoid keeping information for its own sake. Distributed systems give remote users more immediate access to the computer as a dynamic tool of use to them in accomplishing work, rather than as a system for reporting work that is already done. A system approach that fails miserably in one office might work perfectly well in another.

Factors that influence the success of the approach include the fit of the software to the users needs, the degree of training and support and the fit between the company's management style and the system's style. For example, a system that enables salespeople in the field to use the computer for managing their contact schedules, writing orders and communicating with customers directly will work well only if management supports that degree of independence. If communication with customers (mail contact invoicing and the like) is mainly conducted by the central office, the salesperson "ownership" and maintenance of customer names and addresses can impede customer communication.

If sales and tightly controlled by the central company, this software system will frustrate salespeople and management alike and will eventually go unused. The system implementer rarely gets to start from scratch, nor design in a vacuum. Usually a system is being designed in reaction to the failures of the current setup.

System designers often fail to take into account user attitudes shaped by previous systems, but the strength of strong negative assessments of certain programs or styles may preclude otherwise acceptable solutions. The section, which follows, reviews the kinds of database software from which you can choose and issues surrounding their implementation and use.

Database Service and Server-based Applications

Software for DBMSs is undergoing rapid evolution in the industry. Database service and server-based applications are currently hot topics of discussion. Many writers and industry analysts assume that database service is inherently better and faster for shared database access than file service and that file server-based servers are better than other approaches. Currently, the standard approach to retrieving data from a networked database is file service.

With file service, a database program running on a workstation PC requests blocks of files from the file server. With most database files, for example, only the file blocks that contain the requested data records and associated indexes, if any, are downloaded. In most cases that portion of the database is then locked to other users.

The workstation PC can modify and/or update the specific locked records, then upload the file blocks containing them back to the server, at which time they will be unlocked to other users. With file service, database processing takes place at the workstation. Database server systems split up the job of database processing: each user's workstation PC runs the "front end" or user interface software, while another machine on a network processes the database requests. This "back end" processor is called a database engine or database server.

With this approach, only individual records are transmitted from the database server to a workstation. Because individual records are being sent to and from the workstation, traffic on the network may be lessened. On the face of it, it sounds as if database service should be faster and more efficient for database processing than file service; yet this may not always be the case.

A database server can be implemented in several ways:

1. It can be a separate, secondary process on a network file server.
2. It can be a Value-Added Process (VAP) on a file server, working as part of the LAN operating system.
3. It can employ a co-processor in a LAN file server.
4. It can use a dedicated PC on the LAN.
5. It can be a separate background process on a designated LAN workstation.
6. It can employ a co-processor in a LAN workstation.

All of these approaches can be considered server-based applications and each has its own advantages and disadvantages. Remember, server-based does not necessarily mean file server-based, although that is still the current prevalent usage of the term.

Database Service as a Second Task on a File Server

This is the approach that is currently receiving the most attention by the press. The CPU of the server divides its attention between its file server function and its database server function. For example, Microsoft's network operating system LAN Manager runs the database service as a secondary, separate process on the network file server (that should be using the OS/2 PC operating system). The basic idea is that the file server machine is the "logical" place for database service to take place.

What is not often considered sufficiently in this implementation is the degradation on overall performance that can result. With a slow network, a fast server and little traffic, this approach may not worsen performance at all. But on a fast, busy network, sharing the server CPU between the file service and database service can create a performance bottleneck at the server, while workstation processors lie idle.

Database Service as a Value-Added Server Process

A Value Added Process (VAP) is an extension to the file server software. A VAP performs tasks whose results are then integrated with the file server work. Although tighter integration of tasks cold result in less overheads, this approach can have the same potential bottleneck performance problems described above when the database service is performed directly by the file server resources.

Application Co-processor in the File Server

With this approach, a separate processor board is installed in the file server. Workstation database requests are routed to the co-processor. This eases the load on the main processor while eliminating the LAN traffic that would ensue if database requests had to be sent across the cable to individual workstations for processing. All other things being equal, using an application co-processor in a file server probably provides the best performance of the database server designs available.

It does not use file server CPU time or data processing, it does not add to traffic on the LAN cable and it minimizes the time files or records are locked by workstation requests.

Dedicated Database Server

By using a dedicated database server (that is, a second PC separate from the file server and used only for database processing), you can reduce traffic on the LAN cable and free workstations from lengthy database processing. You can store database files on the hard disk of the database server PC or on the file server. (For security and backup reasons, it can be desirable to store the files on the file server.

In that case, the database server has to update the files on the file server, which increases LAN traffic that was supposed to be avoided).

Background Database Server on a Workstation

Under OS/2, you can use a workstation PC as a database server, where the server functions are performed as background tasks. This would have most of the attributes of a dedicated database server, but would provide lower performance due to the sharing of the workstation CPU, bus and network interface.

Application Co-processor in a Workstation

A co-processor in a workstation PC would probably have about the same overall effect on performance as a separate database server. Because the expansion bus and network interface are being shared, performance of the host workstation could be affected in a heavy traffic situation. One additional performance factor to consider is the database server itself.

Multiple requests and updates must be queued by the database server, while update processing with file service is provided by the workstation PC. With a busy system, the database server itself can become a bottleneck, while DBMSs that do not employ a database server distribute the workload to each user's workstation. A serious potential problem with distributed database processing is that each of the workstations has the power to corrupt the entire database.

With database service, since all database processing being handled by a single dedicated CPU, there is less chance of file corruption. System integrity is another factor to consider, especially with applications and/or co-processors running in the file server, What if a server-based application "hands up" the server?

Applications have been known to hang single PCs and they could also hang a file server running a server-based application. One primary advantage of the database server approach is that a "client" workstation can access multiple database servers, so that physically separate database can be treated by the user as one logical distributed database.

A user can request data without necessarily knowing or caring where the data is physically located; the database software locates and delivers the requested data. With this distributed database approach, available databases could include a PC database server on the local LAN, a mini-or mainframe computer on the local LAN or accessed through a gateway or bridge, or a remote database accessed through a remote gateway or bridge. Because you care generally not moving vast amounts of data across a LAN when accessing a database server, low-speed remote LAN bridges (say, 19.2 Kb/sec. or lower) may become more viable.

With database servers, you are only sending requests and retrieving records, not massaging large blocks of data at the client PC. Distributed databases enable you to remain central control and empower remote uses and offices. While many database server systems have been announced, few are actually available for PC LANs and very few benchmark tests have been published.

Most of the forthcoming database server systems are based on Structured Query Language (SQL) is an ANSI standard for data retrieval based on IBM's design and specifications. Most announced SQL servers are based on the ANSI standard. Even after the SQL, database servers reach the market, it will take time to create or modify applications to make use of them. In the long run, standardization on SQL servers will probably mean interchangeability of various vendors' DBMS front ends and applications generators with various database servers. The big advantage of this approach is that user can get many different views of the same data, using familiar front-end DBMS interfaces, like Lotus1-2-3, Paradox, Data Flex, Database and dBase. Initially, however, DBMS vendors may have to choose sides, as each database engine developer attempts to lock front end developers into their "enhanced" standard SQL severs.

This would in turn force users to choose the SQL server that runs their favorite interface and that SQL server might not run other interfaces that they need. Eventually, however, front-end developers will provide their interfaces for all the SQL severs that survive the initial market struggle. They will have to in order to survive themselves. Some DBMS vendors have already announced alliances with particular SQL database server vendors.

For example, Borland's Paradox, Micro Database Systems' MDBS III and Ashton-Tate's (taken over by Borland) dBase IV will front-end the Ashton Tate/Sybase/Microsoft SQL Sever for LAN Manager. Paradox and WorldTech's dBXL will work with Oracle's database server, while dBXL and Gupta Technology's SQL Windows and Oracle's front end will work with Novell's Netware SQL. On the downside, expect the first generation of SQL database servers to be slow performers. There will inevitably be problems to solve, incompatibilities and unexpected bottlenecks.

As SQL database servers are optimized, performance will improve. Like the database, servers may well use specialized operating software (and possibly even specialized hardware) optimized for database service. As the technology matures, however, SQL (or whatever it may evolve into) and database servers will come into their own.

Faster hardware, including machines optimized for database service, more sophisticated server software and optimized applications, could all contribute to the process. Much of the commentary about SQL database servers by the press and by vendors is speculative. It is too early to tell which products will prevail and what their practical shortcoming will be, since so few have actually been released.

LAN Operating Systems

The focus of the book is on SQL Server, that is, PC Workstations connected to servers running some of the Operating Systems, such as OS/2 UNIX and Windows NT. The overwhelming choice for client workstations today is Windows. In the LAN environment there exist a few network operating systems: Novell's, Netware, LAN Manager, Windows NT, BANYAN VINES DIGITAL Network Architecture (DNA). AppleTalk, etc. Depending on your client and server operating system and the Network environment.

Appropriate networking software needs to be loaded on both ends in order for them to communicate. This section introduces several leading protocol stacks for computer networking. To gain a rudimentary understanding of any protocol, try to relate it to the OSI Reference Model and identify the general methods the protocol uses.

You can apply this approach when evaluating real-world computer networking scenarios, industry publications and any other source of information in networking technologies. You should understand that the OSI Reference Model is not tangible. However, computer networks actually require design specifications from which they are built. These specifications are called protocols. A protocol is a statement of formalized rules, conventions and standards.

You will also use the terms protocol suite to indicate a group of specifications that are meant to be used together and protocol stack as the suite that is ordered in a logical hierarchy. Typically, protocols are created by computer networking standards organizations and vendors. Once a protocol has been established, the hardware and software vendors implement it in their various products. Protocols and protocol implementations do not always fit well into the conceptual framework that the OSI Reference Model provide.

Some protocols specify functions corresponding to more than one layer while skipping part or all of another. In many cases this mismatch is not intentional. Many protocols were already in use and quite popular before the OSI Reference Model was developed. Note that the Network communications may be possible when using these non-OSI standard protocols, however it is often more difficult for the corresponding devices to communicate with those of other protocols.

Organizations that attempted to interconnect devices which use differing protocols have driven the industry towards open systems. There is much disagreement as to what entails an open system, but the OSI model remains the most unifying model of network communications. Some vendors have attempted to retrofit their protocols to the OSI model or options of it since not all of the protocols cover the entire seven-layer model. Others have tried to prove the merit of their own protocols and justify their models as being open. As a result, today's protocols demonstrate several degrees of conformance to the OSI model.

Still, the OSI Reference Model serves as a valuable tool for comparing disparate protocols, which are attempting to perform similar functions. The Internet protocol suite specifies functions corresponding to OSI model layers above the Data Link layer. The lower-layer protocols are intentionally open to allow the use of various protocols. The suite was designed to allow the Internet protocols to work with diverse data link and physical technologies. This has been one of the keys to the Internet protocols' success. Similarly, Netware suite specified functions corresponding to OSI layers above the Physical Layer. The lower layer protocols are open to allow the use of various protocols.

The Digital Network Architecture (DNA), Apple Talk and Systems Network Architecture (SNA) functions on all the layers of OSI model, which is one of the major disadvantage of not getting success.

NETWARE (IPX/SPX)

Today, Netware is the most popular and widely used LAN operating system available in the market. Created by Novell, Inc, and introduced to the marketplace in the early 1980s, the NetWare architecture resembles that of an early network system developed in the 1960s by Xerox at its Palo Alto Research Center (PARC). The Xerox Network System (XNS) is the basis for many past and present PC networking systems, including those from 3Com, Ungermann-Bass, and Banyan. The complete NetWare system provides file, print, message, application and database services. It is based on a server-centric network architecture through which remote network devices appear local to the user.

Another Novell product-Personal NetWare-provides similar functionality through a peer-to-peer network architecture. Since its introduction, the marketplace acceptance of NetWare has steadily grown. NetWare's success is at least partially attributable to its flexibility. NetWare runs with a number of different transport protocol stacks, links technologies and computer platforms. NetWare also supports communications with a number of today's most popular local operating systems, including DOS, Macintosh, OS/2 Windows NT, UNIX and VMS. Because of the tremendous variety of protocols and programming interfaces associated with NetWare, mapping NetWare and related technologies to the OSI Reference Model is not trivial.

Although the NetWare protocols are modular and layered, NetWare's architects concentrated on providing a high level of functionality without strict adherence to any existing standard model. Therefore, the protocol suite dose not fit nearly into ISO's seven layers. However, since all computer networks must address similar topics and methods, the NetWare protocols can be assigned or grouped. Multiple Link Interface Driver (MLD) is Novell's name for a network for interface board driver.

Specifically, each MLID is a piece of software (typically created by the board's manufacturer) that complies with Novell's Open Data-Link Interface (ODI) architecture. An MLID is not directly linked to an individual protocol stack so that it can be concurrently bound to various stacks. The Media Access for MLID are contention, token passing and polling. Link Support Layer (LSL) is the interface between an MLID and the various upper-layer protocol stacks. The LSL interprets each packet's protocol identification field and passes the packet to the appropriate protocol stack.

Internetwork Packet eXchange Protocol (IPX) is a connectionless (datagram) Network layer protocol derived from XNS's Internetwork Datagram Protocol (IDP). As a network layer protocol, IPX addresses and routes packets form one location to another on an IPX Internetwork. To do so, IPX performs logical network addressing and Internetwork routing functions. It relies upon the underlying hardware's physical device address for node addressing and upper-layer service addresses (called sockets) to address the ultimate packet destination within the node. In addition, IPX makes route selections based on network reachability information compiled by RIP (Routing Information Protocol). Router Information Protocol (RIP) was also derived from XNS. RIP is a distance-vector route discovery protocol, which uses a hop count to determine cost.

Although RIP is implemented as a service, it is directly based on IPX and performs Network layer functions. NetWare Link Service Protocol (NLSP) is a link-state route discovery protocol modeled after a routing protocol, developed by an ISO standards organization, called Intermediate. System-to-Intermediate System (IS-IS). Due to its inherent link-state features, NLSP supports the highly fault-tolerant mesh, a hybrid mesh networks. Sequenced Packet exchange Protocol (SPX) is an extension of IPX that provides for connection oriented Transport layer packet delivery.

Derived from the Xerox Sequenced Packet Protocol, SPX enhances the IPX protocol by providing reliable delivery. SPX virtual circuits are referred to as connections and have specific connection identifiers (connection IDs), which are placed in the SPX header. Multiple connection IDs can be attached to a single upper-layer process. SPX ensures reliable delivery by retransmitting information that is not received correctly. NetWare Core Protocols (NCP) Many NetWare server application functions (for example, file service, print service, name management, file locking and synchronization) are made available to users through the NetWare Core Protocols (NCP).

NCP is comprised of numerous function calls that support network services. NetWare client software runs on the workstation to provide transparent file and printer access to service clients through NCP function calls. Service Advertising Protocol (SAP) NetWare servers use SAP to advertise their services. Each server running SAP may identify itself and its services each minute by broadcasting a Service Identification Packet. A SAP user can also determine the servers' identities and services on the Internetwork using a Service Query Packet.

By referencing the IPX header information, SAP implementations identify the service addresses required to initiate a session.

Digital Network Architecture(DNA)

Digital Network ArchitectureTM (DNA) is a network architecture created by Digital Equipment Corporation (DEC). Originally announced in 1974, DNA is now in its fifth iteration. Products that implement DNA are referred to as DECnet products.

Although the name DECnet is commonly used to identify this protocol stack, this section specifically discusses DNA as network architecture without dwelling on the specific products classified as DECnet. DNA has evolved over the years to reflect changes in computer networking. It is complex and complete, spanning all seven layers of the OSI Reference Model.

DNA supports both DEC proprietary protocols and standards-based protocols. Most recently, DNA has been focused on supporting ISO standards that are based on the OSI Reference Model. For this reason, DNA can be mapped relatively well to the OSI Reference Model. With DNA Phase V, the DNA architecture becomes two-headed above the Transport layer. Even at and below the Transport layer old DNA and new OSI protocols are supported, but they are reasonably well integrated.

DNA Protocol Summary

Ethernet Version 2 was first co-developed by Digital, Intel and Xerox as Version 1 of the Ethernet Specification, a 10 Mbps Physical and Data Link Layer protocol. It was based on the existing 3 Mbps Xerox Research Ethernet and has since been revised and documented in Ethernet Version 2. Ethernet Version 2 uses CSMA/CD and Manchester encoding and was originally developed using coaxial cable.

The Ethernet v.2 specification provided the design basis for and is very similar to the IEEE/ISO 802.X/8802.X protocol family. However, the Ethernet V.2 frame format is slightly different from the IEEE/ISO frame format. High-level Data Link Control (HDLC) is a Data Link layer protocol which supports both asynchronous and synchronous transmission synchronization using Physical layer modem protocols.

HDLC defines both the format of data frames as well as the command syntax to establish frame transfer. Using the defined commands, HDLC can also achieve LLC-level flow control. Digital Data Communications Message Protocol (DDCMP) was the original DNA Data Link protocol designed in 1974 for WAN links. Like HDLC, DDCMP can operate with synchronous or asynchronous transmissions. It can also be used with full-or half-duplex point-to-point or multi-point configurations. DDCMP uses commands and acknowledgments to provide connection-oriented error control, LLC-level flow control and message sequencing services (DDCMP literature uses the term message for Data Link layer frames).

Connectionless-Mode Network Service (CLNS) is supported at the Network layer DNA. DNA supports both connectionless (OSI CLNS) and connection-oriented network services (OSI CONS). However, DNA Phase V typically uses CLNS. CLNS is supported through the following three ISO protocols:

- ISO 10589, Intermediate System to Intermediate System Intra-Domain Routing Exchange Protocol for Use in Conjunction with the Protocol for Providing the Connectionless-Mode Network Service, which defines the mechanisms for moving data packets between routers (or routing nodes).
- ISO 8473, Protocol for Providing the Connectionless-mode Network Service, which controls data transmission tasks between two end systems
- ISO 9542, End System to Intermediate System Routing Exchange Protocol for Providing the Connectionless-Mode network Service, which is used to perform routing functions.

Since these protocols provide connectionless service, they are limited to performing address, switching, route discovery, and route selection tasks.

Connection-Mode Network Service (CONS) is supported by DNA through the following protocols:

- ISO 8208, X.25 Packet-level Protocol for Data Terminal Equipment is the ISO version of X.25.
- ISO 8878, Use of X.25 to Provide the OSI Connection-Mode Network Service is simply additional protocol required to enable standard X.25 implementations to provide full connection-oriented services.

ISO 8073, Connection Oriented Transport Protocol Specification is used by provider a reliable connection at the Transport layer. Implementation of this protocol determines the level of flow, error and packet sequence control provided by the network.

Network Services Protocol (NSP) was designed by DEC for DNA and has been a part of DNA since its announcement in the mid-1970s. NSP offers a connection-oriented, flow controlled service through normal or expedited full-duplex subchannels. To achieve end-to-end flow control, the Network layer reports congestion to the transmitting NSP, which reduces the number of outstanding messages it will tolerate using either the guaranteed rate or window flow control method. Session Control provides an interface between applications and the Transport layer protocols. It assumes responsibility for the Session and Presentation functions for non-OSI complaint DNA implementations.

It is a proprietary architecture which performs the following functions:

- Address/name resolution
- Protocol stack selection
- Transport connection management
- Connection identifier addressing

ISO 8327, Session Protocol Specification, implements the service definition found in ISO 8326, Session Service Definition. ISO 8327 provides negotiated connection establishment and release as well as half-duplex data transfer.

In addition, the protocol can use one or more Transport layer connections for each session. It organizes data transfers by synchronizing the transfer of packets through major and minor synchronization tokens. Using tokens, a session's dialog can be reset to any synchronization point.

For example, if someone were reading this paragraph to you and you didn't hear or understand what was read, you could ask them to return to the first line of "ISO 8327, Session Protocol Specification." Using the subsection title as a token, both of you know exactly where your dialog would resume. ISO 8824, Abstract Syntax Notation One – ASN.1 with ISO 8825, Specification of Basic Encoding Rules for ASN.1 – BER is a standard character code set that disparate entitles may use as a mutually agreeable code. ASN.1 can perform character code translation. The BER protocol defines the rules to be used when translating to and from ASN.1 notation. It describes the length and location of character code type descriptions. Naming Service and X.500 Directory is the portion of DNA that performs address/name resolution.

X 500 is a directory service recommendation. Some differences exist between these two architectures, but DEC has stated that it intends to eventually convert the naming service to comply with the OSI Directory. ISO 8571 File Transfer, Access and Management – FTAM and DATA Access Protocol (DAP) is a standard protocol for file services. It may be implemented differently by every vendor who chooses to develop an FTAM application; a DECnet FTAM application may look completely different from other applications.

However, the FTAM protocol does specify that each implementation must support some combination of specific document types and service classes. The document types include textual, binary and hierarchical files and service classes include file transfer and file management tasks. DNA provides file transfer through the Data Access Protocol (DAP). DAP offers the usual file system operations, including file retrieval, storage, creation, deletion and renaming. It supports heterogeneous file systems and allows multiple accesses to the same remote file.

Unlike some other file access protocols, DAP allow access to indexed files such as those used for database applications. MAILbus Product Family and X.400 Message Handling System, while not technically protocols, provides the architectural specifications for DECnet message services. MAILbus is a family of proprietary E-mail services developed by DEC. MAILbus products use the X.400 recommendation to interact with their X400 implementations on an Internetwork. Network Virtual Terminal Service (NVTS) By using NVTS, data can be translated from the local terminal format to the network format before it is transmitted to a networked host.

The host then translates the data into its own format. The network command terminal format ensures that heterogeneous systems can communicate.

AppleTalk

Apple Computer, Inc. began development of the AppleTalk protocol suite in 1983. AppleTalk was created as the network architecture for Apple Macintosh computers. Today, AppleTalk provides connectivity for a variety of computer systems including IBM PCs running MS-DOS, IBM mainframes, Digital Equipment VAX and various UNIX computers.

To integrate the Macintosh into enterprise networks, Apple expanded the capabilities of the original AppleTalk with AppleTalk Phase 2. Introduced in 1989, AppleTalk Phase 2 increases the potential size and complexity of AppleTalk networks. Phase 2 allows AppleTalk and other protocol suites to coexist on large, complex networks. The AppleTalk protocol suite was developed after the OSI Reference Model was conceived.

Some of the key architects of AppleTalk mention that the layered approach to designing these network protocols was inspired by the prior use of layered models for "describing various concepts (in particular, operating systems) of stand-alone computers". For these reasons, the AppleTalk protocol stack can be mapped reasonably well to the ODI Reference Model. Local Talk, EtherTalk and TokenTalk ink Access Protocols (LLAP, ELAP and TLAP) are Apple's successful integration of Physical and Data Link layer technologies into AppleTalk.

To maintain consistent naming conventions, Apple refers to AppleTalk protocols over Ethernet as EtherTalk and AppleTalk protocols over token-Ring as Token Talk. The LocalTalk Link Access Protocol is an Apple specific CSMA/CA protocol for shielded twisted pair transmission media. It is best suited for small workgroups because LocalTalk segments are limited to a distance of 300 meters, maximum of 32 devices and a data rate of 230.4 Kbps.

One of the unique features of LocalTalk devices is that they can automatically assign themselves an address. At startup, each device negotiates with the other active devices to determine an acceptable physical device address. EtherTalk (also called ELAP) and TokenTalk (TLAP) are simply implementations of AppleTalk protocols that use the Ethernet and Token-Ring protocols. AppleTalk Address Resolution Protocol (AARP)- Since both ELAP and TLAP use predefined physical device addresses, AARP is used by AppleTalk addresses to the ELAP and TLAP predefined physical addresses.

AARP allows the upper layers of the AppleTalk stack to work with a variety of Data Link layer protocols. Datagram Delivery Protocol (DDP) is AppleTalk's primary Network layer protocol. DDP provides connectionless service between two sockets. Routing Table maintenance Protocol (RTMP) performs route discovery functions to create and maintain AppleTalk routing tables.

It uses a distance vector routing algorithm that is similar to the RIP routing protocol. Zone Information Protocol (ZIP) uses the concept of zones to logically organize service provider names on large Internet works, where the number of service providers can get quite large. However, most users are only interested in some subset of all the service providers. Zones can limit the number of service providers that are presented to the user at one time.

ZIP is used by routers to perform the following functions:

- Coordinate relationships between zone and network names.
- Assign service providers to zones.

Name Binding Protocol (NBP): AppleTalk uses names to identify what this course refers to as an entity. However, computer network devices typically rely upon numbers for identification. AppleTalk, in particular, allows the assigned addresses to change as each device joins the network. To make AppleTalk user friendly, the architects decided to use NBP to map AppleTalk names to these dynamic addresses.

AppleTalk Transaction Protocol (ATP) is an acknowledged connectionless transaction-based transport protocol. ATP acknowledges information delivery and initiates retransmission when data is unacknowledged for a given time period. Unlike most transport protocols, however, ATP is based on the concept of a transaction rather than on simply moving a stream of data across a reliable connection. ATP also divides and combines data packets that are too large for the underlying protocols, provides error control for lost packets and performs segment sequencing to the extent that packets are numbered and messages can be buffered until lost packets are retransmitted. AppleTalk Session Protocol (ASP) is standard OSI Session layer protocol designed to optimize file service functions. ASP establishes, maintains and releases connections or sessions.

ASP allows multiple sessions to be established with one service provider; however, each session must be established or requested by the service requester. ASP is a client of ATP and works with ATP to provide a full-fledged transport service to service requesters and providers.

Printer Access Protocol (PAP) is a very similar to ASP. It is also an OSI Session layer protocol. PAP is actually a much more generic protocol than its name implies. It can be used for connections between workstations and any type of server (print, file and so on). However, it was designed to optimize print service functions.

The following are subtle differences between PAP and ASP:

1. PAP allows either the service requester or service provider to initiate a session.
2. ASP can use multiple ATP transactions to reduce overhead on large date transfers.

AppleTalk Data Stream Protocol (ADSP) is AppleTalk's latest Session layer protocol. ADSP is considered a Session layer protocol since it can establish and release logical relationships between two sockets.

ADSP also performs segment sequencing and sliding window flow control Transport layer functions. ADSP provide a full-duplex, flow-controlled, connection-oriented service that runs on DDP. Unlike ATP, ADSP is not transaction based. It uses a connection identifier and bite stream rather than transactions. Because of this and other differences, ADSP is better suited for low bandwidth channels than ATP-ASP, (or ATP-PAP) implementations.

AppleTalk Filing Protocol (AFP) facilitates the file sharing by translating native local file system commands into an acceptable format for network file service. To accomplish this goal, AFP performs command syntax translation and provides a mechanism for other applications to perform file syntax translation. In addition, AFP verifies and encrypts login names and passwords for file access security.

AppleShare AppleTalk's three primary applications are AppleShare File Server, AppleShare Print Server and AppleShare PC.

AppleShare File Server uses AFP services to access remote files. It provides a way for users to store and access files on network servers. AppleShare File Server registers users and maps them to volumes and directories. Through this application, users log in to servers and access their resources.

AppleShare Print Server uses NBP and PAP to send information to prints on an AppleTalk Network. AppleShare Print Server calls use NBP's name lookup service to find the address of the currently selected AppleTalk printer. PAP then opens a connection to that printer. Information is spooled and maintained by AppleShare Print Server. The AppleShare Print Server interacts with the printer to send files when the printer is ready to print them.

Access to AppleShare file servers is not limited to Apple computer users. Computers running MS-DOS can also use AppleShare file services as long as they run **AppleShare PC**. AppleShare PC provides access to files in the AppleTalk file system and allows MS-DOS computers to print to AppleTalk-compatible printers. AppleShare PC supports a variety of third-party Ethernet and token ring interface cards.

Systems Network Architecture(SNA)

IBM has also announced the Systems Application Architecture (SAA) in 1987. SAA's Common Communication Support (CCS) incorporated only specific portions of SNA. SNA LU 6.2 and PU 2.1 are the strategic architectural components that IBM is promoting for the future. However, due to a large installed base, traditional SNA components and architectures should persist for many years. Systems Network Architecture (SNA) is IBM's proprietary networking architecture. As architecture, SNA does not define a single stack of protocols.

Instead, SNA describes the general characteristics of computer hardware and software required for interconnection. It was a primary basis for the OSI Reference Model, which was established roughly a decade later and is one of the oldest network architectures still in existence. In its initial 1974 release, SNA supported only hierarchically organized networks, with hosts, communications controllers, cluster controllers and terminals.

The original architecture was altered by IBM in 1984 to support distributed processing, internetworking, network management and many other advance features. The new peer-to-peer SNA architecture is called Advanced Peer-to-Peer Networking (APPN).

APPN exploits the computer processing power distributed throughout the network in the form of mainframe, minicomputer and PC systems. Because of its prominent use during the OSI model's formation, the relationship between SNA and the OSI Reference Model can be mapped fairly well.

However, SNA is truly Architecture or a model, not a protocol stack as are the other suites described in this section. Therefore, this section performs the following:

- Compares the two models
- Describes basic architectural components
- Identifies topic methods of select protocols, key products, and marketing terms.

The SNA layers are briefly described as follows:

Physical Control is concerned with electrical, mechanical and procedural characteristics of the physical media and interfaces to the physical media. It is directly analogous to the OSI Physical layer; SNA does not define any specific protocols for this layer. IBM assumed that this layer would be implemented with various international standards. However, IBM has developed its own implementations such as Token-Ring.

Data Link Control is also quite similar to the OSI Data Link layer. SNA defines the SDLC protocol for implementation of communication links where master/primaries communicate with slaves/secondaries and IBM Token-Ring on peer-to-peer networks.

Path Control includes many of the functions of the OSI Network layer, such as routing and datagram fragmentation and reassembly. The Path Control layer also describes some OSI Data Link layer functions, such as flow control.

Transmission Control provides a reliable end-to-end connection service and is therefore quite similar to the OSI Transport layer. The Transmission Control layer also provides encryption and decryption services, a function performed by the OSI Presentation layer.

Data Flow Control roughly corresponds to the OSI Session layer. The Data Flow Control layer control request and response processing, determines whose turn it is to talk, groups messages and interrupts data flow on request.

Presentation Services specifies data transmission algorithms, which is also the principal duty of the OSI Presentation layer. The Presentation Services layer also coordinates resource sharing and synchronizes operations.

NAU Services is analogous to OSI's Application layer which provides application services in the form of programs that implement distributed processing or management services. A good example of a transaction service is SNADS (SNA Distribution Services), which provides a distribution system for use by SNA applications.

SNA was designed to integrate IBM and IBM-compatible products; the architecture was based upon specific units called nodes. The following definitions describe the node types used in SNA:

Host nodes (type 5) include mainframes and midrange systems. A host node controls a domain, which includes one or more subareas, each with subordinate nodes and peripherals. Domains consist of the physical and logical units, links and all associated resources that a host has the ability to control. Subareas are portions of SNA networks-consisting of a communication controller, physical units and logical units. SNA networks typically include multiple host nodes and allow a terminal in one host domain to access applications in another host domain.

Communication controller nodes (type 4), also called front-end processors, are hardware devices that route and control the flow of data in a hierarchical structure. A communications controller can be directly attached via a high-speed data channel to the host or remotely attached via a data link to another communications controller.

Peripheral nodes (type 2) include the many different client devices in a hierarchical structure. Cluster controllers, terminals and printers are examples of peripheral nodes,

To interconnect these nodes, SNA relies upon the following concepts:

(1) Physical units

(2) Logical units

(3) Control points

Physical Units (PU's): Physical units are combinations of hardware, firmware and software that manage and monitor the resources of a node. Several of the PUs was previously described as node types. The following is brief description of the PU types:

- Type 1.0 PUs are terminal nodes.
- Type 2.0 PUs are terminals, printers, cluster controllers, or other peripherals which can only communicate with a mainframe.
- Type 2.1 PU devices are typically minis, cluster controllers, gateway devices and occasionally workstations that can communicate with a mainframe or another type 2.1 device.
- Type 4.0 PUs are communication controllers that link host mainframes and cluster controllers or other type 2 devices.
- Type 5.0 PUs are host computers

Logical Units: Logical units are the "entitles" of the network that provide the means to establish a connection with another logical unit and exchange information. They allow people and applications to access the network and the functions provided by VTAM. The following is a list of LU types:

- Type 0 LUs are general purpose LUs used in program-to-program connections.
- Type 1 LUs batch-type terminals, card readers, and printers (such as 3770 and 3270).
- Type 2 LUs are terminals (such as 3270).
- Type 3 LUs are batch-type terminals, card readers, and printers (such as 3270 printers).
- Type 4 LUs were used in old peer-to-peer connections (such as 6670 and 6670 connections and 5250 printers).
- Type 6.0 and 6.1 LUs are used in CICS to CICS or IMS connections between mainframes.
- Type 6.2 LUs are used in new peer-to-peer connections.
- Type 7 LUs are 5270 display stations.

Control Points: Control Points are used to manage and control data flow on the network. Control points are found in type 5.0 and 2.1 PUs. Type 5.0 PUs operate a System Services Control Point (SSCP) which is the software program and central location point within an SNA network that manages configuration, coordinates requests, and provides session services for users on the network. Multiple SSCPs can divide the network into domains of control, with each SSCP having a hierarchical control relationship to the Physical units and logical units with its domain.

Type 2.1 PUs offer a control point which provides similar services, but on a smaller scale. These control points operate in conjunction with other type 2.1 PU control, points to provide peer-to-peer functionality.

Token-Ring is IBM's LAN specification that was used as a model for IEEE 802.5 with the caveat that Token-Ring specifies a physical start topology. Token-Ring uses a token-passing media access method to provide data rate of 4 and 16 Mbps. The specification defines specific cable and connector types.

Synchronous Data Link Control (SDLC) typically uses specific hardware to interface with dedicated, eased or dialup telephone lines. It can support point-to-point or multi-point and half-duplex or full-duplex connections. SDLC generates its own specific control messages in addition to adding data link level headers to packets received from higher layers.

Network Control Program (NCP) is an IBM product that resides in and controls resources connected to a communication control. It was designed to operate front-end processors and perform data link and limited network layer functions. Now, NCP provides routing and gateway functionality in SNA networks.

Virtual Telecommunications Access Method (VTAM) is another IBM product that controls communication and the flow of data in SNA network. It provides single domain, multiple domain and interconnected network capability. VTAM works with NCP to control network resources. Often VTAM and SSCP are considered synonymous terms. However, VTAM is the program product while SSCP is the main software program in VTAM.

Customer Information Control System (CICS) supports transaction processing applications by generalizing input and output commands for use on a network. Software developers use CICS commands to build applications that carry out transactions on local and remote systems. CICS provides terminal-to-application communication, distributed file access, security, multitasking, storage management, transaction tracking and recovery, transaction reversal and a graceful restart facility.

Advanced Peer-to-Peer Networking (APPC) is a network-and transport-level architecture tat allows SNA to operate networks using only type 2.1 PUs.

Information Management System (IMS) is a similar transaction processing product. It is actually composed of two products: the IMS Transaction Manager and the IMS Database Manager. Using these products, IMS allows multiple applications to share IMS Database Manager databases, provides message switching capabilities and facilities the scheduling of priority transactions.

Advanced Program-to-Program Communication (APPC) is actually a term for the SNA extension that added LU 6.2. This version of SNA was the first to allow peer-to-peer communication between logical units that did not involve a mainframe host.

Distributed Data Management (DDM) provides transparent remote file access to SNA service requestors. It performs this function similar as OS Call Interception, "The OSI Application Layer." DDM receives file requests from applications and executes them though the local OS or through a DDM server across the network.

SNA Distribution Services (SNADS) is an application-level service that initiates store-and-for-ward transfers or "distribution" of messages and documents.

Documents Interchange Architecture (DIA) defines the functions required for exchanging documents between different computer systems. DIA coordinates file services such as the storing and retrieving of documents and file transfer.

LAN Manager and Windows NT

Today, Windows NT is the most popular and widely-used LAN operating system available in the market. Created by Microsoft Inc, and introduced to the marketplace in 1996. The difference between all Network Operating Systems lies in their architecture. As discussed earlier, NetWare uses a proprietary implementation of Xerox Network system (XNS) called SPX/IPX as the underlying transport protocol.

On top of that, it provides Netware Core Protocol (NCP) for access to network services.

NCP spans the session and presentation OSI layers. Hence in Netware environments the file server is reserved for running Netware and providing network services.

Netware is both the NOS and the OS in this case; it does its own file management, task scheduling, I/O and so on. This means you cannot run standard applications written for Windows NT and OS/2 on a traditional Netware file server. The solution is to have a dedicated Windows NT or OS/2 application sever computer on the Netware LAN. A LAN Manager server, however, runs on top of OS/2. In this case, NOS uses all of the underlying facilities of OS/2 for file management, process management, scheduling and so on.

LAN manager itself resides at the OSI presentation layer and is implemented on top of the NetBIOS session protocol stack, an interface defined by IBM. This insulated it form underlying transport protocols and hardware considerations. Therefore, other transport stacks, such as TCP/IP, or other access protocols such as token-ring, can be substituted without affecting any LAN Manager services. Microsoft's Windows NT is client-server operating system that includes all of the key features of OS/2 and includes built-in networking based on LAN Manager. In this sense it acts as both the OS and NOS.

In fact the networking functionality in Windows NT is very similar to LAN Manager and LAN Manager and Windows NT workstations and servers can co-exist and interoperate with each other. This discussion will not dwelve deeper into the architectural differences between these network operating systems. Most NOSs are moving in the direction of providing transport protocol and hardware independence, while retaining control of the network operating system and its features.

In case of LAN Manager and Windows NT, for example this means the adherence to two standards:

(1) Each transport must provide a NetBIOS interface at the session layer.

(2) Each transport is written tc conform to a specific interface based on the network driver interface specifications (NDIS) at the data link layer.

In this way, different transport stacks and network drivers (for network adapter cards) can be substituted, without affecting functionality. For example, LAN Manager supports the TCP/IP and ISO TP4 transport stacks, while there are already network drivers for all of the popular access protocols and hardware.

SQL Server Platforms

This chapter and the preceding chapter have discussed the basics of several different technologies that form the basis for SQL Server. SQL Server is a high-performance SQL-based, relational database server that is based on client/server architecture. Client applications formulate queries in SQL and ship them via the LAN to the SQL Server where they are processed.

SQL Server processes the SQL request and returns to the application only the required data in response to the request. SQL Server is available for several different platforms. They include SQL Server for OS/2 and SQL Server for Windows NT (available today from Microsoft) and SQL Server NLM and SQL Server for UNIX (available from Sybase).

In each case the target OS on which SQL Server runs is different and based on the network environment, the transport protocols and IPC mechanisms supported vary. For SQL Server for OS/2, the IPC mechanism required is named pipes. Thus, SQL Server will run on any LAN as long as the NOS supports named pipes. Currently, support exists for OS/2-based LANs (such as IBM's LAN Server) and for Novell's NetWare and Banyan Vines. Novell and Banyan provide named pipes support in the form of an OS/2 requestor that basically allows a machine running OS/2 on the LAN to run SQL Server on the machine. The named pipes interface frees applications developers from having to write low-level NOS calls to enable IPC between client applications and SQL Server. As discussed earlier, SQL Server for Windows NT has built-in support for multiple IPC mechanism (named pipes, sockets and SPX) running on top of multiple transport protocol stacks and in fact can activated them simultaneously.

Thus SQL Server for Windows NT server can co-exist in a wide variety of network environments (including networks based on Windows NT Advanced Server) and supports a wide range of client workstations including DOS, OS/2, Windows, Windows NT, UNIX and Macintosh. SQL Server NLM (Netware Loadable Module) is an implementation of SQL Server for NetWare servers. It could run concurrently with the file server or may be run on a dedicated computer.

The NLM version supports communication through native SPX/IPX and hence would be a natural choice for all NetWare environments, since additional protocols would not have to be loaded on the client side. SQL Server is available form Sybase for most of the leading UNIX platforms. These include variants for UNIX available from Sub (Solaris), HP (HP-UX), DEC (Ultrix), IBM (AIX) and SCO UNIX. In fact, it was first developed by Sybase for UNIX and VMS minicomputer environments using TCP/IP and DECNET protocols. The basic client/server architecture of the SQL Server, however, is still the same on all the platforms.

The important point is that client/server architecture offers a scalable and open platform. With client support for different protocols stacks and IPC mechanism, you can have a truly heterogeneous solution that allows different client workstations to talk to SQL Servers running under different sever and network environments.

SQL RDBMS Servers

Novell NetWare SQL

Novell is offering Netware SQL as their back-end database "engine" for NetWare 2.1 and above. Netware SQL runs on a file server or Netware External Bridge as a VAP. The workstation runs only the front-end application and the NetWare SQL Requestor, which takes the front-end application requests, translates them into SQL requests and transmits the SQL requests to the database server for processing. NetWare SQL relies on NetWare's System Fault Tolerance (SFT) for error recovery, but it continues transaction recovery and record locking within itself. NetWare SQL uses the NetWare record manager to access the database files.

The NetWare Btrieve server program consists of two VAPs. BSERVER, which directly accesses database files on the server and BROUTER, which routes requests to other servers. When there are multiple database servers on the network, BROUTER determines which server the data is on and routes the request there.

BSERVER user NetWare's Transaction Tracking System (TTS) to provide file roll-back and recovery. NetWare XQL is Novell's application program interface to SQL. XQL provides access to the SQL database through ANSI-standard SQL statements and other lower-level function calls. Using XQL, a C, BASIC, Pascal, or COBOL application can pass requests to the NetWare SQL database. Third-party front-end programs for NetWare SQL include WorldTech's dBXL and Quicksilver, Gupta Technologies' SQL Windows, Revelation Technologies' Revelation, Borland's Paradox and others. Novell itself provides a "blueprint" driver for Lotus 1-2-3 users.

Fox Software FoxServer

Fox Software, has a Microsoft company, provides a version of Novell's NetWare SQL called FoxServer. It incorporates dBase language functions into NetWare SQL. This means that front-end applications can use SQL, XQL, Btrieve and/or dBASE commands to directly access the database server.

Ashton-Tate/Microsoft SQL Server

Another example of SQL server software is Borland/Microsoft SQL Server, developed jointly by Microsoft, Borland and Sybase as their database engine for OS/2 servers. SQL server can run as tasks in an OS/2-based file server, or on a separate machine running OS/2. Network operating systems supported by SQL Server include Novell NetWare, IBM LAN Server and networks based on Microsoft LAN Manager. SQL Server is compatible with Sybase's minicomputer-based SQL server. SQL Server provides on-line, write-ahead transaction logging. This means that transactions are written to a log file before the database is updated. In the event of a system failure, database changes can be recovered from the transaction log. SQL Server incorporates a set of extensions (nearly all SQL databases have their own nonstandard extensions) called TRANSACT-SQL that can store commonly used group of commands at the database server and execute them with a procedure call. This means that a "client" workstation can send a single command to the server to execute complex transactions.

Among others, products that will "front-end" SQL Server include Borland's Paradox, Revelation Technologies' Revelation, Borland Dbase IV and Word Tech's dBXL and Quicksilver.

Gupta SQL Base

Gupta Technologies is a pioneer in SQL database servers. Gupta shipped the first SQL database server for PC LANs. Its SQL back-end engine offerings are SQLBase and SQLBase for OS/2, both of which work on any NetBIOS compatible LAN. Gupta produces a powerful, event-oriented application program developer called SQL Windows. SQL Windows is a Microsoft Windows-based application generator that supports graphics, menus, dialogue boxes, and mice.

Although SQL Windows only works with SQLBase now, Gupta plans to allow it to interface with other SQL DBMSs including ORACLE, Novel's NetWare SQL, Lotus's forthcoming DBMS product (based on Gupta's software and Microsoft's SQL Server). SQL Windows currently run under DOS Windows and will eventually run under the OS/2 Presentation Manager, Since SQL Windows does not (yet) have a built-in report writer, Gupta has licensed SQL, a report writer produced by SQ Software originally intended to enhance the report writing capabilities of the ORACLE DBMS. Gupta also supplies versions of WorldTech's DBXL and Quicksilver dBASE-like products that will access the SQL-Base server. SQL Network is a series of products that provides connectivity between Gupta's SQL products and IBM's mainframe-based DB2. SQL Network uses IBM's Application Program-to-Program Communications (APPC) to provide this connectivity.

Oracle

Oracle Corporation, one of the largest independent vendors of DBMS software, currently provides a XENIX-based SQL database server for use with PC LANs. This means that PCs on NetWare LANs and others must use network interface cards that support NetWare and the TCP/IP protocol concurrently, or a TCP/IP gateway to access the database server. Users on MS-Net and LAN Manager-based LANs and others must be similar methods. A primary advantage of ORACLE is the fact that it currently runs in a wide range of operating environments on microcomputers, minicomputers and mainframes. Like Gupta Technologies, ORACLE supplies versions of World Tech's DBXL and Quicksilver dBASE-like products that will access its SQL database server.

10

TCP/IP

Introduction

So far, we have discussed about networking and its cables and hardware/software. But one another thing very important is the protocols. In fact, there are lots of protocols in the market which makes it very confusing. Not only that even the software has various versions to add to the confusion. So in this chapter we try to solve some of the doubts of the protocols.

Ethernet, for instance, boasts a vast number of protocol suites such as DDCMP, LAT, MOP, XNS, SNS, TCP/IP, VRP, NRP and a slew of other three-letter acronyms for various protocols that will solve all the problems a customer could possibly have. Within the scheme of protocols, however, some still seem to rear their ugly heads, no matter how hard the industry tries to put them down or get rid of them.

One suite, **Transmission Control Protocol/Internet Protocol (TCP/IP)**, is such an occurrence. Every other vendor of networks will claim that their protocol is better and that (TCP/IP) is going away. Some will point to the decisions made by the US department of defense (DOD) to eventually migrate to internationally recognized and standardized communications hardware and protocols, obviating the need for TCP/IP and eventually replacing it.

Some view TCP/IP as a workhorse whose time has come to be put out to pasture. Then there are the zealots—those that think that the only communications protocol suite for use in the world is TCP/IP and all other are fluff. These folks are dangerous because they not only are vocal about TCP/IP; many times they are UNIX zealots as well. Some where in the middle of the camps are those who do not know what to do with TCP/IP or, worse, do not even really understand its significance to networks.

Unfortunately, these individuals are usually the managers of such diverse camps of attitudes and must make decisions on whether to use TCP/IP on a project or not. Although it is the ISO open systems protocols which have received most recent publicity, there are other well-established protocols sets, particularly on Ethernet, which have a large share of the current LAN market. Some argue that these protocols offers a better alternative to the largely untried and potentially cumbersome ISO set, but most manufacturers indicate a willingness to adopt ISO protocols at some point of time in future. The non ISO protocol described in this chapter illustrate different approach from the ISO protocol set to open system working . TCP/IP, is a vendor –independent wide are network protocol set, which has been widely used on LANs for peer-to-peer communication.

Here, we all examine the TCP and IP networking protocols and some implementation that have become de-facto standards in the military area as well as academic and UNIX areas. In recent years, knowledge of the capabilities of Transmission Control Protocols/Internet Protocol (TCP/IP) has spread far in the globe. IT managers in all types of organization have begun to research its suitability as an internetworking.

TCP/IP seems to be a ready-made solution to the commercial information systems requirements of intercommunication and interoperation. In US, government officials and research communities and many UNIX aficionados are already well versed in the vocabulary and configuration issues of this set of protocols. But for the newcomers to TCP/IP, the existing sources of information are, in many cases, written by developers apparently for developers.

Most information is primarily technical with detailed description of the bits, flags and fields of the protocols. But less information is given about the practical problems of implementing TCP/IP from scratch. For example, in a commercial rather than a technical or research environment; here the skills and constraints may be very different. The information needed does exist, but one has to read a considerable quantity of material before finding what one needs.

What is TCP/IP?

A comprehensive set of 'ready-made' communication protocols called TCP/IP became widely available and well known only when Berkeley Software Distribution released Berkeley UNIX 4.2 BSD in September 1983. This was not a coincidence; its inclusion in this release was funded by the US government TCP/IP protocols are based on standards originally developed for the US government and US research community. With the release of UNIX 4.2BSD, these communication standards emerged from the confines of the US Departments of defense and the US University and research networks; TCP/IP became the way to interconnect UNIX system. Berkeley UNIX 4.2 BSD and subsequent releases spread quickly throughout the US University and commercial communities.

With UNIX achieving wide popularity as an 'open system' the frame of TCP/IP has continued to spread. But TCP/IP is not and never has been, narrowly confined to UNIX. It was developed to allow free interchange of data among all machines, independent of type, manufacturer, hardware or operating system. In the late 1980s, TCP/IP received a further boost to its fortunes when Sun Microsystems published the specification for Open Network Computing (ONC), often called the Network File System (NFS). NFS adds important functions to TCP/IP and is now very widely available and regarded as an integral part of the TCP/IP protocol suite.

It is particularly valuable for the commercial implementer because of the simple user interfaces that it provides. TCP/IP was developed to satisfy the need to interconnect various projects that included computer networks and also allow for the addition of dissimilar machines to the networks in a systematic and standardized manner. While it is quite true that smaller defense projects may not have warranted the use of TCP/IP for project aspect, edicts from various DOD concerns such as the Undersecretary of Defense for Research and Development forced many government contractors and in-house developed projects to use the suite to conform with DOD requirements. The suite of protocols commonly referred to as TCP/IP (US Military Standards 1778 and 1777) was developed by the United States Department of Defense for its A.R.P.A (Advanced Research Project Agency) network. This is a very large scale wide area network linking many major commercial, university and military establishments.

The relevance of TCP/IP to LANs is two–fold. First, as it is a data gram based protocol, it is well suited to LAN access method, particularly Ethernet. Secondly, it is particularly popular within the UNIX community, giving it a large user base, many of whom wish to use LANs. Cost effective implementations of TCP/IP are now available for all types and sizes of machines from the largest a mainframe to personal computers and workstations. This has brought TCP/IP and its capabilities to the attention of a very wide audience.

Computer managers and users in commercial organizations throughout the world have begun to implement TCP/IP as a way of solving the problems of networking between machines of different manufacture. TCP/IP provided all the facilities for two computer systems to exchange information (intercommunication), interpret it properly and present it in a format which can be understood by the local machine and its users (interoperation). NFS gives a simple and locally-familiar representation of a set of remote and possibly unfamiliar computer filing system; like the original components of the TCP/IP suite, NFS is now available for many different computers.

How TCP/IP Works?

Most networks provide some sort of connection mechanism to get from point A to point B. Other networks worry about how to get from node A on network X to node B on network Y. If a program wishes to send information from itself on node A to another node on the same network, TCP will provide the packet sequencing, error control and other services that are required to allow reliable end-to-end communications.

This does not mean that IP is required. In fact, some implementations of TCP connect directly to the network services layer and bypass IP altogether. If, however, a program on node A on an Ethernet wished to connect to a destination program on node B on an X.25 network, an internet routing function would be necessary to get data packets sent properly between the two dissimilar network services.

IP would take the packet from TCP, pass it through a gateway that would provide conversion services and then send the packet to the IP layer at the remote node for delivery to the remote TCP layer and subsequently, the destination program. A good comparison would be as follows:

(a) Program A on node ALPHA wishes to connect to program B on node BET on the same network. Program A would send a data packet to TCP with the proper destination address. TCP would then encapsulate the data with the proper header and checksums in accordance with whatever services the program requested and pass the TCP packet to the IP layer. IP would then determine, from network directory information, that the remote node is on the same network as itself and simply pass the packet through to the network services layer for local network routing and delivery.

(b) Program A on node ALPHA on network X wishes to connect to program B on node BETA on network Y. In this situation, data would be handled as in case (a) above, but IP would determine that the destination is not on the local network. As a result, the IP layer in node ALPHA would determine the best route to get to the remote node and send the TCP packet to the next IP node in the path to get to the remote. IP does not care which program the source wants to connect to; all it cares about is which node to send the packets to.

IP nodes in the path from node ALPHA to node BETA will examine the packet to determine the destination and will forward the packet to the proper IP until it reaches the destination network IP. That IP determines that the node is on its local network and the packet is handed to the network services layer for the network on which BETA resides for delivery to node BETA. Once the packet is received at the final destination IP, it is passed up to the TCP layer, which breaks out the packet header to figure out which program on the destination node is to receive the data.

First, however, the packet header is examined carefully to insure that it has arrived in the proper sequence and that there are no special handling issues that need to be serviced. Once TCP is satisfied that everything is reasonable, the data is delivered to the destination program. While all of this seems pretty straightforward, there are some implementation issues that make this entire complex. Since TCP and IP allow many service options such as message priority, security classification, data segmentation at the TCP level, packet segmentation at the IP level and other issues that some network architectures, such as DECnet, need not concern themselves with, there can be some considerable overhead associated with packet processing.

As a result, TCP/IP performance varies significantly from network hardware to network hardware as well as from machine implementation to machine implementation. Now that we have examined the generalized delivery model, let us look at some of the specifics.

What is TCP supposed to do?

One of the base problems that TCP was built to address is the issue of connection from a particular program on a particular node on a particular network to a remote program destination that may or may not be on the same network as the originator. As such a method of addressing nodes needed to be developed that identified a particular program on a particular node in a particular network. A possible solution is to develop hard addresses for all entities on a particular network.

While this solves the problem, it is inflexible and usually does not provide an upwardly flexible network architecture. Another problem is that some networks have their own proprietary (and sometimes bizarre) addressing scheme that must be considered as TCP/IP are above the local network addressing scheme mechanism in the network architecture and will need to use the local mechanism on packet delivery.

To solve the problem, TCP/IP uses a three-layer addressing mechanism that allows for delivery of packets across dissimilar network architectures. To begin with, each program (called a PROCESS in TCP) has a unique one-up address on each machine. That unique local program address is combined with a particular node address to form something called a port. The port address is further combined with the local network address, forming a new entity called a socket. There can be many, many sockets on a TCP/IP network but each socket identifies, exactly, one specific application on a specific node on a specific network.

Through this mechanism, IP will get the packets to the proper node and TCP will deliver the packet to the proper program on that node. Some nodes provide a standard process type (such as type 23 for remote log-ins) that are "known" to other network entities and that provide certain standard services. Through this mechanism TCP provides a multiplexing capability that is essential in the efficient use of the network resource.

From One Socket to Another

As with any network, two sockets that wish to connect to each other must have a mechanism by which this happens. TCP provides this in various ways. One of the more common ways connections are established is via an ACTIVE/PASSIVE network OPEN. A PASSIVE OPEN is when a receptive socket declares itself to be open and available for incoming connections (this would typically be the mode used by something like a database server). A PASSIVE OPEN, however, may be set up in various ways. First, the PASISVE OPEN may be set up to be FULLY SPECIFIED, which means that the socket issuing the PASSIVE OPEN tells the network exactly which socket may connect to it, including security levels allowed and other related details.

Another type of PASSIVE OEPN is the UNSPECIFIED PASSIVE OPEN in which the socket will accept any connection request from any remote socket provided that the remote system requesting connection meets prescribed security and other criteria. In both types of network OPENS, it is pertinent to point out that the socket OPENing the network may also declare timeout values for all data received from the originator of the connection.

This allows for the expeditious handling of data as well as providing a means by which "old" messages are handled in a reasonable fashion and messages requiring special handling (in terms of time) are processed correctly. Another type of OPEN is the ACTIVE OPEN.

Unlike the PASSIVE OPEN, the ACTIVE OPEN aggressively seeks a connection to a particular socket. An ACTIVE OPEN will only be successful if there is a cooperating and corresponding PASSIVE OPEN or other ACTIVE OPEN from the destination socket. Once a connection has been established between two sockets, data may be transferred between the sockets.

TCP provides several mechanism for data transfer, but the two most popular are segmented data transfer and PUSH mode. Segmented data transfer allows TCP to end user data in chunks across the network. As such, TCP may send the data in such a manner that allows for the best efficiency for the network being used. This means that even if the user has transferred 25 blocks of use data to TCP, TCP may not send it all at once, opting to segment the data in such a manner as to provide optimal flow of data on the network. While this technique is great for data flow issues and network congestion issues, it can be troublesome for transfers in which the data needs to get to the remote system NOW! In such cases, the user may specify the PUSH flag.

A PUSH request forces TCP to end whatever has been passed from the user to TCP right away with no consideration for optimal flow control. In addition to the PUSH flag, the user may specify the urgency of the data being transferred to keep the remote system on its toes. How much data is allowed to be sent from one socket to another is a function of the network and programs involved. Since TCP was developed with multiple network architectures in mind, it allows some level of link negotiation on connection and data transfer that provides for maximum buffer sizes (somewhat dynamically) and maximum buffer allocation.

TCP Sequencing

To insure that everything gets to where it is going and in the proper order, TCP provides packet sequencing services as well as error detection functions utilizing a 16-bit checksum in the TCP header area. It is also interesting to note that TCP presumes the IP layer to be unreliable and therefore, includes a 96-biy pseudoheader in front of the actual TCP packet header that includes the source address, destination address, protocol being used and segment size.

Through the use of the pseudoheader, TCP protects itself from IP delivering the packet to the wrong place (or not at all) by misinterpreting TCP header fields. The checksum in the TCP header also includes the pseudoheader bits to insure that everything is clean when it hits the remote side. After the connection is established and all data has been transferred, the link may be shut down via user request. This is the clean way. It is very possible that the link may also be abruptly aborted due to link from or some catastrophic failure of the network or socket-to-socket linkage.

TCP provides mechanisms to handle both situations. A CLSOE primitive issuance tells TCP that the user is finished with the network link and to close down the link gracefully by sending all remaining data in local buffers and notifying the remote socket that the sending user wishes to CLOSE the link. The remote TCP socket notifies the user that a CLOSE has been issued. The user may then send any remaining data and issue a CLOSE to the sender. When the sender received the CLSOE acknowledgement from the receiver, it sends a TERMINATE to the user and notifies the remote TCP that a TERMINATE has been issued.

The remote TCP socket sends a TERMINATE to the remote user and the links is closed completely. If a network link abort occurs, for whatever reason, the ABORT primitive is sent to the remote TCP, which tells the remote user that a TERMINATE has occurred. No more data of any kind is transmitted on the link and the link is closed immediately on both sides. Obviously, a link termination of the ABORT kind is not desirable, as data may be lost and other integrity issues may be involved.

TCP Needs Not an IP

It is important to understand that TCP need not be connected to an IP, although that is frequently the case. TCP provides the essential network connection and data transfer features which a sure would require to connect with a particular program on a remote system. Some companies use TCP as the protocol of choice when setting up simple direct-connect network connections (where the remote node is hard-wired to the originating node) or when performing tasks such as downline system loading.

In any case TCP is a powerful and full-featured protocol that provides reasonable network services for user data. Many times, however, just getting the data from one socket to another may involve the connection to various types of network technologies.

A TCP packet coming in from an asynchronous link may need to be routed on to an Ethernet to reach its ultimate destination, Because of the need to connect and properly route data through to its proper network and destination socket, the IP layer was developed.

What is an IP?

IP is a datagram service. It basically provides rudimentary internetwork routing, services without any regard to the destination program, TCP formats, error control, packet sequencing etc. Its function in life is to get the packet to the right network and eventually, to the right node. Further, IP allows for expedited routing of packets that need to get to a destination quicker than other, routine packets. In many respects, with the exception of routing priority, IP functionality is similar to Ethernet packet handling. If a packet arrives that is damaged (there is an IP checksum), the packet is discarded.

What is in the data field of the packet is of no interest to IP. IP could be sending a TCP packet or some other protocol for all it cares. As long as the proper SEND (user sending to the network) primitive fields have been filled in, IP will send the packet on its merry way. When the packet reaches the remote node and the checksum figures out OK, IP sends the packet to TCP (or whatever the receptor protocol is) via DELIVER directive and all is well with the universe. If the packet gets trashed in the process of being delivered, so be it. If the packets arrive out of sequence, that is not IP's problem. If a packet is missing, again, IP does not care. IP gets the data packet (usually a TCP packet) form point A on network X to point B on network Y. That is all, nothing more.

Gateways and IP

To provide the internetwork routing function, IP makes use of special nodes called gateways. A gateway, in IP terms, is a machine that allows two dissimilar networks to be connected to each other. The two networks may or may not be the same type (Ethernet, X.25, token ring, etc.), as IP operates above the hardware itself and is only interested in the virtual connection function, not the physical path or hardware used. As such, there may be a need to segment large messages from the upper software layers into sizes that are applicable to the remote network's allowances.

To do this, IP will segment large messages into proper-sized chunks (such as when going from 1500 byte Ethernet packets to 128 byte X.25 packets) for the destination network and reassemble them at the remote destination IP layer before delivery to the user. If a packet gets destroyed in the segmented message and the remote IP detects the packet loss, the entire segment is killed off by the remote IP. Obviously, TCP would detect that a segment is missing and request a retransmission from the remote TCP for any missing packets.

TCP has the option of forcing IP NOT to segment packets, but this is usually not implemented as it can cause routing problems where differing network technologies are concerned. IP also provides for proper security classification of packets being sent to a remote site. If an intermediary gateway or network is not at the same security level as the transmitted packet, the packet will not be sent through that network. As a result, some strange routing of data may occur sometimes as IP must contend with the problem of expeditious routing but also the problem of security-oriented routing. Finally, IP has some different terminology than that typically used in a network. In many networks, the concept of a "hop" is the routing of a data packet through a node on its way to its final destination point.

In IP, a hop is when a data packet goes through a gateway to another network. Therefore, it is quite possible that a packet may wander through various nodes in a local network before it actually gets to the remote network gateway, depending, of course, upon previously discussed variables. If the packet does not incur a route through a gateway, it, in IP terms, has not incurred a hop.

If it transverses through two gateways, it would be considered to have incurred two hops on its path to the final destination. Hops, therefore, are not referred to in the same manner as many other popular communications architectures. As can be seen, TCP and IP are not the same and may actually be implemented totally independent of each other for separate uses. More often than not, however, they are both included in many offerings from various vendors.

TCP/IP Applications

In any network architecture, the protocols and transmission methods are not enough. Users frequently want and need utilities that implement the protocols in the network architecture to allow file transfer, program communication, virtual terminal support and electronic mail. Most TCP/IP implementations are the same and a few standard applications exist.

File Transfer

File Transfer facilities are usually provided for by a mechanism known as the File Transfer Protocol (FTP). FTP is a simple featured file-moving utility that allows a record-oriented (one record at a time) transfer, a block transfer (which moves chunks of a file), or an image transfer (which does not look in any way at the file contents). Further, FTP knows about EBCDIC and ASCII (also NVT-ASCII) and may provide some rudimentary conversion facilities BEFORE a transfer begins.

As file systems are very complex and the need for file transfer between systems is growing, FTP has evolved in some cases to special implementations that know how to convert specific file formats between certain types of machine architectures. This conversion facility is not within the defined scope of FTP, but some vendors include the conversion features anyway. To transfer a file, the user invokes the host. FTP utility, specifies file name, type (if necessary), remote destination and off it goes. One interesting feature on some FTP implementation is the recovery facility.

Networks, as most are well aware, will fail from time to time. In the case of failure, any transfers in process will usually have to be restarted from scratch. If the file is being transferred with FTP in block mode, it may be possible to resume the transfer at a later time by specifying which block was the last transmitted. FTP would then continue to send the file as if nothing had happened.

This feature is not available on all FTP would then continue to send the file as if nothing had happened. This feature is not available on all FTP implementations and has some host and remote system software considerations involved with it, but, all in all, it is a useful feature to have when transferring very large files.

Telnet

Another popular utility is known as TELNET. TELNET is a virtual terminal facility that allows a user to connect to a remote system as if the user's terminal were hard-wired to that remote system. As with file systems, virtual terminals may need to emulate a wide variety of terminals, which may be impractical on larger, complex networks. As such, TELNET provides a basic protocol handling facility and a negotiation facility that allows for the inclusion of different types of terminal protocols and signaling mechanisms.

There are four ways of using Telnet. The terminal could be a simple 'dumb' terminal connected to a TCP/IP terminal server with a standard communications interface (V.24/

V.28 or EIA232). Equally, that simple terminal could be a workstation or PC running a terminal emulator and connected to the same terminal server in the same way.

A minicomputer can run Telnet software which provides the terminal server capability from within the minicomputer. Alternatively, a PC or other workstation could run a version of TCP/IP and a terminal emulator and connect directly to a LAN. The,Telnet service was one of the first to be provided in a standard way by the TCP/IP architecture. It delivers a similar service to that provide by the switching statistical multiplexers of the early to mid-1980s which provided many companies with their first example of flexible access to information. Telnet allows terminal or workstation users to gain access to a host system and to display host data on their screens.

It is a remote terminal service; any terminal user must know how to operate the host system or host application from a terminal of that type. No attempt is made to map the user interface environments from one system to the other. The Telnet service is most commonly used with ASCII asynchronous terminals such as the ANSI standard terminal or the DEC VT series. Most manufacturers of other terminal types have registered them with the Internet assigned Numbers Authority (IANA) so that they can be identified to the Telnet protocol. That does not mean that a particular implementation of workstation Telnet will necessarily match the host software.

Any-to-any protocol conversion is not necessarily a feature; systems which match must be carefully chosen. The advantage of the Telnet terminal server is that it provides a low cost connection. But the interface often operates in asynchronous character-by-character mode; the terminal is strictly limited in its capabilities with little possibility of upgrading the service in the future. Asynchronous interfaces can involve large management overheads. Cabling for the terminals may require only three wires, but for some terminal types and uses, it could be more. A structured cabling system with centrally located terminal servers can reduce management costs.

At each interface, a number of parameters must be configured—speed, parity, flow control method and type of terminal, to ensure the correct control sequences are used. Unless a single standard for these parameters can be enforced throughout the organization, any apparent cost savings can be quickly allowed up in increased management costs. This is particularly so in the larger installation, where the unit costs of supporting large numbers of terminal servers may not reduce with increasing size. Where terminal servers can be remotely configured from a central network management system, support costs may be more easily contained.

Trivial File Transfer Protocol

The **Trivial File Transfer Protocol** (TFTP) is a simple program with minimal facilities, designed to be implemented in permanent memory (PROM), so that diskless computers may perform their initial loading of an operating system. It is often used in conjunction with the boot protocol. It is not usual for it to be used for other purposes. TFTP lacks the security features of FTP and it is normal to disable the TFTP server on hosts which do not provide a BOOTP service.

Simple Mail Transfer Protocol (SMTP)

A final utility that is somewhat popular is the Simple Mail Transfer Protocol or SMTP as it is more affectionately known. SMTP provides a mechanism by which a user can specify a destination address (or addresses if to more than one remote user), a particular path to follow (if desired) and a message. Like other electronic mail systems, SMTP provides for return receipts, forwarding of mail, and other similar features. The only odd issue has to do with the problem of the term "simple". Having used SMTP for some years now, it is not intuitive and the routing issues can get strange. Yet, it is a useful utility and heavily used in the defense area.

Some of the organizational issues of SMTP arise because of the association of a person with a particular computer. Those computers are the .MDBO/ mail servers. MDNM/of SMTP and they must always be available to receive mail. An individual workstation or PC is unlikely to make a satisfactory mail server as its availability cannot be guaranteed.

A mail server is more likely to be a part-time task carried out by another server machine. Building on SMTP protocol, some manufacturers have introduced the mail relay or mail store, which receives and stores mail on behalf of workstation users until they access the store using an SMTP client on their workstation.

A workstation can be a satisfactory generator of SMP mail, but it is a poor and inattentive recipient. Staff who travel must be able to access the mail system they are registered on, for that is where their mailbox resides. Alternatively, a method of mail forwarding can be devised, but such features are beyond the SMTP itself and are implementation dependent. If mail users change location permanently, their mail addresses may change. They will have to advise all their correspondents for that change.

TCP/IP standards do not include a directory service to relate people to mail addresses or for that matter to relate application servers to network addresses. Worldwide research into directory services has concentrated on perfecting and implementing the CCITT X.500 recommendations which are accepted as part of OSI. Indeed, the US Internet is said to be the biggest trial of X.500 directory services in the world. Several RFCs describe how X.500 is to be used on the Internet and the adaption needed to operate over TCP/IP protocols.

Network File System

The Network File System (NFS), as it is still commonly known, or Open Network Computing (ONC), as its creator Sun Microsystems Inc, now calls it, is one of the more recent standard additions to the TCP/IP protocol suite. ONC was developed by Sun Microsystems Inc. for its high performance UNIX workstations and later released to the 'public domain' as three RFCs which describe the major protocol components. Recognizing the importance of the

IBM PC, SUN also developed NFS software for the IBM PC, the PC-NFS client. This allows PCs to use UNIX workstations as remote file and print servers.

NFS client and server software is now available for most computer systems. NFS provides user services familiar to any user of a proprietary resource-sharing LAN such as NetWare, LAN Manager or Banyan VINES. Files directories and peripherals on a remote NFS server are mapped to 'virtual' drives directories peripherals on the local system. For most purposes these virtual drives and printers area indistinguishable from and are used identically to local resources. On a UNIX system each remote directory appears as an additional directory of the main local directory structure. For a PC, with PC-NFS, the remote directories appear as additional disk drives. From the perspective of the commercial information system manager, this is ideal, for unlike other TCP/IP applications described below, most business users need no new training to use NFS; they merely have a access to more information with bigger disks and better printers. But NFS can go beyond simple resource sharing. It provides the mechanism for true distributed computing, where processing power, not just data, is shared among networked machines.

These client/server applications can reduce the load on busy networks significantly. The major management issues of NES can be hidden from the users. These issues centre on the security and mapping of user identifiers and access rights between different operating system. NFS works in conjunction with the Network Information Services (NIS), a distributed database system for NFS security which provides for centralized management of a highly distributed system.

Technically, the tools have been provided by Sun; the administration of a large user population still requires careful organization, with the correct clerical procedures in place to ensure that security meets the requirements of the organization. It must not be so lax as to compromise data integrity and not so tight that no one can get work done. NFS uses the UDP transport protocol. Remote disk data transfer rates can be reduced significantly by delay, particularly in wide area links.

There is at least one implementation providing the same services as NFS, which uses TCP transport. An alternative solution is to buy more servers and place them close to the users. Where the main NFS activity is resource sharing, poor configuration options in the workstations can have a dramatic effect on network traffic. The use of print spoolers, temporary files backup files, PC batch files and the format of the 'path' statement can all influence the traffic, a workstation generates on the network. To make NFS completely invisible to end users, each workstation should have a script or batch file which executes the NFS 'mount' commands to make the remote resources locally available.

The details of the command line can be totally hidden. In the past, memory requirements for PC network software have left too little of the available 640k to run some of the more demanding PC applications. Some implementations of PC-NFS require in excess of 130 kbytes to load a LAN card driver, the TCP/IP core software and the NFS client application.

By reducing the number of file systems which may be mounted and by tuning other parameters, this figure can be reduced by a few kilobytes.

As 80386 processors with large amounts of memory and the MS DOS 5.0 operating system replace older configurations and software, the PC memory will become less of a restriction. Where replacement cannot be considered, careful memory sizing will be required for NFS systems.

TCP/IP Implementations

Some vendors of TCP/IP have made a cozy living out of providing their wares to defense contractors and UNIX/Ultrix shops that need to connect and communicate with their compatriots supporting TCP/IP. How the vendors have implemented TCP and IP varies greatly, which also means that features and performance vary significantly. Some vendors, such as Excelan, have chosen to implement much of the protocol suite in a controller card, effectively offloading the host from the duties of running TCP and IP programs and utilities and yet providing the necessary connectivity.

This is nice as it offloads the host and makes the overall system more cost effective and less bogged down in the network mire. Other companies, such as Wollongong, have chosen to implement TCP/IP in software on the host. This degrades the host system, sometimes severely, but has the advantage of being able to function as a true IP node, allowing connection to various network technologies simultaneously. Each implementation has its benefits and drawbacks. Which one is best for a particular system depends heavily upon cost factors, system loading expectations and how many different kinds of networks a site may be connected to.

Some vendors have begun to introduce TCP/IP routers that allow IP services to different types of networks by connecting the networks through a dedicated IP router (sometimes referred to as an IMP) and allowing TCP messages to be created by a particular network protocol, translated into TCP and sent to a destination node on either the same or another network. Such routing and translation trickery is beginning to become more and more prevalent in environments where TCP and other types of networking software exist. In the quest to TCP/IP, the bottom line is how long can it last? A few years ago it would have been said that it was a safe bet that usage of TCP/IP would last a company for some years to come. Now that the DOD no longer requires the absolute use of TCP/IP, opting, instead, to go with OSI, such is not a safe bet for all sites.

There are enough TCP sites installed that it would be foolish and expensive to haul off and convert all sites to something else. It is also prudent to remember that the number of networked machines that will appear in near future will far eclipse anything currently installed in such a way as to make protocols such as TCP/IP become a minority. Much has to do with who is buying what as to how long it will last. However, TCP/IP will be around for a while, if to do nothing else than support current systems.

As those systems cut over to OSI, however, fewer and fewer nodes will be seen running TCP or IP in favour of OSI. What would we do if we had to buy today? Buy TCP/IP, of course. Why? Because it works and it is now. It would server very nicely for the short term (2-4 years) and give the OSI packages sometime to mature before diving in headlong. A nice side benefit is that the OSI transport service and TCP's capabilities are very similar, as are the OSI network layer routing service and the IP services. Further, TCP/IP prescribes standardized network hardware, so OSI-compliant hardware is given in many TCP/IP environments, allowing a nice migration path to OSI at a future date. If one installs OSI-compliant hardware, then conversion to OSI from TCP/IP is not as traumatic as it could be.

TCP/IP Communication Architecture

An interconnected set of lines and terminals allowing processing to take in one or several locations is usually viewed as a network. A network may have several hosts interacting with multiples of terminals. To bring structure to this view of a network, the concept of network Architecture is proposed; this is a structured hardware and software design that supports the interconnection of a number of physical and logical components. A network architecture is a way to define the set of rules to which these interconnecting elements must conform. It is not however, a definition of how the internal design is made or how the functions in the network operate or how a rule is actually implemented.

A network architecture is a statement of what services need to be provided to enable the network to follow one set of rules. In the past several years the International Organization for Standardization (ISO) has developed a model of network architecture. The goal of this model is to promote the interconnecting of networks of all types. The underlying principle exploited by the OSI model is layering. The idea is to create network architecture with several layers where each layer provides certain unique functions which are not provided by any of the other layer is strictly defined.

Based on some standard structuring techniques, the OSI model defines seven distinct layers. Each layer need only interact with the adjacent layers and has no knowledge about any other layers. Information flows down through the layers of the sending host and then up through the layers of the receiving host. Because the layers are isolated from each other by strict interfaces, information that is added by a layer in the sending host will only be used by the matching layer in the receiving host. In this sense the matching layers of the sending and receiving hosts communicate with each other in a peer-to-peer relationship. Each layer adds value to the services provided by the set of lower layers in such a manner that the highest layer is offered the set of services needed to run an application distributed over several networks.

Each layer provides services to the layer above and requests services from the layer below. Thus, the total network problem is divided into a set of smaller problems. Intermediate networks that merely relay information from one network to another will only need to implement some of the lower three layers to act as transferal agents. In the standard which describes the reference model, OSI standard developers state that they will exclude any details which would be implementation dependent. The result is that while the standards have been kept 'pure', many details which would aid they would aid development of viable OSI products are excluded from the standards themselves. While some would argue that OSI is more rigorous in its standardization that TCP/IP, the OSI development process seems to have become enmeshed in procedures weighed down by the difficulties of obtaining consensus in large committees and dogged by supplier politics.

By confining OSI standards to abstract definitions in a complex vocabulary, defined just for the purpose and then charging considerable sums for copies of those standards, ISO committees have, undoubtedly, if unintentionally, slowed the OSI development process and the delivery of useful conforming products. With a more restricted geographic and technical scope, TCP/IP developers adopted a pragmatic approach. TCP/IP standardization was based on the Request For Comments (RFC), a flexible and fast standardization process using electronic mail to publish and exchange comments and ideas and to update drafts.

Developers often outlined parts of a standard in a familiar computer language, usually 'C' which, while not intended to be implemented directly, gave a very good starting point for an initial implementation. TCP/IP standards are freely available on-line from a number of computer systems, originally without full drawings or graphics, but today with all the quality of a laser-printed, desktop-published document as Postscript files. For manufacturers of communications and computing products, the contrast with OSI could not be more stark; it is just so much easier to obtain TCP/IP information than OSI.

Standards were produced more quickly and they are written in a readable and comprehensible form by developers for developers. The US government demanded TCP/IP for all systems, thereby ensuring every US government computer supplier provided it. They also funded universities to implement the standards. In the USA, such publicly funded work enters the public domain and if not of a military nature, is freely available to all citizens.

While it may not be used directly for commercial purposes, having a working example in 'C' source code certainly assists future developments by commercial suppliers! Neither OSI nor TCP/IP has been developed in isolation. There has been a considerable interchange of ideas and techniques, particularly evident in the changes in OSI since the mid-1980s with the development of the connectionless OSI suite. Nor have the OSI standards been ignored by suppliers. As with TCP/IP in the USA, universities have been busy developing OSI implementations and governments have, since the mid-1980s, required OSI-conforming products.

But this activity has not as yet created a general market demand and the same level of fully developed OSI computing products, except perhaps with the notable exception of X.25 network equipment. The 'pump priming' of TCP/IP has been more successful and has ensured, thereby, that it has moved ahead much faster than OSI. Governments and commercial organizations worldwide have waited patiently for OSI to become available and to reap the benefits of the promised flexibility of an international standard for computer communications and inter operation.

In short, the development of OSI has lagged considerably behind TCP/IP despite support from a number of governments (including since 1985, the US government and Department of Defense). When it comes to breaking down communications barriers between different computer suppliers, information systems managers in commercial companies now see TCP/IP as a fully functional, proven and low-cost alternative to open systems interconnection. OSI is still immature and almost unavailable.

This may change in near future but the explosive interest in TCP/IP will, on the one hand, delay OSI implementation and on the other, encourage it as larger organizations come up against some of the known fundamental limitations of TCP/IP. As with much of the specialist vocabulary which surrounds computers and telecommunications networks, the term TCP/IP will conjure up different concepts to different readers. TCP/IP is used as shorthand for a large set of standards with many different features and functions. The letters 'TCP/IP' stand for two communications protocols, Transmission Control Protocol (TCP) and Internet Protocol (IP).

These were developed during the late 1970s and early 1980s as the key communications protocols for the US 'Internet', the collected set of interconnected communications networks (originally comprising ARPAnet, but now including UFSnet, and NYSERnet and the Department of Defense Network among many others). Today these support the US government. Department of Defense, US military and the university, education and commercial organizations conduct research on behalf of those bodies. (Use of the US Internet for commercial traffic between commercial organizations is not allowed.) TCP and IP, are but two of the building blocks required for a complete communications 'architecture', but the term 'TCP/IP' is most often used as a **shorthand** term of the whole communications 'architecture' specified originally by the US Department of Defense.

This architecture is a much bigger set of standards than just TCP and IP. We shall also use 'TCP/IP' to mean the complete architecture, except where this will cause confusion. **Communication architectures** have been developed by computer manufacturers since the mid 1970s. An architecture describes three facets of communications in an abstract way which is independent of particular hardware or technology. The three aspects are:

(1) Data exchange (intercommunications)

(2) Data interpretation (interoperation)

(3) System management

Like the OSI reference model, communications architectures are described in layers; each layer providing its own functions but using the functions of the layer below. This layering decouples the functions of one layer from another making layered architectures flexible; their designers can respond to changes in technology and in application software without a major upheaval for existing users. The implementation and existing installations can be extended, as new, often faster techniques and technologies become available. It is important to realize that the standards do not specify the interfaces seen by computer users.

Though suppliers often base their implementations on a competitor's successful product, one must expect that user interfaces will differ, in major or minor ways, from supplier to supplier. For TCP/IP, the architectural standards and the operational US Internet are controlled by the Internet Activities Board (IAB). The IAB devolves its responsibilities for development, operations and management to a number of subcommittees and working groups which it controls and to other commercial companies specializing in communications and computing research and consultancy.

TCP/IP The Complete Suite

The TCP and IP, explain only the communication aspects, the movement of data across a set of interconnected physical networks. The complete architecture must include standard mechanisms for interpreting and converting data for the common tasks that users of computers have come to expect. As these tasks sit on top of and depend on the communications protocols, they are sometimes called the **Upper Layer Protocols (ULPs).**

- Generally, computer users have needed three major functions:
- File Transfer
- Terminal access (virtual terminal protocols)
- Mail preparation and transfer

In commercial environments other tasks have become equally important.

- Resource sharing (for example: files, printers, plotters)
- Diskless workstations
- Transaction processing
- Management
- Directory services
- Security

Those familiar with the resource-sharing Local Area Network (LAN) (such as Microsoft LAN Manager and Novell NetWare) must have seen the power of remote or distributed file and disk sharing and of peripheral sharing; and of peripheral sharing; for some companies, diskless workstations have a number of advantages. In a complete, modern architecture, standard protocols are needed for all these new distributed systems as well as for the proven minicomputer and mainframe-based architectures. The TCP/IP protocol suite addresses these issues comprehensively.

The standards are not static but are being added to at a steady rate. Current activities relate to new facilities in directory services at the application layer and improvements in routing and addressing mechanism at the lower layers.

Upper Layer Protocols

Beginning with the well-known application layer protocols, File Transfer Protocol (FTP), Telnet (TCP/IPs virtual terminal protocol), and Simple Mail Transfer Protocol (SMTP), NFS adds a disk/file system resource-sharing capability, LPR deals with printing, the BOOT Protocol (BOOTP) provides the basis for diskless workstation operation and Simple Network Management Protocol (SNMP) is the Internet Standard for management.

Lower Layer Protocols

IP is not the lowest level of the layered architecture. TCP/IP does not explain new standards for low-level communications but TCP/IP standards include descriptions of how IP operates over the commonly available long-distance and local physical communications networks. These descriptions include many proprietary networks as well as CCITT and other international standard transmission mechanisms. For long-distance operation over public telecommunications circuits, the standards include point-to-point leased and dial up, synchronous and asynchronous links and X.25 connections.

For local communications. Ethernet Version 2 (as specified by DEC, Intel and Xerox) is by far the most widely used. ISO/IEEE networks (ISO 8802.3, 8802.4, 8802.5) and FDDI (ISO 9314) are also specified as are proprietary networks such as ARCNET.

TCP/IP Protocol Set Structure

The TCP/IP suite is not a single protocol. Rather, it is four-layer communication architecture that provides some reasonable network features, such as end-to-end communications, unreliable communications line fault handling, packet sequencing, internetwork routing and specialized functions unique to DOD communications needs such as standardized message priorities. The bottom layer, network services, provides for communication to network hardware. Network hardware used in the various networks throughout the DOD typically reflects the usage of FIPS (Federal Information Processing Standard) compliant network hardware (such as IEEE 802 series of LANs and other technologies such as X.25). The layer above the network services layer is referred to as the Internet protocol (IP) layer.

The IP layer is responsible for providing a datagram service that routes data packets between dissimilar network architectures (such as between Ethernet and say, X.25). IP has a few interesting qualities, one of which is the issue of data reliability. As a datagram service, IP does not guarantee delivery of data. Basically, if the data gets there, great. If not, that's OK too. Data concurrency, sequencing, and delivery guarantee is the job of the TCP protocol. TCP provides for error control, retransmission, packet sequencing and many other capabilities.

It is very complex and provides most of the features of the connection to other applications on other systems. To understand properly what TCP/IP is all about, it is important to understand that: (a) it is not OSI in implementation (although some argue that there are substantial similarities) and (b) it is a unique network architecture that provides what are considered traditional network services in a manner that can be overhead intensive in some implementations. The structure of the TCP/IP protocol set is shown in Figure 13.1.8, alongwith the approximately equivalent ISO model layers. It can be seen that this is essentially a four layer model, although the layers are not as clear cut as in the ISO model and the model has been drawn from analysis of what is used, rather than being defined first and then the protocols specified.

The TCP/IP philosophy is the antithesis of the ISO philosophy. In ISO protocols, everything appears to be put into the protocol, but parts are made optional. In TCP/IP, the protocols are kept very simple. If more functionality is required, then another protocol is added to deal with the situation.

The main protocols are as follows:

IP The Internet Protocol, which provides a connectionless datagram 'network' layer.

ICMP The Internet Control Message Protocol is an example of the bolt-on approach mentioned above. It adds functionality to the IP protocol and can be considered as an extension to that protocol.

UDP The User Datagram Protocol provides the rough equivalent of the ISO connectionless transport service.

TCP The Transmission Control Protocol is a connection oriented, reliable, end-to-end transport protocol.

The protocols which run above TCP include TELNET, a terminal access protocol and a file transfer protocol FTP. The four main protocols are now examined further as a contrast to the ISO approach.

Internet Protocol

There is a second difference in philosophy between ISO and the TCP/IP approach, which revolves around the word 'network'. In the TCP/IP model, a network is an individual packet switched network which may be a LAN or a WAN, but is generally under the control of one organization.

These networks connect to each other by gateways, and the resulting collection of such networks is called a catenet (from concatenation). The internet protocol provides for the transmission of datagrams between systems over the whole catenet. It specifically allows for the fragmentation and reassembly of the datagrams at the gateways, as the underlying networks may demand different packet sizes.

The Internet Protocol (US Military Standard 1771) is a very simple protocol, with no mechanism for end-to-end data reliability, flow control or sequencing. The header is quite complex, the fields being as follows:

Version

The version number of IP. There have been several new releases, which (given the size of ARPANET) must co-exist for some time.

IHL

The IP header length. Because of the options field, the header is not a fixed length. This field shows where the data starts.

Type of

This field allows for a priority system to be imposed, plus service indication of the desired, but not guaranteed, reliability required.

Length

The total length of the IP packet. Although there is a theoretical maximum of 64 Kbytes, most networks operate with much smaller packets, though all must accept at least 576 bytes.

ID/flags/offset

These fields enable a gateway to split up the datagram into smaller segments. The ID field ensures that the receiver can place together the fragments from the correct datagrams, as fragments from many datagrams may arrive in any order. The offset tells how far down the datagram this fragment is and the flags can be used to mark the datagram as non-fragmentable.

Time to live

This is a count which limits the lifetime of a datagram on the catenet. Each time it passes through a gateway, the count is decremented by one. If it reaches zero, the gateway does not forward it. This prevents permanently circulating datagrams.

Protocol

This indicates which higher level protocol is being carried, e.g. TCP or UDP

Checksum

This checksum covers the header only. It is up to the higher layers to detect transmission errors in the data.

Source/dest address

To assist the gateways to route datagrams by the most efficient path, each IP address is structured into a Network Number and a local address. There are three classes of network providing different numbers of locally administered addresses.

Options

The final part of the header is a variable number of optional fields, which are used to enforce security or network management.

Padding

This field is used to align the header to the next 32-bit boundary.

Because there is not facility for error reporting in IP, for example, the sender of a datagram is not informed if the intended recipient is available, an extra protocol is used particularly to help gateways between networks. This is called the Internet Control Message Protocol (ICMP) which, although it is carried over IP, is considered to be an integral part of it. It does not help in making IP reliable, however, it merely reports errors without trying to recover from them. Examples of ICMP messages include TIME EXCEEDED when the lifetime of a datagram expires and DESTINATION UNREACHABLE when a gateway or network has failed.

The gateways also exchange routing information using another extra protocol, called the gateway-to-gateway protocol. This enables the gateways to have up-to-date information on the loading on certain routes, so that bottlenecks can be avoided.

User Datagram Protocol

The User Datagram Protocol (UDP) provides a connectionless transport service to applications. Unlike the ISO protocols, which are layer independent, it assumes that IP is running below and implementations must have access to incoming IP headers. The UDP header, is very simple and can be considered as an extension of the IP header to permit multiple services to be addressed within the same IP network address.

Transimission Control Protocol

TCP (US Military Standard 1781) provides a highly reliable, connection oriented, end-to-end transport service between processes in end systems connected to the catenet. TCP only assumes that the layer below offers an unreliable datagram service and thus could run over any such protocols. In practice, however, it is invariably linked to IP. TCP provides the types of facility associated with the ISO Class 4 transport service, including error recovery, sequencing of packets, flow control by the windowing method and the support of multiplexed connections from the layer above. The operational procedures are similar to the ISO connection oriented protocols, such as LLC Type 2. The fields in the header are as follows:

Source/dest ports

These fields identify multiple streams to the layer above

Sequence/ack number

These are used for the windowing acknowledgement technique.

Data Offset

This is the number of 32-bit words in the TCP header which like the IP header has a variable length options field.

Flag bits

There are several bits used as status indicators to show, for example, the resetting of the connection.

Window

This field is used by the receiver to set the window size.

Checksum

Again this covers only the header.

Urgent pointer

The sender can indicate that an urgent datagram is coming and urges the receiver to handle it as quickly as possible.

Options

This variable-sized field contains some negotiation parameters to set the size of the TCP packets, for example.

Padding

To align to the next 32-bit boundary.

The procedures used by the TCP protocol are too complex to describe here. It can be seen however, that the catenet style of networking has benefit for linking LANs— hence the widespread use of TCP/IP on LANs. It should not be assumed, however, that TCP/IP networks are immune from the compatibility problems discussed earlier for ISO networks. Differences in interpretation of the protocols can drastically reduce interoperability and there are reports of deficiencies in many of the protocols. One interesting recent development, however, is an experimental implementation of the ISO transport service on top of TCP, which means that ISO applications could be carried over IP catenets. TCP/IP can also co-exist with ISO and other protocols on a LAN and it can be expected that the production of protocol converters should ease the transition between TCP/IP and ISO for many users.

Internet Architecture

Two networks can only be connected by a computer that attaches to both of them. A physical attachment does not provide the interconnection we have in mind, because such a connection does not guarantee that the computer will cooperate with other machines that wish to communicate. To have a viable internet, we need computers that are willing to shuffle packets from one network to another.

Computers which interconnect two networks and pass packets from one to the other are called internet gateways or internet routers. The idea of a gateway seems simple, but it is important because it provides a way to interconnect networks, not just machines. Note that in a TCP/IP Internet, computers called gateways provide all interconnections among physical networks. You might suspect that gateways, which must know how to route packets to their destination are large machines with enough primary or secondary memory to hold information about every machine in the internet to which they attach.

However, gateways used with TCP/IP internets are usually minicomputers; they often have little or no disk storage and limited main memories. The concept of building a small internet gateway is gateways route packets based on destination network, not on distinction host. If routing is based on networks, the amount of information that a gateway needs to keep is proportional to the number of networks in the internet, not the number of machines. Note that TCP/IP is designed to provide a universal interconnection among machines independent of the particular networks to which they attach.

Thus, we want the user to view an internet as a single, virtual network to which all machines connect despite their physical connections. In addition to gateways that interconnect physical networks, internet access software is needed on each host to allow application programs to use the internet as if it were a single, real physical network. The advantage of providing interconnection at the network level now becomes clear. Because application programs that communicate over the internet do not know the details of underlying connections, they can be run without change on any machine. Because the details of each machine's physical network connections are hidden in the internet software, only that software needs to change when new physical connections appear or old ones disappear. It is possible to optimize routing by altering physical connections without event recompiling application programs. A second advantage of having communication at the network level is more subtle: users do not have to understand or remember how network connect or what traffic they carry.

Application programs can be written that operate independent of underlying physical connectivity. In fact, network managers are free to change interior parts of the underlying internet architecture without changing application software in most of the computers attached to the internet.

It may be necessary for traffic traveling from one machine to another to pass across several intermediate networks. Thus, networks participating in the internet are analogous to highways in the US interstate system: each net agrees to handle transit traffic in exchange for the right to send traffic throughout the internet.

Typical users are unaffected and unaware of extra traffic on their local network. It is important to understand a fundamental concept: from the internet point of view, any communication system capable of transferring packets counts as a single network, independent of its delay and throughput characteristics, maximum packet size, or geographic scale. Note that the TCP/IP internet protocols treat all network equally. A local area network like an Ethernet, a wide area network like the NSFNET backbone, or a point-to-point link between two machines each count as one network.

TCP/IP Network Planning

The aim of TCP/IP network planning and design is to provide a communications infrastructure that meets the requirements of the organization with readily available equipment and skills. It must provide the correct level of performance for different functions within the organization, at different places and at acceptable costs. In setting up a local and wide are structure for TCP/IP, the first task of the designer is to consider what each of these terms means for that situation. Each case is unique but the overall size of the organization and its network requirement will determine the complexity of the problems to be solved.

Growth Rate

Whatever aspect of human communications you consider, it could be said that a measurement of success is often that the size and usage grows rapidly. As a result of experience in road network planning, this has become known as the 'motorway (or highway) effect'. If a system is useful, people change their travel habits and use the system in new ways that the planners never envisaged.

Traffic grows to fill the space available. In an organization a successful network has been seen to grow at a rate which was totally unexpected and to expand rapidly to cover the company. It is advisable to consider the initial size of the network while planning a TCP/IP installation and have some indication of maximum size and growth rate.

This measure of size has two dimensions:

(i) The total number of attached ports, that is, computer and router connections to the network

(ii) The geographic coverage.

It is important to consider what ways the network could grow—by addition of devices on the same network or by connection to other TCP/IP installations. In the first case, all the issues are under the control of one organization; in the second, they may not be. The problems to be solved will be different in each case.

Today's computer applications and systems are distributed on workstations and PCs throughout the sites and buildings where the computer users sit. Some types of change cannot be centrally managed and must be carried out at each machine. These changes are always difficult and labour-intensive and hence costly. As far as possible, they must be predicted and eliminated.

These considerations can affect the detailed planning process the LAN and WAN links, the planning of the address space and of the bridges and routers which interconnect LANs and sites. Planners will wish to determine solutions to the following questions. How many cable systems will there be?

How should the address plan for the network evolve? Is there a requirement for the Domain Name Service? Is responsibility split with one person or body? If it is split, is the division by function, by location, or by technology? Is there a need to split application management from communications management? Is there a need to split communications management into more than one subfunction?

Existing Standards

To avoid duplication of effort and perhaps more importantly to avoid choosing incompatible solutions to the same TCP/IP options and problems, it is quite important to determine if there are any other existing TCP/IP implementations in the organization. Some systems may hide their use of TCP/IP; the banyan VINES resource-sharing LAN or any communications management system which uses the simple network management protocol are current examples.

If other examples do exist and will share the same cables or TCP/IP equipment at any time, the developments must be coordinated. In some situations there may already be a central authority for TCP/IP implementation which has set local standards for the use of TCP/IP.

These standards should relate to:

- Addressing conventions
- Host-naming conventions
- Local area network
- Choice of equipment
- Choice of network software
- Configuration and management of the network
- Configuration and management of the applications

It is easier if these standards can be used rather than starting from scratch.

Traffic Flows and Capacity

While planning the network layout and capacity it is important to know the volume of information which will be carried. At the simplest level, high-performance routes in the network must follow the high traffic flows in the organization. Faults on those major arterial routes will affect more users, so they, if any, may need to be protected against failure. Judging future traffic flows is always one of the most difficult estimates in installing new TCP/IP systems.

One of the great successes of modern software development techniques is to provide an effective barrier between the application developer and the underlying network. But it leaves the network planners with a major problem. Some people can relate the use of an application to the traffic it will generate. Given the continued growth in workstation performance, existing LAN implementations already seem slow. For many commercial environments, a single physical LAN can support only 20 to 50 workstations and one or two file servers before the network must be partitioned with bridges or routers.

The need for 100 Mbps Fiber Distributed Data Interface (FDDI) or even higher network speeds (1 Gbps—10 Gbps) is evident, particularly for backbone networks and image systems, but the costs of such a system are not yet within the budgets of most network operators. In the absence of such speeds, planners must ration the limited resource of normal speed LANs.

They must understand how particular applications use the network and what the traffic flow between different user groups and applications processor are at different times of the day and business year.

Key questions are as follows:

- What will be the total volume of data on different parts of the network at the busiest time of the day? Is this traffic seasonal?
- How will the traffic grow with time, taking into account the changing and improving user perception of the network services and the increase in number of attached devices and a move towards more demanding applications?
- How is the traffic distributed among adjacent machines and to more remote machines?

The only way of obtaining such information is to measure the operation of real applications and extrapolate the results. Armed with the traffic information and its growth, it is time to consider the network structure.

Partitioning the Network

Bridges and **routers** partition the network and improve performance for workstations on the same cable. The majority of network traffic should be local to the group of users and a small percentage (15-30%) should cross the bridges into a backbone network which interconnects different user groups. If this traffic split cannot be achieved, then the bridge is not used in the optimum way. Splitting a network into small pools of users interconnected by routers and bridges is always a poor substitute for that single, reliable, large, high-speed network, for at any time a high proportion of the traffic is less than optimum.

By adding bridges and routers to a network the cost per user, the administrative and the technical difficulties all increase and the reliability and performance between some remote portions of the network can fall to unacceptable levels. So why do it? In local area networks it is justified by the **containment of traffic** to physical networks which that traffic must traverse; this reduces the load on the local LAN segment and there is a dramatic improvement in performance for local traffic to local file servers.

For long-distance wide-area interconnection, there must be a convertor between different link layer technologies. The prime purpose of a bridge in a LAN is to prevent traffic flowing where it does not need to, rather than to allow traffic to flow where it will. In many networks, it is only secondary function of the bridge to provide communications where none existed by translating to a different type of cable and extending the cable length limits of the basic LAN specification.

In network partitioning, routers have few advantages and few disadvantages over bridges. They have a more positive role to play. Routers relay only what they are specifically told to relay. They are part of the IP protocol and are designed to interconnect network technologies of different performance.

Routers are particularly useful at matching the high speeds of LANs to the much lower speeds of intersite communications circuits that are now available. On the other hand they have a higher cost and lower performance and need more careful management than bridges.

Using Bridges

Bridges filter traffic by Media Access Control (MAC) address. They must examine each frame received on each port and build a table of frame source addresses with the port on which the frame was received. When the bridge learns that a source and destination are on the same port, it will not pass traffic for that destination to any other cable.

- The important performance factors of bridges are described as follows:
- Filtering rate – the ability to examine frames for possible relaying.
- Forwarding rate – the ability to relay frames which have to be relayed
- 'Routing' algorithm that allows bridges to be connected redundantly in parallel and in loops but prevents frames circulating round the loops.
- Transit delay—normally related to forwarding rate.
- Filter table size
- Variations in performance with filter table occupancy.

Bridges Filtering Rate

Bridges can filter at the theoretical maximum rate for Ethernet of 14880 frames per second. Even in busy operational networks the offered traffic will not be this demanding, for this figure is based on all minimum-sized frames. The true demand depends on the type of TCP/IP services in use. Networks used mainly for character-by-character TCP/IP Telnet terminal server traffic have a much higher number of small frames than those used for file transfer and NFS.

The importance of a bridge operating at this theoretical maximum figure is not that it can examine the number of frames per second but that there is no limitation to the number of successive short frames that can be captured by the bridge, since it can capture at the maximum possible rate. The frame rates on Token Ring systems are theoretically much higher than on Ethernet (20,000 fps on 4 Mbps and 80,000 fps on 16 Mbps Token Ring) but the overheads of TCP/IP mean that the absolute maximum practical frame rates are approximately 7700 and 31,000, respectively.

Bridges for TCP/IP traffic could be chosen accordingly. For multi-port hub bridges, one must ensure that each bridge port can examine all frames on every port simultaneously and that the specification does not just give some aggregate figure.

Limited Horizon

A TCP/IP application working through a bridge has a limited horizon. A bridge isolates two cable segments so that systems have no knowledge of the traffic on the other cable, that is, on the other side of the bridge. A bridge is more likely to be unable to relay all traffic, not because it does not have the power, but because the output cable is continuously busy. Frames will queue in the bridge but bridges eventually throw away any frames that are older than about one second.

Most low-level protocols – those which carry data over bridges – do not have any error correction or flow control. End stations may retransmit these lost frames from higher level software but, in an extreme case, this may just add to the network congestion that caused the problem in the first place. It is up to the network manager to design the network so that traffic is distributed correctly and does not concentrate on one work area or in one bridge.

Using a high-speed FDDI or Token Ring backbone or a hub bridge may complicate the design of the network. Traffic flows can become more critical, for they may arrive on the high-speed backbone successfully but focus on one work area where a number of key resources are located. High-performance resources, such as ONC (NFS) servers, should either be directly attached to the backbone or must be distributed on a number of feeder work area LANs.

Broadcasts, Broadcast Stroms and Multicast Frames

TCP/IP protocols use two techniques which impact on the performance of a bridged network. They use **broadcast** and **multicast frames** for discovering the locations of resources and for communicating between systems which cooperate to provide a common service. Multicast frames take capacity on the cable but are not processed by every station.

They become a problem only on slower wide area bridge links. 'Slow' is a relative term; for today's LANs, 'slow' could be 256 kbps, 128 kbps or less. Broadcast frames are much more detrimental to performance. They are generated by ARP, RARP, BOOTP and RIP. Every system on an Ethernet or Token Ring network must process every broadcast frame. If the number of broadcast frames increases, the performance of every system will degrade noticeably. A frame takes some time to process, independent of its size.

Each broadcast frame can reduce the performance of a PC by almost one normal data frame of 1000 to 1450 bytes. PCs slow down noticeably with 10 to 15 broadcast packets per second. Bridges relay broadcast frames everywhere.

To try to filter broadcasts is to destroy the possibility of any-to-any communication. So networks which are interlinked only with bridges reach a size where the percentage of broadcast traffic from all the devices is unacceptable. Unless the broadcast traffic can be reduce, it becomes impossible to manage the network or to grow it further successfully. It has been known for in-house application programmers who do not appreciate the potential harmful effects to write applications using broadcasts.

On more than one occasion a complete LAN including powerful minicomputers, has been brought to a standstill by a **broadcast storm** of about 100 packets per second. Broadcast storms are sometimes attributed to Ethernet design limitations; it is often not realized that the broadcast storm is usually caused by a combination of bad software design and a poor bridged network structure of any type of LAN.

Bridging to a Backbone

As an aid to structuring the distribution of data between work areas it is common practice to use a **backbone** LAN to carry the transit traffic. This backbone may be built with the same technology as the work area, though often on a more robust cable (Thick Ethernet, 10Base5, rather than Thin Ethernet, 10Base2, or Unshielded Twisted Pair, 10BaseT), or it may use a different technology (16 Mbps Token Ring or 100 Mbps FDDI). This topology places a minimum of two bridges in series between any two work areas.

Unless application processor or file servers are directly attached to the backbone, the performance for demanding file transfer applications is affected by this double hop. This is most noticeable if the backbone is no faster than the work areas. Those applications using TCP as their transport layer will need an increase in window size; applications which use UDP protocols with a small datagram size may suffer badly.

Hub Bridges

Hub and **multiport bridges** replaces the backbone network with a single internal high-speed bus of greater speed than any LAN.

This reduces the double hop effect but requires more extensive cabling and potentially reduces the backbone to a single point of failure.

Identifying a Network Connection

Connections to a TCP/IP network are often known to each other and to users in three different ways, which identify the same connection to the network but at different levels of TCP/IP.

- As names: in the **fully qualified host** and **domain** name

  Vax1.icds.com.in

- Using the domain name scheme is often not considered early enough in the planning of commercial networks; users of larger networks will find it invaluable.
- As a group of four numbers separated by full stops. This is the IP or network address used by the IP layer of TCP/IP.

  164.120.9.61

- On a shared LAN by its network interface card address the 48-bit MAC address. (Medium Access Control address often called the physical address)

  02 60 8C 12 34 56

The three levels of address is required, since they all refer to the same connection to the TCP/IP Internet. The reason is that while at any one time these addresses identify the same location, over a period of time, each may change for different reasons. The three types of address allow a degree of flexibility where none would exist if the functions were not separated:

- The host and domain name should remain unchanged for the longest time, it is completely determined by the system designers and managers, though it will often change if there is a major change in machine location.
- The IP address may change due to network growth and reconfiguration, for instance, if a machine is moved from one location in a building to another.
- The MAC address may change for similar growth or performance reasons, or because the network card is replaced following a card failure. The shortest lived address is likely to be the MAC address.

The fully qualified domain name is for 'human consumption' and consists of a set of identifiers, separated by full stops, which describe a computer in a hierarchical relationship to all others. For example:

machine.departmet.site.organization.org_type.country

Introducing flexibility brings with it the possibility of error and communications failure if the flexible functions are not managed and controlled correctly.

Planning the IP Address Scheme

To plan an IP addressing scheme you must have the following information:

(i) The maximum number of host ports that your organization could ever wish to interconnect. The whole of your organization is not just your particular department, but the whole organizational structure, if necessary worldwide, which may at any time be interconnected.

(ii) An understanding of the number of devices at each location and in each building on each site. Assume one address per member of staff in those buildings and leave some 25% spare.

(iii) An understanding of the different departments, their geographic locations and the likelihood that they will need to communicate. An estimate of the amount of information that is exchanged is useful but it has a very short-lived value.

(iv) A knowledge of any other current users of TCP/IP and any standardization decisions that have been taken already

In a small organization of a few hundred people, getting this information is straightforward in comparison to a large corporation; but it is the large corporation that must have accurate figures and which must derive centralized standards that are adhered to everywhere.

Internet Protocol

The Internet Protocol (IP) may be described as the network layer protocol of TCP/IP. IP is operated and interpreted by each intermediate relay in an interconnected set of LANs and WANs which is using the TCP/IP protocol suite co communicate.

Such a collection is often called an **internetwork** and the intermediate relays are routers. IP provides a best efforts delivery service based on a technique called **datagram transmission;** 'best efforts' and 'datagram' because no attempt is made by IP to recover any errors which may occur in transmission.

IP supports routing and relaying of information between communicating hosts or end devices according to the Type or quality Of Service (TOS) they require. IP allows routing errors to be trapped and reported and their effects on system performance to be minimized. IP does not make assumptions about the underlying network of physical cables. LAN hardware (Ethernet, Token Ring or FDDI) or the point-to-point wide area links (PTT circuits).

IP Addressing

The IP address is one component in the Internet protocol. The IP address is a number that uniquely identifies the connection of a host computer or end system as OSI would call it, to a physical network as it communicates with other computers or end systems. Hosts with more than one connection have a different IP address for each one.

IP routers also have their own IP addresses for they can be the source and destination of IP datagrams. The purpose of the IP address is twofold: to identify each connection to the internetwork in a way that is independent of the underlying physical network (LAN or WAN) technology and to collect a group of connections together to simplify routing. Internetwork routers use IP addresses to make routing decisions. IP addresses must be unique in the communicating internetwork. If not, communications will fail erratically.

Since TCP/IP protocols do not directly provide any technical means by which IP addresses can be automatically made unique, it is up to network managers to configure and manage them correctly by traditional manual methods aided by database and network management technology.

MAC Addresses

Where TCP/IP systems are connected to a shared cable such as an Ethernet or Token Ring LAN, communication between stations must take place using MAC addresses, normally built into the network adapter card. Since the IP address is configured independently of the MAC address, it remains unchanged even if the network card fails and is replaced. Every Ethernet or token Ring card comes with a preconfigured 48-bit MAC address, its universally managed address. LAN standards also allow locally managed addresses; network cards can be loaded with a 48-bit address chosen by the network manager.

Locally managed addresses are not normally used in TCP/IP systems. AS IP addressed in TCP/IP must be controlled and managed, there is little value in adding a second layer of management by also configuring and controlling MAC addresses. But the issue of MAC address management does not disappear completely from the TCP/IP story; some of the facilities of TCP/IP such as the Boot Protocol, BOOTP, use the MAC address as a fixed reference point for obtaining other information. If you wish to use these features, you must at least have a record of the MAC address of each computer for which the facility will be used.

These addresses appear as a reference point in look-up tables in information servers. But as discussed above, the MAC address can change if the network card is replaced. In a large network, keeping an up-to-date record of MAC addresses and ensuring that all servers have the correct record can be time-consuming. Few advanced star wiring systems have management facilities that can record the MAC address attached to each user drop cable.

Such systems make it easier to record the location of particular MAC addresses.

Characteristics of the IP Address

The IP address is a 32-bit number which must be unique in internetwork. Devices which must have an IP address include every connection of each application processor and of each network router. As mentioned previously, computers with more than one network connection have a different IP address for each connection.

In TCP/IP literature, such computers are referred to as **multihomed.** These connections are usually on different networks. This is the reason for sizing the network-by-network connections rather than the number of computers, though these numbers will often be very similar. Unlike some other network addressing schemes, the IP address does not necessarily convey any information about geographic location.

Given an IP address you can only deduce a management authority; that authority could manage one corporate network which in itself has global coverage and meshes with many other global networks. This has interesting implications for routing between two worldwide networks. In other way, the IP addressing scheme is not hierarchical unlike the telephone or telex network or for that matter the CCITT X.121 addressing scheme for the X.25 interface to public packet switched networks. The 32-bit IP address has two components a **network number** or network identifier and a **host number** or host identifier.

Some 'class bits' can be extracted from the network number, but trying to examine these on their own can lead to confusion. It is safer always to think of the network number as containing the class bits.

It is the network number which identifies the controlling organization and the port number which identifies the particular connection within the authority of that organization. The term 'host number' is historic and this name could cause confusion for, as we have seen, a multihomed host has more than one IP address and hence more than one host number.

For reasons that will become apparent later, it would be unusual for two ports on the same machine to have the same network number.

Class bits + Network number Host number

The terms **net id.** and **host id**. are in common usage for network number and host number. IP addresses are divided into five address classes (A to E). It is important to understand that these divisions were conceived to ease the management of addresses by the Internet Activities Board (IAB); they have less immediate significance for the network manager.

The first three classes, A, B, C, are available for normal allocation and for host-to-host communications. Class D and class E addresses are not for general use; class D is reserved for special use by IAB designated protocols and class E is reserved for future use. One use of class D addresses is by routers, so network managers may encounter them while monitoring router protocols. There are no practical distinctions in the way in which computer systems with class A, class B or class C addresses use those addresses.

With some noted exceptions, which are discussed further below, any address from any class is equivalent for communications purposes. In principle, any host can communicate equally well using an address is the number of network numbers and the number of host connections which each network number can support.

The limitations of each class are described as follows:

Network class	Max. number of network numbers	Max. number of hosts on Each network number
A	126	16 777 214
B	16 382	65 534
C	2 097 150	254
D	Not applicable—reserved for multicast systems	
E	Reserved for IAB use	

Network Numbers and Host Numbers

The choice of network numbers is most important. Network connections with the same network number should communicate directly on the same physical LAN.

Network connections with different network numbers do not communicate directly; they must use the services of a router.

This router either is directly connected between the two LANs to which the hosts connect or it in turn knows of a router which can relay the message towards its ultimate destination.

These factors determine the basic rules for choosing network numbers and host numbers. They may alternatively be stated as:

- Computers separated only by bridges or repeaters will have the same network number
- Computers or workstations separated by routers have different network numbers.

For the network implementor, the most important factor is the choice of IP address for a particular host is affected by the presence of routers. The positioning of routers is determined by the exact geography of the underlying physical networks which connect computers, floors, buildings, sites and countries into a complete internetwork.

It is also heavily influenced by organizational needs, traffic flows and traffic volume. The layout will change as the network grows and matures. If a bridge is replaced by a router, the network number on one side of the new router must change. A TCP/IP addressing scheme evolves as the needs of users are better understood during the design process.

Adding a TCP/IP addressing scheme to a LAN must take into account the existing layout of that LAN. One factor is key. Network planners must attempt to design an addressing scheme that can remain substantially unchanged in a changing environment.

This can be achieved using subnetwork addressing. The convention is the address is written down, or described to software, in **dotted decimal notation.** Each eight bits of the address (each **octet)** is converted to a decimal number in the range 0 to 255 and separated by a dot (.).

While the US standards initially specified 'dotted decimal notation' some computer staff are more at home with hexadecimal notation. **Dotted hexadecimal** (and UNIX or C-style hexadecimal) and **octal** notations are sometimes used and will be accepted by some (though by no means all) implementations.

Occasionally it is useful, it somewhat long-winded, to represent these numbers in binary. Leading zeros in each octet, which have no significance, need not be included. 128.1.0.9 is valid and more usual than 128.001.000.009, though this is also perfectly acceptable; however, 128.1.0.9 or 128...9 are not valid.

Table: Distinguishing the class of address

Address Class	*Class bits*	*Number of network bits*	*First usable value*	*Last usable*	*Remark*
A	0	7	1	126	Value 0 and 127 are reserved
B	10	14	128.1	191.254	
C	110	21	192.0.1	223.255.254	
D	1110	—	224.0.0.0	239.255.255.254	Not available for general use
E	1111	—	240.0.0.0	255.255.255.254	Not available for general use

Distinguishing the Class of Address

The five classes of address have already been mentioned. The class of address is determined by certain bits in the first eight bits, that is, in the first decimal number of the four. The magnitude of the first number that defines the class of the address is given in the table.

There are two important features of this system:

(i) The division between one class and the next is always at an octet boundary. This simplifies finding the boundaries between the classes of address, since each decimal number represents one octet.

(ii) When the network number is written down the 'class bits' are always included in the first octet, to ensure that the class of address and hence the true network number are unambiguous.

It is important that users of TCP/IP, planners and implementors would be fully familiar with the different classes of address and the limitations that they place on network growth. Many people new to the subject at first find the technique of dotted decimal notation a little eccentric.

But it should become second nature to recognize the class of address, the network number and the host id. As compared to other network addressing schemes the TCP/IP addressing range is quite limited. Current work in the IAB is investigating the options for extending the address range.

IAB and Network Number Registration

The address in an internetwork must be unique, there has to be a registry which ensures that such a policy can be enforced. TCP/IP was developed for use on the US Internet. This collection of networks is managed by many different authorities, with the IAB as overall design authority. In this environment of devolved management, the network number has two functions.

First, since each IP address on the whole set of interconnected networks must be unique, the network number is used to identify one addressing authority, often called an autonomous system, responsible for issuing unique connection ids in that part of the address space. The second function is to support routing. The IAB ensures that IP addresses on the Internet are unique, by registering and issuing network numbers to organizations that have reasons to connect to the Internet.

Such organizations don't choose their own network number, it is issued to them. They agree to undertake certain network management responsibilities when they request an official IAB address allocation. They must then issue host Ids so that they are unique within their own network number address space. If they fail to issue unique host numbers, only the services of that organization will be affected. The IAB has devolved the clerical tasks of registering and issuing IP network numbers to the Internet Registry, part of the Internet assigned Numbers Authority (IANA) which controls all numbers in the TCP/IP protocol suite, which must be managed if correct operation is to be guaranteed.

The Internet Registry is operated by the Department of Defense Network Network Information Center (DDNNIC), now located in Chantilly, Virginia.

Configuring the IP Address

Every computer, workstation, personal computer, network router and network management station which 'speaks IP' must have a different IP address for each of its connections. The IP address is entered through the normal configuration management processes. IP addresses are usually represented and entered in dotted decimal notation; occasionally dotted hexadecimal notation is accepted.

The address is usually stored in non-volatile memory, either RAM or on a disk file when available. Diskless workstations often have no nonvolatile storage. They obtain their IP address across the network at start-up time using BOOTP or RARP. Visiting each device to change the IP address is time-consuming, particularly in dispersed networks. BOOTP provides a mechanism for centralizing the distribution of IP addresses and other useful TCP/IP parameters, even for machines which do have storage.

The key to distributing the correct IP address and other information via BOOTP is the MAC address of the interface card. It is then essential to record accurately the MAC address used by each machine on the network that uses the BOOTP service. This is excellent policy for fault diagnosis and security in any case, though it is often neglected. In an operational network, IP addresses become recorded in distributed tables and in software in machines.

While this is bad practice, it is unavoidable. Frequent wholesale changes to IP addresses must not occur, so preplanning is essential. Such changes are labour-intensive because of the widespread distribution of addresses; the change introduces errors and has unpredictable consequences for the integrity of operational applications and for the time taken to restore any-to-any communications.

Reserved IP Addresses

Certain IP network numbers and host numbers are reserved for the use of particular aspects of TCP/IP communication. Not all these protocols are regularly used. Once you configure a connection with a reserved IP address, the faults caused are likely to be obscure, apparently intermittent and difficult to isolate. No all host software checks that the IP address it is requested to use is invalid.

The following addresses are reserved:

- Network number 127.X.X.X, where X.X.X is any set of numbers. This is used for a local software loopback test.
- A network number of all 0s is classless and means ‘my current network which I do not know the number of –sometimes referred to as ‘this network’
- A network number of all 1s.
- Host number 0 is reserved to refer to a particular network number. For example, 192.0.0.1 is the first class C network address which could be allocated.
- Host number ‘all 1s’ is reserved to broadcast to all hosts on a specific network; it can only be used as a destination address.
- The full address 0.0.0.0 is reserved. It is used in two ways: as a source address when the host does not know its genuine address, for example during bootstrapping of a diskless workstation and by routers in a list of addresses to advertise the default route, the route to all networks which are not explicitly listed.
- The full address 255.255.255.255 is reserved as a destination address to mean ‘broadcast to all hosts on my network’. 0.0.0.0 as a destination is an obsolete form of 255.255.255.255.

IP Addresses with Routers an Dial-up Devices

Few older router implementations need a point-to-point wide area PTT or dial-up link between two LANs should be identified with its own unique IP network number with only two connections attached.

In the larger network that is wasteful of the limited resource of IP network numbers. Check with your router manufacturer that the most modern techniques, which conserve network and subnetwork numbers, are used in their implementation.

11

Protocol Suites

Models and Protocols

In computing, a **protocol** is a convention or standard that controls or enables the connection, communication, and data transfer between two computing endpoints. In its simplest form, a protocol can be defined as **the rules governing** the syntax, semantics, and synchronization of communication. Protocols may be implemented by hardware, software, or a combination of the two. At the lowest level, a protocol defines the behaviour of a hardware connection.

A protocol is a convention or standard that controls or enables the connection, communication, and data transfer between two computing endpoints.

Typical properties

It is difficult to generalize about protocols because they vary so greatly in purpose and sophistication. Most protocols specify one or more of the following properties:

- Detection of the underlying physical connection (wired or wireless), or the existence of the other endpoint or node
- Handshaking
- Negotiation of various connection characteristics
- How to start and end a message
- How to format a message
- What to do with corrupted or improperly formatted messages (error correction)
- How to detect unexpected loss of the connection, and what to do next
- Termination of the session or connection.

Importance

The widespread use and expansion of communications protocols is both a prerequisite to the Internet, and a major contributor to its power and success. The pair of Internet Protocol (or IP) and Transmission Control Protocol (or TCP) are the most important of these, and the term TCP/IP refers to a collection (or protocol suite) of its most used protocols. Most of the Internet's communication protocols are described in the RFC documents of the Internet Engineering Task Force (or IETF).

Object-oriented programming has extended the use of the term to include the programming protocols available for connections and communication between objects.

The pair of Internet Protocol (or IP) and Transmission Control Protocol (or TCP) are the most important of these, and the term TCP/IP refers to a collection (or protocol suite) of its most used protocols.

Generally, only the simplest protocols are used alone. Most protocols, especially in the context of communications or networking, are layered together into protocol stacks where the various tasks listed above are divided among different protocols in the stack.

Whereas the protocol stack denotes a specific combination of protocols that work together, a reference model is a software architecture that lists each layer and the services each should offer. The classic seven-layer reference model is the OSI model, which is used for conceptualizing protocol stacks and peer entities. This reference model also provides an opportunity to teach more general software engineering concepts like hiding, modularity, and delegation of tasks. This model has endured in spite of the demise of many of its protocols (and protocol stacks) originally sanctioned by the ISO. The *OSI model* is not the only reference model, however.

Common Protocols

- IP (Internet Protocol)
- DHCP (Dynamic Host Configuration Protocol)
- TCP (Transmission Control Protocol)
- HTTP (Hypertext Transfer Protocol)
- FTP (File Transfer Protocol)
- POP3 (Post Office Protocol 3)
- SMTP (Simple Mail Transfer Protocol)
- IMAP (Internet Message Access Protocol)

Network IPX/SPX

IPX/SPX stands for **Internetwork Packet Exchange/Sequenced Packet Exchange**. It is a networking protocol used by the Novell NetWare operating systems. Like UDP, IPX is a datagram protocol used for connectionless communications. IPX and SPX are derived from Xerox Network Services' IDP and SPP protocols.

SPX is a transport layer protocol (layer 4 of the OSI Model) used in Novell Netware networks. The SPX layer sits on top of the IPX layer (layer 3 - the network layer) and provides connection-oriented services between two nodes on the network. SPX is used primarily by client/server applications.

IPX and SPX both provide connection services similar to TCP/IP, with the IPX protocol having similarities to IP, and SPX having similarities to TCP. IPX/SPX was primarily designed for local area networks (LANs), and is a very efficient protocol for this purpose (typically its performance exceeds that of TCP/IP on a LAN). TCP/IP has, however, become the *de facto* protocol. This is in part due to its superior performance over wide area networks and the Internet (which uses TCP/IP exclusively), and also because TCP/IP is a more mature protocol, designed specifically with this purpose in mind.

Novell is largely responsible for the use of IPX as a popular computer networking protocol due to their dominance in the network operating system software market (with Novell Netware) from the late 1980s through to the mid-1990s.

Because of IPX/SPX's prevalence in LANs in the 1990's, Microsoft added support for the protocols into Windows' networking stack, starting with Windows for Workgroups and Windows NT. Microsoft even named their implementation "NWLink", implying that the inclusion of the layer 3/4 transports provided NetWare connectivity. In reality, the protocols were supported as a native transport for Windows' SMB/NetBIOS, and NetWare connectivity required additional installation of an NCP client (Microsoft provided a basic NetWare client with Windows 95 and later, but it was not automatically installed, and initially only supported NetWare bindery mode). NWLink is still provided with Windows (up to and including Windows 2003). However, it is neither included on nor supported in Windows Vista, Novell will be starting a closed beta in March 2007, but its use is strongly discouraged, because it cannot be used for Windows networking except as a transport for NetBIOS, which is deprecated.

For the most part, Novell's 32-bit Windows client software have eschewed NWLink for an alternative developed by Novell, although some versions permit use of Microsoft's IPX/SPX implementation (with warnings about potential incompatibility).

IPX usage has declined in recent years as the rise of the Internet has made TCP/IP ubiquitous. Novell's initial attempt to support TCP/IP as a client protocol, called NetWare/IP, simply "tunnelled" IPX within IP packets, allowing NetWare clients and servers to communicate over pure TCP/IP networks. However, due to complex implementation, and a significant loss in performance due to the tunnelling overhead, NetWare/IP was largely ignored except as a mechanism to route IPX through TCP/IP-only routers and WAN links. NetWare 5.x introduced native support for NCP over TCP/IP, which is now the preferred configuration.

Both Microsoft and Novell have provided support (through Proxy Server/ ISA Server and Border Manager, respectively) for IPX/SPX as an intranet protocol to communicate through a firewall.

This allows a machine using client software to access the Internet without having TCP/IP installed locally; the client software emulates a native TCP/IP stack and provides WinSock support for local applications (e.g. web browsers), but actually communicates with the firewall over IPX/SPX. In addition to simplifying migration for legacy IPX LANs, this provides a measure of security, as the use of the IPX protocol on the internal network provides a natural barrier against intruders, should the firewall be compromised.

One area where IPX remains useful is to sidestep VPNs that force all TCP/IP traffic to traverse the VPN, preventing any access to local resources such as printers and shared disks.

Intranet Protocols

An **intranet** is a private computer network that uses Internet protocols, network connectivity to securely share part of an organization's information or operations with its employees. Sometimes the term refers only to the most visible service, the internal website. The same concepts and technologies of the Internet such as clients and servers running on the Internet protocol suite are used to build an intranet. HTTP and other Internet protocols are commonly used as well, FTP. There is often an attempt to use Internet technologies to provide new interfaces with corporate 'legacy' data and information systems.

Briefly, an **intranet** can be understood as "**a private version of the Internet,**" or as a version of the internet confined to an organization.

Extranets

Intranets differ from "Extranets" in that the former is generally restricted to employees of the organization while extranets can generally be accessed by customers, suppliers, or other approved parties.

There does not necessarily have to be any access from the organization's internal network to the internet itself. When such access is provided it is usually through a gateway with a firewall, along with user authentication, encryption of messages, and often make use of virtual private networks (VPN's). Through such devices and systems off-site employees can access company information, computing resources and internal communications.

Increasingly, intranets are being used to deliver tools and applications, e.g., collaboration (to facilitate working in groups and teleconferencing) or sophisticated corporate directories, sales and CRM tools, project management etc., to advance productivity. Intranets are also being used as culture change platforms. For example, large numbers of employees discussing key issues in an online forums could lead to new ideas.

Intranet traffic, like public-facing web site traffic, is better understood by using web metrics software to track overall activity, as well as through surveys of users. Intranet "User Experience", "Editorial", and "Technology" teams work together to produce in-house sites.

Most commonly, intranets are owned by the communications, HR or CIO areas of large organizations, or some combination of the three.

Advantages

1. Workforce productivity: Intranets can help users to locate and view information faster and use applications relevant to their roles and responsibilities. With the help of a web browser interface such as Internet Explorer or Firefox, users can access data held in any database the organization wants to make available, anytime and - subject to security provisions - from anywhere within the company workstations, increasing employees' ability to perform their jobs faster, more accurately, and with confidence that they have the right information. It also helps to improve the services provided to the users.
2. Time: With intranets, organizations can make more information available to employees on a "pull" basis (ie: employees can link to relevant information at a time which suits them) rather than being deluged indiscriminately by emails.
3. Communication: Intranets can serve as powerful tools for communication within an organization, vertically and horizontally. From a communications standpoint, intranets are useful to communicate strategic initiatives that have a global reach throughout the organization. The type of information that can easily be conveyed is the purpose of the initiative and what the initiative is aiming to achieve, who is driving the initiative, results achieved to date, and who to speak to for more information. By providing this information on the intranet, staff have the opportunity to keep up-to-date with the strategic focus of the organisation.
4. Web publishing allows '***cumbersome'*** corporate knowledge to be maintained and easily accessed throughout the company using hypermedia and Web technologies. Examples include: employee manuals, benefits documents, company policies, business standards, newsfeeds, and even training, can be accessed using common Internet standards (Acrobat files, Flash files, CGI applications). Because each business unit can update the online copy of a document, the most recent version is always available to employees using the intranet.
5. Business operations and management: Intranets are also being used as a platform for developing and deploying applications to support business operations and decisions across the internetworked enterprise.
6. Cost-effective: Users can view information and data via web-browser rather than maintaining physical documents such as procedure manuals, internal phone list and requisition forms.
7. Promote common corporate culture: Every user is viewing the same information within the Intranet.

8. Enhance Collaboration: With information easily accessible by all authorised users, teamwork is enabled.
9. Cross-platform Capability: Web browsers that support Java under Windows, Mac, Unix are supported.

Disadvantages

1. Inappropriate or incorrect information can be posted on an intranet which can reduce its credibility and effectiveness.
2. In a devolved and highly interactive intranet there is freedom to post abusive and possibly illegal materials. There is a balance to be struck between taking advantage of this freedom to achieve corporate goals and having appropriate controls in place to meet an organization's legal or moral responsibilities.
3. Training is required to educate people of what intranet can do.
4. Need expertise in field to administer and develop Intranet information within the organization.
5. Security of the intranet becomes an issue. Other users may post sensitive information which may appear to another user. Furthermore, in an industry with high turnover there is the potential for an employee to acquire sensitive information which may significantly benefit their new position at a competing company.
6. As information can be posted by any user, information overload may occur during the cause if it is not controlled well.

Planning and creating an intranet

Most organizations devote considerable resources into the planning and implementation of their intranet as it is of strategic importance to the organization's success. Some of the planning would include topics such as:

- What they hope to achieve from the intranet
- Which person or department would "own" (take control of) the technology and the implementation
- How and when existing systems would be phased out/replaced
- How they intend to make the intranet secure
- How they'll ensure to keep it within legislative and other constraints
- Level of interactivity or interactivity (eg on-line forms) desired.
- Is the input of new data and updating of existing data to be centrally controlled or devolved.

These are in addition to the hardware and software decisions (like Content Management Systems), participation issues (like good taste, harassment, confidentiality), and features to be supported.

The actual implementation would include steps such as

1. User involvement to identify users' information needs.
2. Setting up a web server with the correct hardware and software.
3. Setting up web server access using a TCP/IP network.
4. Installing the user programs on all required computers.
5. Creating a homepage for the content to be hosted.
6. User involvement in testing and promoting use of intranet.

Industry examples

- KPMG moved all of its information assets to an intranet called KWorld.
- Calor Gas uses an Intranet called Interact Intranet to share documents and communicate with staff. They also use it for electronic forms and workflow.
- "The success of Cisco Systems has been largely attributed to its innovative corporate intranet"
- The People's Republic of China (PRC) is attempting to build a national intranet while limiting access to information forbidden by Chinese Internet regulations. If they are successful in their attempt, it will be the largest intranet.
- North Korea controls access to the internet among its people by using a country-wide intranet called "Kwangbyong" ('Bright'), while those with actual access to the internet are controlled by a government agency called the Korean Computer Centre. They are employed in searching the web for useful information, which is then copied and moved onto the Kwangbyong.
- Ford Motor Co has more than 175,000 employees in 950 locations worldwide, each of whom had access to the company's intranet. The intranet gave employees information about benefits, demographics, salary history, general company news and human resources forms.
- ShoreBank's branch, affiliate, and consulting service employees around the world communicate and collaborate using SIREN. SIREN is an intranet, extranet, and knowledge management solution implemented in 2006 using Intranet DASHBOARD.
- The Australian National University uses an Intranet called Claromentis to maintain one of its external sites.

Apple Talk

AppleTalk is a proprietary suite of protocols developed by Apple Inc for computer networking. It was included in the original Macintosh (1984) and is now deprecated by Apple in favour of TCP/IP networking.

Design

The design **fairly** rigorously followed the OSI model of protocol layering. Unlike most other early LAN systems, AppleTalk was not built on the archetypal Xerox XNS system, as the intended target was not Ethernet and did not have 48-bit addresses to route. Nevertheless many portions of the AppleTalk system have direct analogs in XNS.

One key differentiator for AppleTalk was that the system contained two protocols aimed at making the system completely self-configuring. The **AppleTalk address resolution protocol** (**AARP**) allowed AppleTalk hosts to automatically generate their own network addresses, and the **Name Binding Protocol** (**NBP**) was essentially a dynamic Domain Name System (DNS), system which mapped network addresses to user-readable names. Although systems similar to AARP existed in other systems, Banyan VINES for instance, nothing like NBP has existed until recently.

Both AARP and NBP had defined ways to allow "controller" devices to override the default mechanisms.

The concept here was to allow routers to provide all of this information, or additionally "hardwire" the system to known addresses and names. On larger networks where AARP could cause problems as new nodes searched for free addresses, the addition of a router could dramatically reduce "chattiness".

Together AARP and NBP made AppleTalk perhaps the easiest to use networking system yet developed. New machines were added to the network simply by plugging them in, and optionally giving them a name. The NBP lists were examined and displayed by a program known as the **Chooser** (originally because it allowed you to choose your default printer) which would display a list of machines on the local network, divided into classes such as fileservers and printers. All of this was completely automated.

One problem for AppleTalk was that it was originally intended to be part of a project known as **Macintosh Office**, which would consist of a host machine providing routing, printer sharing and file sharing. However, this project was cancelled in 1986, although the LaserWriter included AppleTalk built-in. Apple did eventually release a File and Print Server known as the AppleShare File and Print Servers.

For some the old AppleTalk protocol was considered clunky and often called 'chatty', notably on larger networks and Wide area networks (WAN) where the naming services generated considerable unwanted traffic. AppleTalk Phase 2, included with System 7, reduced the chattiness significantly.

Today AppleTalk support is provided for backward compatibility in many products, but the default networking on the Mac is TCP/IP. Starting with Mac OS X v10.2, Bonjour (originally named *Rendezvous*) provides similar discovery and configuration services for TCP/IP-based networks. Bonjour is Apple's implementation of ZeroConf, which was written specifically to bring NBP's ease-of-use to the TCP/IP world.

Addressing

An AppleTalk address was a 4-byte quantity. This consisted of a two-byte network number, a one-byte node number, and a one-byte socket number. Of these, only the network number required any configuration, being obtained from a router. Each node dynamically chose its own node number, according to a protocol which handled contention between different nodes accidentally choosing the same number. For socket numbers, a few well-known numbers were reserved for special purposes specific to the AppleTalk protocol itself. Apart from these, all application-level protocols were expected to use dynamically-assigned socket numbers at both the client and server end.

Because of this dynamism, users could not be expected to access services by specifying their address. Instead, all services had *names* which, being chosen by humans, could be expected to be meaningful to users, and also could be sufficiently long enough to minimize the chance of conflicts.

Note that, because a name translated to an address which included a socket number as well as a node number, a name in AppleTalk mapped directly to a *service* being provided by a machine, which was entirely separate from the name of the machine itself. Thus, services could be moved to a different machine and, so long as they kept the same service name, there was no need for users to do anything different to continue accessing the service. And the same machine could host any number of instances of services of the same type, without any network connection conflicts.

Contrast this with *A records* in the DNS, where a name translates only to a machine address, not including the port number that might be providing a service. Thus, if people are accustomed to using a particular machine name to access a particular service, their access will break when the service is moved to a different machine. This can be mitigated somewhat by insistence on using *CNAME records* indicating service rather than actual machine names to refer to the service, but there is no way of guaranteeing that users will follow such a convention. Some newer protocols, such as Kerberos and Active Directory use DNS *SRV records* to identify services by name, which is much closer to the AppleTalk model.

Protocols

AppleTalk Address Resolution Protocol

AARP resolves AppleTalk addresses to physical layer, usually MAC, addresses. It is functionally equivalent to ARP.

AARP is a fairly simple system. When powered on, an AppleTalk machine broadcasts an **AARP probe packet** asking for a network address, intending to hear back from controllers such as routers. If no address is provided, one is picked at random from the "base subnet", 0. It then broadcasts another packet saying "I am selecting this address", and then waits to see if anyone else on the network complains. If another machine has that address, it will pick another address, and keep trying until it finds a free one.

On a network with many machines it may take several tries before a free address is found, so for performance purposes the successful address is "written down" in NVRAM and used as the default address in the future. This means that in most real-world setups where machines are added a few at a time, only one or two tries are needed before the address effectively becomes constant.

AppleTalk Data Stream Protocol

This was a comparatively late addition to the AppleTalk protocol suite, done when it became clear that a TCP-style reliable connection-oriented transport was needed. Significant differences from TCP were:

- a connection attempt could be rejected
- there were no "half-open" connections; once one end initiated a tear-down of the connection, the whole connection would be closed (*i.e.*, ADSP is full-duplex, not dual simplex).

Apple Filing Protocol

The Apple Filing Protocol (AFP), formerly AppleTalk Filing Protocol, is the protocol for communicating with AppleShare file servers. Built on top of AppleTalk Session Protocol, it provides services for authenticating users (extensible to different authentication methods including two-way random-number exchange) and for performing operations specific to the Macintosh HFS filesystem. AFP is still in use in Mac OS X, even though most other AppleTalk protocols have been deprecated.

AppleTalk Session Protocol

ASP was an intermediate protocol, built on top of ATP, which in turn was the foundation of AFP. It provided basic services for requesting responses to arbitrary *commands* and performing out-of-band status queries. It also allowed the server to send asynchronous *attention* messages to the client.

AppleTalk Transaction Protocol

ATP was the original reliable transport-level protocol for AppleTalk, built on top of DDP. At the time it was being developed, a full, reliable connection-oriented protocol like TCP was considered to be too expensive to implement for most of the intended uses of AppleTalk. Thus, ATP was a simple request/response exchange, with no need to set up or tear down connections.

An ATP *request* packet could be answered by up to eight *response* packets. The requestor then sent an *acknowledgement* packet containing a bit mask indicating which of the response packets it received, so the responder could retransmit the remainder.

ATP could operate in either "at-least-once" mode or "exactly-once" mode. Exactly-once mode was essential for operations which were not idempotent; in this mode, the responder kept a copy of the response buffers in memory until successful receipt of a *release* packet from the requestor, or until a timeout elapsed.

This way, it could respond to duplicate requests with the same transaction ID by resending the same response data, without performing the actual operation again.

Datagram Delivery Protocol

DDP was the lowest-level data-link-independent transport protocol. It provided a datagram service with no guarantees of delivery. All application-level protocols, including the infrastructure protocols NBP, RTMP and ZIP, were built on top of DDP.

Name Binding Protocol

NBP was a dynamic, distributed system for managing AppleTalk names. When a service started up on a machine, it registered a name for itself on that machine, as chosen by a human administrator. At this point, NBP provided a system for checking that no other machine had already registered the same name. Then later, when a client wanted to access that service, it used NBP to query machines to find that service. NBP provided browseability ("what are the names of all the services available?") as well as the ability to find a service with a particular name.

As would be expected from Apple, names were truly human readable, containing spaces, upper and lower case letters, and including support for searching.

Printer Access Protocol

PAP was the standard way of communicating with PostScript printers. It was built on top of ATP. When a PAP connection was opened, each end sent the other an ATP request which basically meant "send me more data". The client's response to the server was to send a block of PostScript code, while the server could respond with any diagnostic messages that might be generated as a result, after which another "send-more-data" request was sent. This use of ATP provided automatic flow control; each end could only send data to the other end if there was an outstanding ATP request to respond to.

PAP also provided for out-of-band status queries, handled by separate ATP transactions. Even while it was busy servicing a print job from one client, a PAP server could continue to respond to status requests from any number of other clients. This allowed other Macintoshes on the LAN that were waiting to print to display status messages indicating that the printer was busy, and what the job was that it was busy with.

Routing Table Maintenance Protocol

RTMP was the protocol by which routers kept each other informed about the topology of the network. This was the only part of AppleTalk that required periodic unsolicited broadcasts: every 10 seconds, each router had to send out a list of all the network numbers it knew about and how far away it thought they were.

Zone Information Protocol

ZIP was the protocol by which AppleTalk network numbers were associated with zone names. A *zone* was a subdivision of the network that made sense to humans (for example, "Accounting Department"); but while a network number had to be assigned to a topologically-contiguous section of the network, a zone could include several different discontiguous portions of the network.

Physical implementation

The initial default hardware implementation for AppleTalk was a high-speed serial protocol known as **LocalTalk** that used the Macintosh's built-in RS-422 ports at 230.4 kbit/s. LocalTalk used a splitter box in the RS-422 port to provide an upstream and downstream cable from a single port. The system was slow by today's standards, but at the time the additional cost and complexity of networking on PC machines was such that it was common that Macs were the only networked machines in the office.

Other physical implementations were also available. One common replacement for LocalTalk was **PhoneNet**, a 3rd party solution (from a company called Farallon) that also used the RS-422 port and was indistinguishable from LocalTalk as far as Apple's LocalTalk port drivers were concerned, but ran over two unused wires in existing phone cabling. PhoneNet was considerably less expensive to install and maintain.

Ethernet and TokenRing was also supported, known as **EtherTalk** and **TokenTalk** respectively. EtherTalk in particular gradually became the dominant implementation method for AppleTalk as Ethernet became generally popular in the PC industry throughout the 1990s.

Networking model

OSI Model	Corresponding AppleTalk layers
Application	Apple Filing Protocol (AFP)
Presentation	Apple Filing Protocol (AFP)
Session	Zone Information Protocol (ZIP)
	AppleTalk Session Protocol (ASP)
	AppleTalk Data Stream Protocol (ADSP)
Transport	AppleTalk Transaction Protocol (ATP)

	AppleTalk Echo Protocol (AEP)
	Name Binding Protocol (NBP)
	Routing Table Maintenance Protocol (RTMP)
Network	Datagram Delivery Protocol (DDP)
Data link	EtherTalk Link Access Protocol (ELAP)
	LocalTalk Link Access Protocol (LLAP)
	TokenTalk Link Access Protocol (TLAP)
	Fiber Distributed Data Interface (FDDI)
Physical	LocalTalk driver
	Ethernet driver
	Token Ring driver
	FDDI driver

Cross Platform Solutions

The BSD and Linux operating systems support AppleTalk through an open source project called Netatalk, which implements the complete protocol suite and allows them to both act as native file or print servers for Macintoshes, and print to LocalTalk printers over the network.

In addition, Columbia University released the Columbia AppleTalk Package (CAP) which implemented the protocol suite for various Unix flavours including Ultrix, SunOS, *BSD and IRIX. This package is no longer actively maintained.

Digital Network Architecture

DECnet is a proprietary suite of network protocols created by Digital Equipment Corporation, originally released in 1975 in order to connect two PDP-11 minicomputers. It evolved into one of the first peer-to-peer network architectures, thus transforming DEC into a networking powerhouse in the 1980s.

Initially built with four layers, it later (1992) evolved into a seven layer OSI compliant networking protocol, around the time when open systems (POSIX compliant, i.e. Unix-like) were grabbing marketshare from the proprietary OSes like VAX/VMS and AlphaVMS.

DECnet was built right into the DEC flagship operating system VAX/VMS since its inception. Digital ported it to its own Ultrix variant of UNIX, as well as Apple Macintosh computers and PCs running both DOS and Windows under the name **DEC Pathworks**, transforming these systems into DECnet end-nodes in a network of VAX machines. More recently, an open-source version has been developed for the Linux OS.

Brief overview of the evolution of DECnet

DECnet refers to a specific set of hardware and software networking products which implement the **DIGITAL Network Architecture** (DNA). The DIGITAL Network Architecture is essentially a set of documents which define the network architecture in general, state the specifications for each layer of the architecture, and describe the protocols which operate within each layer. Although network protocol analyzer tools tend to categorize all protocols from DIGITAL as "DECnet", strictly speaking, non-routed DIGITAL protocols such as LAT, SCS, AMDS, LAST/LAD are not DECnet protocols and are not part of the DIGITAL Network Architecture.

To trace the evolution of DECnet is to trace the development of DNA. The beginnings of DNA were in the early 1970s. DIGITAL published its first DNA specification at about the same time that IBM announced its Systems Network Architecture (SNA). Since that time, development of DNA has evolved through the following phases:

Phase I (1974)

Support limited to 2 PDP-11s running the RSX-11 operating system only, with communication over point-to-point (DDCMP) links between nodes.

Phase II (1976)

Support for networks of up to 32 nodes with multiple, different implementations which could interoperate with each other. Implementations expanded to included RSTS, TOPS-10 and TOPS-20 with communications between processors still limited to point-to-point links only. Introduction of file transfer (FAL), remote file access (DAP), task-to-task programming interfaces and network management features.

Phase III (1980)

Support for networks of up to 255 nodes over point-to point and multi-drop links. Introduction of adaptive routing capability, downline loading (MOP), record access, a network management architecture, and gateways to other types of networks including IBM's SNA and CCITT Recommendation X.25.

Phase IV and **Phase IV+** (1982)

Phase IV was released initially to RSX-11 and VMS systems, later TOPS-20, TOPS-10, ULTRIX, VAXELN, and RSTS/E gained support. Support for networks of up to 64,449 nodes (63 areas of 1023 nodes), datalink capabilities expanded beyond DDCMP to include Ethernet local area network support as the datalink of choice, expanded adaptive routing capability to include hierarchical routing (areas, level 1 and level 2 routers), VMScluster support (cluster alias) and host services (CTERM). CTERM allowed a user on one computer to log into another computer remotely, performing the same function that Telnet does in the TCP/IP protocol stack. Digital also released a product called the PATHWORKS client, and more commonly known as the PATHWORKS 32 client, that implemented much of DECnet Phase

IV for DOS, and 16 and 32 bit Microsoft Windows platforms (all the way through to Windows Server 2003).

Phase IV implemented an 8 layer architecture similar to the OSI (7 layer) model especially at the lower levels. Since the OSI standards were not yet fully developed at the time, many of the Phase IV protocols remained proprietary.

The Ethernet implementation was unusual in that the software changed the physical address of the Ethernet interface on the network to AA-00-04-00-xx-yy where xx-yy reflected the DECnet network address of the host. This allowed router-less LAN operation because the LAN address could be deduced from the DECnet address.

The initial implementations released were for VMS and RSX-11, later this expanded to virtually every operating system DIGITAL ever shipped with the notable exception of RT-11. DECnet stacks are found on Linux, SunOS and other platforms, and Cisco and other network vendors offer products that can cooperate with and operate within DECnet networks. Full DECnet Phase IV specifications are available.

At the same time that DECnet Phase IV was released, the company also released a proprietary protocol called LAT for serial terminal access via Terminal servers. LAT is entirely separate from DECnet, though many DECserver LAT terminal servers did use MOP for the server image download and related bootstrap processing.

Enhancements made to DECnet Phase IV eventually became known as DECnet Phase IV+, although systems running this protocol remained completely interoperable with DECnet Phase IV systems.

Phase V and **Phase V+** (1987)

Support for very large (architecturally unlimited) networks, a new network management model, local or distributed name service, improved performance over Phase IV. Move from a proprietary network to an Open Systems Interconnection (OSI) by integration of ISO standards to provide multi-vendor connectivity and compatibility with DNA Phase IV, the last two features resulted in a hybrid network architecture (DNA and OSI) with separate "towers" sharing an integrated transport layer. Transparent transport level links to TCP/IP were added via the IETF RFC 1006 (OSI over IP) and RFC 1859 (NSP over IP) standards.

It was later renamed **DECnet/OSI** to emphasize its OSI interconnectability, and subsequently **DECnet-Plus** as TCP/IP protocols were incorporated.

DECnet Phase IV protocol suite

Application	DAP: Data Access ProtocolCTERM: Command Terminal
Network Management	NICE: Network Management protocolMOP: Maintenance Operation Protocol
Session	SCP: Session Control Protocol

Transport	NSP: Network Service Protocol
Network	DRP: DECnet Routing Protocol
Data link	DDCMP: Digital Data Communications Message ProtocolEthernet, Token ring, HDLC, FDDI, ...
Physical	Ethernet, Token ring, FDDI, ...

12

Network Troubleshooting Techniques

Troubleshooting Process

Network troubleshooting means recognizing and diagnosing networking problems with the goal of keeping your network running optimally. As a network administrator, your primary concern is maintaining *connectivity* of all devices (a process often called *fault management*). You also continually evaluate and improve your network's *performance*. Because serious networking problems can sometimes begin as performance problems, paying attention to performance can help you address issues before they become serious.

As a network administrator, your primary concern is maintaining* connectivity *of all devices.

About Connectivity Problems

Connectivity problems occur when end stations cannot communicate with other areas of your local area network (LAN) or wide area network (WAN). Using management tools, you can often fix a connectivity problem before users even notice it. Connectivity problems include:

- **Loss of connectivity** - When users cannot access areas of your network, your organization's effectiveness is impaired. Immediately correct any connectivity breaks.
- **Intermittent connectivity** - Although users have access to network resources some of the time, they are still facing periods of downtime. Intermittent connectivity problems can indicate that your network is on the verge of a major break. If connectivity is erratic, investigate the problem immediately.
- **Timeout problems** - Timeouts cause loss of connectivity, but are often associated with poor network performance.

About Performance Problems

Your network has performance problems when it is not operating as effectively as it should. For example, response times may be slow, the network may not be as reliable as usual, and users may be complaining that it takes them longer to do their work. Some performance problems are intermittent, such as instances of duplicate addresses. Other problems can indicate a growing strain on your network, such as consistently high utilization rates.

If you regularly examine your network for performance problems, you can extend the usefulness of your existing network configuration and plan network enhancements, instead of waiting for a performance problem to adversely affect the users' productivity.

Solving Connectivity and Performance Problems

When you troubleshoot your network, you employ tools and knowledge already at your disposal. With an in-depth understanding of your network, you can use network software tools, such as "Ping", and network devices, such as "Analyzers", to locate problems, and then make corrections, such as swapping equipment or reconfiguring segments, based on your analysis.

Transcend provides another set of tools for network troubleshooting. These tools have graphical user interfaces that make managing and troubleshooting your network easier. With "Transcend Applications", you can:

- Baseline your network's normal status to use as a basis for comparison when the network operates abnormally
- Precisely monitor network events
- Be notified immediately of critical problems on your network, such as a device losing connectivity
- Establish alert thresholds to warn you of potential problems that you can correct before they affect your network
- Resolve problems by disabling ports or reconfiguring devices.

Network Troubleshooting Framework

The International Standards Organization (ISO) Open Systems Interconnect (OSI) reference model is the foundation of all network communications. This seven-layer structure provides a clear picture of how network communications work.

Protocols (rules) govern communications between the layers of a single system and among several systems. In this way, devices made by different manufacturers or using different designs can use different protocols and still communicate.

By understanding how network troubleshooting fits into the framework of the OSI model, you can identify at what layer problems are located and which type of troubleshooting tools to use. For example, unreliable packet delivery can be caused by a problem with the transmission media or with a router configuration.

If you are receiving high rates of "FCS Errors" and "Alignment Errors", which you can monitor with Status Watch, then the problem is probably located at the physical layer and not the network layer.

Table below describes the data that the network management tools can collect as it relates to the OSI model layers.

Network Data and the OSI Model Layers

Layer	Data Collected	Transcend NCS Tool Used
Application Presentation Session Transport	Protocol information and other Remote Monitoring (RMON) and RMON2 data	• LANsentry Manager • Traffix Manager(for more detail)
Network	Routing information	• Status Watch • LANsentry Manager (for more detail) • Traffix Manager(for more detail)
Data Link	Traffic counts and other packet breakdowns	• Status Watch • LANsentry Manager (for more detail)
Physical	Error counts	• Status Watch

Troubleshooting Strategy

How do you know when you are having a network problem? The answer to this question depends on your site's network configuration.

If you notice changes on your network, ask the following questions:

- Is the change expected or unusual?
- Has this event ever occurred before?
- Does the change involve a device or network path for which you already have a backup solution in place?
- Does the change interfere with vital network operations?
- Does the change affect one or many devices or network paths?

After you have an idea of how the change is affecting your network, you can categorize it as critical or non-critical. Both of these categories need resolution (except for changes that are one-time occurrences); the difference between the categories is the time that you have to fix the problem.

By using a strategy for network troubleshooting, you can approach a problem methodically and resolve it with minimal disruption to network users. It is also important to have an accurate and detailed map of your current network environment. Beyond that, a good approach to problem resolution is:

- Recognizing Symptoms
- Understanding the Problem
- Identifying and Testing the Cause of the Problem
- Solving the Problem.

Recognizing Symptoms

The first step to resolving any problem is to identify and interpret the symptoms. You may discover network problems in several ways. Users may complain that the network seems slow or that they cannot connect to a server. You may pass your network management station and notice that a node icon is red. Your beeper may go off and display the message: WAN connection down.

User Comments

Although you can often solve networking problems before users notice a change in their environment, you invariably get feedback from your users about how the network is running, such as:

- They cannot print.
- They cannot access the application server.
- It takes them much longer to copy files across the network than it usually does.
- They cannot log on to a remote server.
- When they send e-mail to another site, they get a routing error message.
- Their system freezes whenever they try to Telnet.

Network Management Software Alerts

Network management software can alert you to areas of your network that need attention. For example:

- The application displays red (Warning) icons.
- Your weekly Top-N utilization report (which indicates the 10 ports with the highest utilization rates) shows that one port is experiencing much higher utilization levels than normal.
- You receive an e-mail message from your network management station that the **threshold** for broadcast and multicast packets has been exceeded.

These signs usually provide additional information about the problem, allowing you to focus on the right area.

Analyzing Symptoms

When a symptom occurs, ask yourself these types of questions to narrow the location of the problem and to get more data for analysis:

- To what degree is the network not acting normally (for example, does it now take one minute to perform a task that normally takes five seconds)?
- On what subnetwork is the user located?
- Is the user trying to reach a server, end station, or printer on the same subnetwork or on a different subnetwork?
- Are many users complaining that the network is operating slowly or that a specific network application is operating slowly?
- Are many users reporting network logon failures?
- Are the problems intermittent? For example, some files may print with no problems, while other printing attempts generate error messages, make users lose their connections, and cause systems to freeze.

Understanding the Problem

Networks are designed to move data from a transmitting device to a receiving device. When communication becomes problematic, you must determine why data are not traveling as expected and then find a solution. The two most common causes for data not moving reliably from source to destination are:

- The physical connection breaks (that is, a cable is unplugged or broken).
- A network device is not working properly and cannot send or receive some or all data.

Network management software can easily locate and report a physical connection break (layer 1 problem). It is more difficult to determine why a network device is not working as expected, which is often related to a layer 2 or a layer 3 problem.

To determine why a network device is not working properly, look first for:

- **Valid service** - Is the device configured properly for the type of service it is supposed to provide? For example, has Quality of Service (QoS), which is the definition of the transmission parameters, been established?
- **Restricted access** - Is an end station supposed to be able to connect with a specific device or is that connection restricted? For example, is a firewall set up that prevents that device from accessing certain network resources?
- **Correct configuration** - Is there a misconfiguration of IP address, subnet mask,

gateway, or broadcast address? Network problems are commonly caused by misconfiguration of newly connected or configured devices. Identifying and Testing the Cause of the Problem

After you develop a theory about the cause of the problem, test your theory. The test must conclusively prove or disprove your theory.

Two general rules of troubleshooting are:

- If you cannot reproduce a problem, then no problem exists unless it happens again on its own.
- If the problem is intermittent and you cannot replicate it, you can configure your network management software to catch the event in progress.

For example, with "LANsentry Manager", you can set alarms and automatic packet capture filters to monitor your network and inform you when the problem occurs again.

Although network management tools can provide a great deal of information about problems and their general location, you may still need to swap equipment or replace components of your network until you locate the exact trouble spot.

Sample Problem Analysis

This section illustrates the analysis phase of a typical troubleshooting incident.

On your network, a user cannot access the mail server. You need to establish two areas of information:

- **What you know** - In this case, the user's workstation cannot communicate with the mail server.
- **What you do not know and need to test** -
- Can the workstation communicate with the network at all, or is the problem limited to communication with the server? Test by sending a "Ping" or by connecting to other devices.
- Is the workstation the only device that is unable to communicate with the server, or do other workstations have the same problem? Test connectivity at other workstations.
- If other workstations cannot communicate with the server, can they communicate with other network devices? Again, test the connectivity.

The analysis process follows these steps:

1. Can the workstation communicate with any other device on the subnetwork?

- If **no**, then go to step 2.
- If **yes**, determine if only the server is unreachable.

- If only the server cannot be reached, this suggests a server problem. Confirm by doing step 2.
- If other devices cannot be reached, this suggests a connectivity problem in the network. Confirm by doing step 3.

2. Can other workstations communicate with the server?
   - If **no**, then most likely it is a server problem. Go to step 3.
   - If **yes**, then the problem is that the workstation is not communicating with the subnetwork. (This situation can be caused by workstation issues or a network issue with that specific station.)
3. Can other workstations communicate with other network devices?
   - If **no**, then the problem is likely a network problem.
   - If **yes**, the problem is likely a server problem.

When you determine whether the problem is with the server, subnetwork, or workstation, you can further analyze the problem, as follows:

- **For a problem with the server** - Examine whether the server is running, if it is properly connected to the network, and if it is configured appropriately.
- **For a problem with the subnetwork** - Examine any device on the path between the users and the server.
- **For a problem with the workstation** - Examine whether the workstation can access other network resources and if it is configured to communicate with that particular server.

Identifying and Testing the Cause of the Problem

To help identify and test the cause of problems, have available:

- A laptop computer that is loaded with a terminal emulator, TCP/IP stack, TFTP server, CD-ROM drive (to read the online documentation), and some key network management applications, such as LANsentry® Manager. With the laptop computer, you can plug into any subnetwork to gather and analyze data about the segment.
- A spare managed hub to swap for any hub that does not have management. Swapping in a managed hub allows you to quickly spot which port is generating the errors.
- A single port probe to insert in the network if you are having a problem where you do not have management capability.
- Console cables for each type of connector, labeled and stored in a secure place.

Solving the Problem

Many device or network problems are straightforward to resolve, but others yield misleading symptoms. If one solution does not work, continue with another.

A solution often involves:

- Upgrading software or hardware (for example, upgrading to a new version of agent software or installing Gigabit Ethernet devices)
- Balancing your network load by analyzing
- What users communicate with which servers
- What the user traffic levels are in different segments.

Based on these findings, you can decide how to redistribute network traffic.

- Adding segments to your LAN (for example, adding a new switch where utilization is continually high)
- Replacing faulty equipment (for example, replacing a module that has port problems or replacing a network card that has a faulty jabber protection mechanism).

To help solve problems, have available:

- Spare hardware equipment (such as modules and power supplies), especially for your critical devices
- A recent backup of your device configurations to reload if flash memory gets corrupted (which can sometimes happen due to a power outage).

Troubleshooting Tools

To help you isolate the source of network problems you can employ two useful tools - ping and traceroute.

Ping

Ping is a useful tool for testing to see if a host is responding, among other things. On machines running Windows 95, 98, ME or 2000, ping can be accessed via a DOS prompt. Select "Run..." from the Start menu and type "command" ("cmd" for Win2K) or click on the MS-DOS Prompt shortcut in your Start Menu. Once you're at the DOS prompt, type "ping Host-Address*".

For those who use *nix systems (BSD, Linux, Solaris etc.), ping should have been installed with the OS. Access it by typing "ping Host-Address*" at your command line. Due to the configuration of our network, you will not be able to ping or traceroute directly to your account. Instead, you will have to ping use the address "router.dmvnoc.com" for these tools.

This program uses the Internet Message Control Protocol (IMCP) to send data packets to a host you specify and responds with the amount of time, in milliseconds, it took for the packet to return. Here is an example of a ping dialog:

```
# ping yahoo.com
PING yahoo.com (204.71.202.160): 56 data bytes
64 bytes from 204.71.202.160: icmp_seq=0 ttl=246 time=108.0 ms
64 bytes from 204.71.202.160: icmp_seq=1 ttl=246 time=102.3 ms
64 bytes from 204.71.202.160: icmp_seq=2 ttl=246 time=102.6 ms
64 bytes from 204.71.202.160: icmp_seq=3 ttl=246 time=105.5 ms
64 bytes from 204.71.202.160: icmp_seq=4 ttl=246 time=103.9 ms
-- yahoo.com ping statistics -
5 packets transmitted, 5 packets received, 0% packet loss
round-trip min/avg/max = 102.3/104.4/108.0 ms
```

Reading the results from a ping is simple. The only information you really need to take note of is the time=108.0 ms which tells you how many milliseconds it took for the packet to reach the host and return. There isn't any concern unless these numbers are close to 1000 (one second) or an asterisk "*" appears. If the results do exceed 1000, it may mean that there are some problems with your connection to the Internet, the server's connection, or a connection between you and the server. If an asterisk is displayed, there was no response and that also signifies a problem with the connection between you and the server. The other information in the results includes the time to live, the lowest, average and most time it took the packets to complete their trips and the sequence in which the packets were sent.

Traceroute

Traceroute works much like ping in that it sends data packets to a host you specify. However, rather than simply giving you the time it takes for the packets to return, traceroute sends back results for each hop the packet makes. Because of this, traceroute is the perfect tool to see where network problems are occuring. Here is what your average traceroute dialog looks like:

```
traceroute to yahoo.com (204.71.202.160), 30 hops max, 40 byte packets
1  151.196.82.1  461.177 ms  765.824 ms  9.107 ms
2  151.196.149.1  2.773 ms  2.8 ms  2.321 ms
3  207.68.20.1  5.059 ms  3.735 ms
4  208.46.126.181  5.785 ms  8.225 ms  7.994 ms
5  205.171.24.117  7.085 ms  10.513 ms  10.155 ms
6  205.171.24.38  9.932 ms  6.092 ms  5.844 ms
7  206.132.150.161  6.138 ms  6.944 ms  6.858 ms
8  208.178.174.53  6.505 ms  6.19 ms  5.25 ms
9  208.50.169.86  67.832 ms  69.224 ms  67.641 ms
10  206.132.254.41  67.499 ms  68.637 ms  67.437 ms
```

```
11  208.178.103.62   67.882 ms   71.674 ms   68.942 ms
12  204.71.202.160   70.85 ms   73.649 ms   69.539 ms
```

Like ping's results, deciphering traceroute's dialog is easy. Each hop in the route the packet has travelled will be displayed in order with the hostname and/or IP address. Next, the results, in milliseconds, of the three probes that are sent to each hop. The rules for ping results also apply here. Numbers near 1000 and asterisks represent network problems. For example, the following traceroute results shows that there are some problems on the 7-11 hops:

```
traceroute to yahoo.com (204.71.202.160), 30 hops max, 40 byte packets
1  151.196.82.1   461.177 ms   765.824 ms   9.107 ms
2  151.196.149.1   2.773 ms   2.8 ms   2.321 ms
3  207.68.20.1   5.059 ms   3.735 ms
4  208.46.126.181   5.785 ms    8.225 ms   7.994 ms
5  205.171.24.117   7.085 ms   10.513 ms   10.155 ms
6  205.171.24.38   9.932 ms   6.092 ms   5.844 ms
7  206.132.150.161   6.138 ms   6.944 ms   6.858 ms
8  * * *
9  * * *
10  * * *
11  * * *
12  * * *
```

If you then performed a WHOIS query against the American Registry for Numbers (ARIN) database on the last IP before the packet loss, you'd see that it's owned by Global Crossing, who happens to provide network-related services including backbone access for many dial-up and website hosting providers. In this case, the network problems would most likely be due to a problem on their network.

On machines running Windows 95, 98, ME or 2000, traceroute can be accessed via a DOS prompt. Select "Run..." from the Start menu and type "command" ("cmd" for Win2K) or click on the MS-DOS Prompt shortcut in your Start Menu. Once you're at the DOS prompt, type "tracert Host-Address*".

Running the Network Diagnostics tool

The Network Diagnostics tool is used in conjunction with Guided Help.

To run the Network Diagnostics tool in Internet Explorer 7

- When presented with the error "Internet Explorer cannot display the webpage," click **Diagnose Connection Problems**.

If you're still running Internet Explorer 6, as I am on my main Windows XP machine, then you'll receive a somewhat different error message. This error message does not include a direct link to Diagnose Connection Problems.

To run the Network Diagnostics tools in Internet Explorer 6

- From the **Tools** menu, select **Diagnose Connection Problems**

After you've started the Network Diagnostics tool, follow the steps to troubleshoot your problem. While the Network Diagnostics tool is actually pretty smart about what it can identify and often fix, especially wireless problems, the tool isn't perfect. But when Network Diagnostics can't fix a problem, you can still use the tool to get enough information to fix the problem yourself. Even if you need help fixing the problem, the log file that the Network Diagnostics tool generates is invaluable to the support personnel when you call for help. Next figure shows the final message I received when I had misconfigured the Domain Name Service (DNS) setting.

The Network Diagnostics tool message advised me to call my Internet Service Provider (ISP) for help. But, more importantly, the tool also created a detailed diagnostics log, as shown in next figure, which provided more than enough information for my ISP's help desk to solve the problem. The diagnostic log clearly shows that I somehow managed to set the IP address of my DNS provider to 127.0.0.1, and that address isn't responding to my DNS queries. The result is not surprising because I don't run a DNS server on my Windows XP laptop.

What the Network Diagnostics tool does?

So what sorts of tests does the new Network Diagnostics tool run and what kinds of problems can it solve? The basic tests are as follows:

- Verify HTTP, HTTPS, and FTP connectivity against Microsoft.com.
- Check for network adapter issues.
- Verify wireless functionality.
- Validate IP configuration.
- Check DNS and gateway settings and functionality.

The Network Diagnostics tool uses four levels of repair automation to solve problems.

- **Automatic repair automation** is only used when the repair is both easily automated and safe to perform automatically. An example is flushing the Address Resolution (ARP) cache.
- **Approval repair automation** is used when the repair can be automated but where it could cause configuration issues. You're prompted for approval before the repair is performed. An example is changing from static IP addresses to automatic DHCP generated addresses.
- **Manual repair automation** is used whenever the steps can't be automated, usually because external hardware is involved. An example is restarting your router or modem.

- **Contact Support repair automation** is used when the tool can't easily identify the issue or point directly to the correction. In these cases, the generated log file will help support personnel identify the issue.

The Network Diagnostics tool can correct many common network issues, but its real strength is in wireless networking, an area that still causes more network problems than any other. The tool builds on the underlying Wireless Zero Configuration architecture to detect and repair many of the most common wireless problems. Some of the most common tests include:

- **Wireless ad hoc check.** The Network Diagnostics tool checks that the wireless connection is linking to an access point and not to another wireless computer.
- **Wireless available networks.** The Network Diagnostics tool checks both novice and advanced views of available networks.
- **Wireless compatibility check.** The Network Diagnostics tool verifies that the access point is using a security method that Windows XP supports; the tool will provide instructions on how to download the WPA2 update for Windows XP if needed.
- **Wireless hardware issue help.** The Network Diagnostics tool identifies hardware issues with the router or adapter and provides help.
- **Wireless out of range check.** The Network Diagnostics tool identifies a weak signal.
- **Wireless security config check.** The Network Diagnostics tool displays the wireless security settings, including authentication settings so the user can verify that the router or access point matches the adapter settings.
- **Wireless security key help.** The Network Diagnostics tool identifies mismatched keys and provides help to match them.
- **Wireless service status check.** The Network Diagnostics tool identifies whether the Wireless Zero Configuration service is running or not and starts the service if necessary. (If third-party configuration software is running, the Network Diagnostics tool will not attempt to troubleshoot the connection—another reason to not use third-party tools for wireless configuration.)
- **Wireless setup help.** The Network Diagnostics tool provides links to Windows Help topics on how to setup a wireless network.
- **Wireless signal strength check.** The Network Diagnostics tool identifies a weak signal and suggests you move closer to the access point or router.
- **Wireless SSID check.** The Network Diagnostics tool provides help on setting the priorities of preferred wireless networks.
- **Wireless turned off check.** The Network Diagnostics tool provides help when turning on any hardware wireless switch on the computer. Many newer laptops have a switch to enable you to turn off the wireless completely to save battery and comply with airline regulations.